With Friends Like These

With Friends Like These

THE AMERICAS WATCH REPORT ON HUMAN RIGHTS AND U.S. POLICY IN LATIN AMERICA

Edited by Cynthia Brown
Preface by Jacobo Timerman
Introduction by Alfred Stepan

PANTHEON BOOKS
NEW YORK

Portions of this work first appeared, in slightly
different form, in reports published by Americas Watch.

Grateful acknowledgment is made to the University of
Wisconsin Press for permission to reprint the map on pages
xvi–xvii from Cathryn L. Lombardi, *Latin American
History: A Teaching Atlas*. Copyright © 1983 by the Board
of Regents of the University of Wisconsin System.

Library of Congress Cataloging in Publication Data
Main entry under title:

With friends like these.

Includes index.
1. Civil rights—Latin America—Addresses, essays,
lectures. 2. Latin America—Foreign relations—United
States—Addresses, essays, lectures. 3. United States—
Foreign relations—Latin America—Addresses, essays,
lectures. I. Brown, Cynthia.
JC599.L3W58 1985 323.4′9′098 84-26410
ISBN 0-394-72949-8

Designed by Naomi Osnos

Manufactured in the United States of America
First Edition

CONTENTS

ACKNOWLEDGMENTS

Like any project undertaken by Americas Watch, this book is the product of many people's efforts. We acknowledge first of all our debt to the Latin Americans who have assisted us, in particular human rights monitors and victims of human rights abuse, whose courage and tenacity we greatly admire.

To the extent that we have relied on past Americas Watch reports for background and analysis, we are grateful to the authors of those reports, including members of the Americas Watch Committee, consultants, and colleague organizations with which we have collaborated, such as the Helsinki Watch and the Lawyers Committee for International Human Rights.

For proposing this project, our thanks to André Schiffrin, and for guiding it, to Wendy Wolf. Fernando Torres, Annette O'Donnell, and Alita Paine provided valuable research assistance.

Finally, a personal word of thanks to my husband, for his encouragement, and to my daughter, for getting well.

CYNTHIA BROWN
New York City

CONTRIBUTORS

JACOBO TIMERMAN, an Argentine newspaper editor and human rights advocate, returned to his country in 1984.

ALFRED STEPAN is dean of the School of International Relations at Columbia University and the author of many books and articles on Latin American affairs.

CYNTHIA BROWN, a writer specializing in Latin America, has been a consultant to the Americas Watch since 1982 and in that capacity has written and edited numerous reports on human rights and U.S. policy. For this volume she is author of "A Rhetoric of Convenience" and the discussions of Chile and Colombia.

HOLLY BURKHALTER is Washington representative of the Americas Watch Committee. For this volume she is co-author of "Recommendations."

ROBERT K. GOLDMAN is Louis C. James Scholar at the Washington College of Law, American University, and a member of the Americas Watch Committee. For this volume he is author of the discussion of Uruguay.

JUAN MENDEZ, an Argentine lawyer, is director of the Washington office of the Americas Watch. In this volume he is author of the discussions of Honduras, Nicaragua, and Argentina.

ALLAN NAIRN is a journalist who writes on Central America and author, for this volume, of the discussion of Guatemala.

ARYEH NEIER is vice-chairman of the Americas Watch. For this volume he is author of "The Law and Lawlessness," the discussions of El Salvador and Peru, and coauthor of "Recommendations."

THE AMERICAS WATCH has monitored human rights conditions in Latin America, and U.S. policy with regard to human rights there, since 1981. The essays in this book address issues relevant to U.S. human rights policy under the Reagan administration and the histories and current conditions of nine countries. We have selected these nine based on the criteria that, first, human rights have been a major domestic issue during the past four years, and second, the administration's diplomatic and aid policies, in particular U.S. relations with the military, have had an effect on human rights. We document U.S. policy as well as these nations' internal conditions in the interests of promoting adherence to U.S. law, thus respect for international law and for the meaning of human rights accepted by that law.

PREFACE

A new phenomenon in recent years has been the emergence of several organizations—Americas Watch, Helsinki Watch, Amnesty International—that publish detailed accounts of human rights abuses. The victims are named; their murderers and torturers are named; their methods are examined; the systems and ideologies that lead to abuses are considered in the light of those abuses; the responsibility of the international community is assessed.

This volume brings together the findings of Americas Watch about nine countries in Latin America that have endured, and still endure, particularly painful conflicts over human rights. As the chapters that follow make clear, there are common elements throughout the region, but the differences from country to country are as great as the similarities.

My own country, Argentina, is living through a unique experience today, one unprecedented in this last half century. The majority of its inhabitants have something to decry, and suddenly all can do so out loud and without fear. Once again, that which is normal in a democracy came as a surprise to Argentines.

In the tumult of changes that accompanied the recent end of seven and a half years of military dictatorship, Argentina had only one expectation that was met immediately by the arrival of democracy: that dissent could be a public activity. Argumentative stances no longer must be taken clandestinely. The other expectations—economic, social, legal, political—are now firing impassioned and open debates. In one sphere, however, that of human rights, the expectations were higher and the debate is even more intense.

The human rights violations suffered by the Argentines

began modestly at the end of the 1960s, and were incorporated into an organized system of state terrorism from 1976 to 1983. After December 10, 1983, when a civilian president, Raul Alfonsin, assumed the government following free elections, the victims—thousands of them—had much to demand: information on what happened to the disappeared; freedom for those who were still to be found in the jails; punishment of the guilty; economic reparations for those who were robbed.

The government could only offer to put in motion the gears of democratic justice, which are necessarily slow, and to try to discover what happened to the disappeared. Such information is of value in securing legal redress, of course, only to the extent that it can become evidence in court. After almost a year of intermittent progress and reversals, the government has discovered how little can be done: that is, how slowly a democratic government functions when it is trying to fulfill a whole range of juridical demands.

Human rights organizations have secured only minimal satisfaction for the victims and for the families of the disappeared; too often they can only aid them in applying to the various tribunals where they might find a positive reaction from the judges. The extent of prosecution is very limited— only ten high officials of the armed forces are now in jail awaiting trial for their deeds. It is estimated that over two thousand acted in direct violation of human rights. Moreover, as the human rights organizations charge, civilian officials who functioned during the military dictatorship, between 1976 and 1983, also knew what was happening and may be considered moral accomplices. But this is difficult ground, because all of Argentine society knew what was happening, and very few protested. This was particularly true of those who normally have as their charge the care of peace and of coexistence—religious groups, the press, political parties, workers' unions.

Here, then, is the crux of the matter: the government can do no more than guarantee the fullest functioning of democracy—that is, for the nation as a whole. For individual citizens, though, the machinery of justice can be exceedingly slow; much that is common knowledge must be disregarded by the courts because it is not available in a form that is legally admissible and sufficient. Human rights organizations find this frustrating, and demand that things advance at greater speed.

One consequence is the debate in Argentina today over the measures that should be taken to prevent another repressive system from emerging in the future. The positions in the debate have various shadings, but the basic argument focuses on the differences between doing justice—that is, punishing the guilty—and determining truth—that is, disclosing all. Some believe that punishment of the guilty will deter future violators of human rights. Others insist that only if all of society is conscious of the crimes that were committed, knows how they were committed, and understands how to ensure that the democracy cannot be destroyed again, can the violators be kept from returning. In essence, they feel that the future of Argentina will be less influenced by the incarceration of the guilty than it will be by the awareness of the whole society.

This question touches on one of the most stirring debates enveloping human rights activists today. How can their energy and organizations be best utilized in the struggle to defend democracy, given the unpromising historical experience of a country like Argentina?

Ideas and opinions cross once more. Some activists want to leave this battle to political parties, workers' unions, and the government. Others point out that these people were not able to guarantee freedoms in the past, and assert that the human rights organizations are in a position to lead in creating a civil power such as has not existed in Argentina for almost sixty years.

After a year of intense discussion and controversy, it appears that the majority have joined the active struggle to organize and support civil power. Their commitment to the political process assumes that a democratic society, if alive and active, will resolve the subject of punishment for the guilty and reparations for the victims. Satisfactory results will take time, of course, but it would be worse to leave the democracy vulnerable to a new assault by military men still unconvinced that they made any mistakes, much less committed any crimes.

The Argentine experience helps define what the struggle for human rights implies in the rest of the world today. If the pursuit of guaranteed freedoms is not integrated into a larger, even global, struggle for democracy and against totalitarianism, the good intentions of rights activists may be reduced to mere philanthropy. In this way, the specter of a new military coup, always present in Argentina, is bringing human rights activists to a more militant attitude in the defense of democracy, via the formation of a civil power.

Could this mean that many people in need of help from the human rights organizations—prisoners serving sentences for common crimes, minority religious groups, the ancient indigenous populations in the north and south of the country—will be left without aid?

The limits of what the struggle for human rights shall embrace in Argentina are still undefined, for the simple reason that for many years the battle was dedicated to confronting the largest repressive massacre in national history. The Argentine experience in 1984 and 1985 will without doubt affect the decisions of activists in Uruguay and Chile in the immediate future. But there is a growing consciousness among activists in Argentina, and perhaps in all of Latin America, that the forces for human rights cannot reach their goals without also ensuring that all the tenets of democracy are secure. It is a painful debate, but inevitable.

JACOBO TIMERMAN
Buenos Aires, Argentina
December 1984

INTRODUCTION

In the early 1960s, several prominent American scholars studying developing countries became convinced that in the face of fractious civilian elites and the growing pressures of poverty and underdevelopment, the nation-building potential of the modernizing military was greater than that of civilian politics. They argued that politicians placed self-interest and their parties' tactical priorities ahead of national development. The military, they said, was quite different—not only democratic in its social character, but disinterested in its social alliances; it recruited from all sectors of society and favored none. Its allegedly nonpolitical approach to social conflict was contrasted to the short-sightedness of civilian political parties and their inefficiency as social architects.

Implicit in these analyses was the assumption that democracy—in the sense of representative government and open debate about social and political issues, the free play of ideas and agendas—carried a risk of chaos, and that a system of tighter control was more capable of resolving social challenges. Implicit too—sometimes even explicit—was the belief that only control would preclude the kind of unrest and open polarization that could lead developing countries leftwards. For such development theorists and policy activists, the world needed a "bulwark" against chaos and communism, and the military was this indispensable "bulwark."

The flaws in an analysis that elevated military officers to social redeemers were evident even at the time. The institutional portrait had been touched up. The military's composition, for example, was neither random nor class-blind; empirical research showed that the regional, educational, and class origins of the officers were in fact often highly

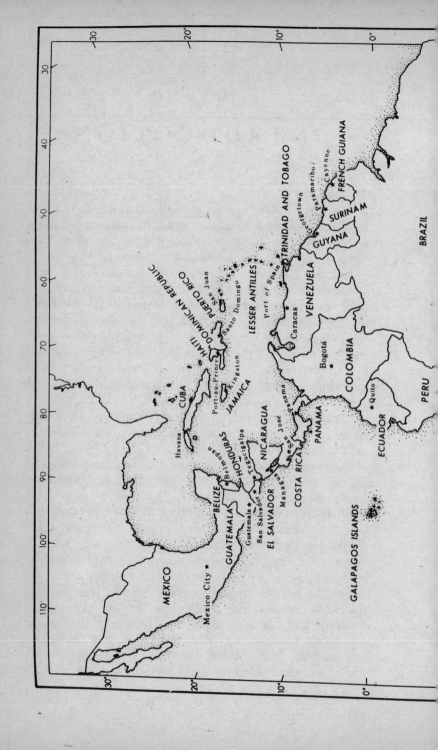

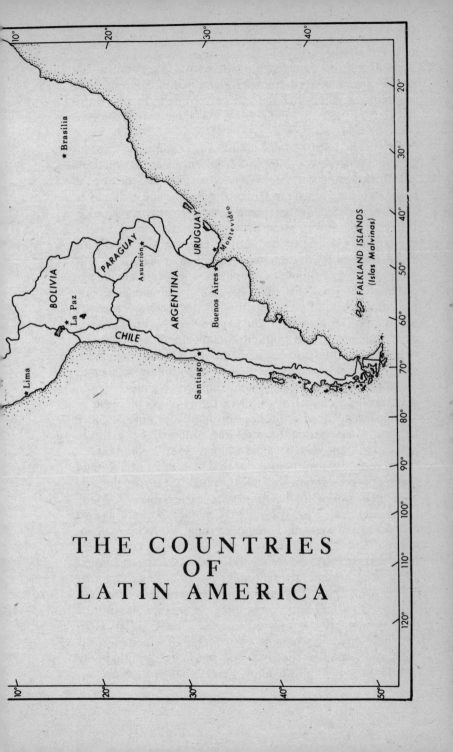

THE COUNTRIES
OF
LATIN AMERICA

skewed. Also the fact that the military was a situational elite whose power derived from its place within a strong state apparatus implied that the officers normally had powerful interests of their own and entered into their own alliances to promote these interests.

Events in Latin America have since painted a portrait of the military very different from the one the theorists sketched twenty years ago. We have seen, to our sorrow, the results of military rule in Chile, Argentina, and Uruguay in the last decade. We have witnessed the activities of a less bureaucratic, but in some ways even more vicious, form of militarism in El Salvador and Guatemala. Along with the moral bankruptcy of these modern military regimes, we note their failure to promote development; their intimate links to national elites and their corollary antagonism to the poor; their promotion of economic models that favor openness to world financial markets at the expense of domestic production, basic needs, and long-range employment; and their corruption, whether discreet or flamboyant. Most essentially, we cannot fail to recognize the cost of forfeiting democracy for the illusion of order that a military regime imposes. Whether one counts this cost in terms of people dead or "disappeared," or of institutions dismantled, or of ignorance fostered by censorship, or of reforms nullified, it amounts to a devastation no society would willingly bring upon itself.

Two decades ago, before the Brazilian coup of 1964 and the era of "civic action" programs, scholars were not the only ones who looked to the armed forces for stability. Many Latin Americans, too, considered them a bulwark against confusion and welcomed their occasional intervention in political affairs. This was the case in Brazil, as well as in Argentina in both 1966 and 1976, and in Chile and Uruguay in 1973. Such promilitary sentiment no longer exists in that region. How could it, after what has happened? In my recent visits there, what I have found instead is a new commitment to democracy, not as a means to some other end, but as an end in itself, a permanent value. This new commitment takes as a given that the "bulwark" has failed, and that only democracy, in its most ample sense, can protect nations from the suffering so many in Latin America have experienced or are still experiencing. This means democracy not merely as a mechanical voting process or as a limited-membership association of the powerful, but as a national project for the fullest possible debate, participation, and responsiveness.

The efforts through force of arms to thwart such democratic evolution lie at the heart of the overthrow of Somoza and the revolts now underway in Central America. And while much of the attention on Latin America in our country is focused on the Reagan government's adventurous military policies in the isthmus, events elsewhere in Latin America, though they do not receive front-page attention, suggest another model for escape from militarism. In the Southern Cone, the era of "bureaucratic-authoritarian" regimes in Brazil, Argentina, and Uruguay has ended. The military regime in Chile is under severe strain. With the utter failure of national-security states, with the elections in Argentina, Uruguay, and Brazil and the continuing protests in Chile, we see new possibilities for development and democracy. Without underestimating the problems confronting these countries—and the debt crisis is clearly a burden for any government, military or democratic—there is reason for some optimism if—a crucial if—the armed forces can be discouraged from taking power once again. To construct stable, unthreatened bases for civilian government is the critical challenge facing the Southern Cone. The ways these countries meet this challenge will have an influence in the rest of Latin America, for no nation can count itself completely free of the threat of militarism.

Since 1973, the nations of the Southern Cone experienced authoritarian rule that was without question more traumatic than any they had endured in their past; indeed, for Chile and Uruguay there was little in the past with which to make a comparison. To reconstruct democracy out of political, moral, and economic ruin is a new task for them. It is therefore disturbing that the Reagan administration has so consistently refused to acknowledge the changes brought about in the past decade, or to abandon a strategy that favors the military far more often than its civilian critics and opponents. In Central America the administration's military alliances are directed more towards winning wars than towards building peace; in the Southern Cone these alliances were often maintained despite the existence of civilian alternatives. The central fact is that the real struggle in Brazil, Uruguay, Argentina, and Chile in the early 1980s has been not between authoritarianism and totalitarianism (a dichotomy that all too often provides the U.S. rationale for supporting authoritarian regimes), but between authoritarianism and democracy.

When Jeane Kirkpatrick remarks that democracy in the Southern Cone and Brazil would signify no more nor less than the swing of the pendulum, she is claiming that history does not move but merely ticks back and forth. The Reagan administration's failure to recognize and respond to the basic facts of change is reducing the United States, in many Latin Americans' eyes, from a multidimensional world power—respected for a dynamic culture, a diverse economy, a tolerance of dissent, and a tradition of open government—to a one-dimensional power which, like the Soviet Union in Eastern Europe, derives its influence largely through possession of, and willingness to use, military force. The message of the 1983 Grenada invasion read by Latin Americans, regardless of their opinion of the former Grenadian government, was that invasion had ceased to be a dirty word in Washington. The policies in Nicaragua and El Salvador, in their different ways, have made that message doubly clear, as the administration consistently chooses military alliances and tactics rather than seriously trying nonviolent measures.

It may be the administration's definition of friendship that is at fault. Friendship among nations is, or should be, more than shared fear; it should be the sharing of goals, of which democracy would logically seem foremost. But if many Latin Americans no longer view democracy as just a tactic, the Reagan administration has not noted the change. Its exaggerated claims for the democracy of some countries—El Salvador, for one—and its praise for the "transition to democracy" in others, as in Guatemala now or in Argentina under the generals, apparently exist merely as complements to a military alliance. As the essays in this book demonstrate, the administration has failed in every case to favor democratic *forces* over the military, despite rhetoric to the contrary. The marked U.S. preference for military means and its apparent continuing faith in the institutions of national security go against the grain of civilian governments in Argentina, Peru, Uruguay, Colombia, and even Duarte's El Salvador, governments that are seeking to cement confidence in civilian rule despite great political and economic difficulties.

An example of the difficulties facing such countries is well illustrated in Argentina. This nation has recently emerged from seven years of dictatorship characterized by torture, the disappearance of possibly 25,000 people, legal manipulation, the suppression of all forms of dissent and political debate; none of its several previous military governments could equal the recent period for either brutality or economic mismanagement. In Argentina, new civilian government is attempting to make the armed forces more accountable to elected authority. The issue of accountability for the crimes against humanity committed during the 1976–1983 military period has provoked legal resistance from the military. Through a series of institutional changes, however, the government has succeeded in acting in other areas. For example, it has dispersed an army corps formerly stationed in the city of Buenos Aires, thus removing a significant military element from the environs of political power and influence. The government has also begun to take control of Fabricaciones Militares, a manufacturer of weapons, steel, and other strategic products, which had formerly been managed by the military and kept off the public record. The military's budget has been reduced, in real terms, by 40 percent—significantly more than the average (25 percent) real reduction for the national budget as a whole. The government's actions suggest both the complexity of military-civilian relations at this moment and the pressure to redefine those relations. Nonetheless, the Reagan administration has been unresponsive to the civilian government's principal requests for political support, which involve its debt negotiations.

Even where U.S. policy tends to support civilian leaders along with the military, the narrowness of that support causes friction. The recent attempts of Honduran civilian officials to distance themselves from the Reagan administration is an expression of this conflict. More dramatic still, Duarte's decision to negotiate for peace in El Salvador was apparently made without advising the United States, which has supported negotiation tepidly, only as a matter of rhetoric.

This book brings together portraits of the armed forces and their excesses in nine countries, along with analyses of the Reagan administration's policies towards these military establishments. Beyond the suffering described in the chapters, and the criticisms of U.S. policy they offer, the essays suggest the positive value our government ought to embrace: a friendship with Latin America based on the strengths of our common ideals and mutual beliefs—that responsive government, free associations, and open debate, and the ability to demand these things without risk of murder, torture, or other harm, are a more secure basis for social progress than armed force. Such an approach would have several residual benefits for the United States, including the recovery of moral stature and the compliance with our own laws regarding respect for human rights. Moreover, it would signify a recognition of what Latin America's recent history has meant—that if a new, broader democracy cannot take hold and control the threat of militarism, the human loss in all the Americas may be yet more devastating.

ALFRED STEPAN
Columbia University, New York
January 1985

With Friends Like These

1

A RHETORIC OF
CONVENIENCE

Following the 1980 presidential election, a group of Republican advisers calling itself the Committee of Santa Fe produced a blueprint for the new administration's policy in the Americas. Contending that "the third phase of World War III"[1] was under way by proxy in Latin America, the authors accused the Carter administration of "strategic indifference while calling for social, economic, agrarian, and human rights reforms. . . ."[2] The world, they argued, was divided in half, and the Western Hemisphere was our half. To preserve its security from Soviet expansion, the United States would have to strengthen traditional military ties and emphasize regional security arrangements, shelter its Latin America policy formulation from the media (due to their liberal bias), systematically counter liberation theology, and recognize that internal and external subversion were one and the same. In this context "Human rights . . . must be abandoned and replaced by a noninterventionist policy of political and ethical realism."[3]

Their analysis echoed that of an influential essay by Jeane Kirkpatrick, soon to be the new administration's ambassador to the U.N. In her 1979 article "Dictatorships and Double Standards," Kirkpatrick had criticized the Carter administration for what she viewed as its tendency to let revolutionary movements get the better of U.S. interests, as in Nicaragua and Iran. Her argument had rested on the general assertion that "traditional authoritarian governments are less repressive than revolutionary autocracies . . . are more susceptible of liberalization and . . . are more compatible with U.S. interests." She further criticized the Carter administration's "apolitical view of contemporary events" as a source of U.S. "passivity" in the face of Third World change.[4]

Kirkpatrick's tolerance of friendly authoritarians and her claim that they were, *ipso facto*, less repressive than revolutionary or Communist states would become the key to the Reagan approach to human rights. The assumption that the United States must bolster the one in order to frustrate the expansion of the other determined policy formulation on Latin America in general and, with it, the outlines of a human rights argument that has excused or overlooked the abuses committed by friends on grounds that even such friends are better than the alternative—an example of "ethical realism" in practice. Without weakening this conceptual essence, the administration's human rights policy—or, more precisely, its response to pressure for a human rights policy —has undergone three permutations.

At first the new administration sought to discredit the Carter-era emphasis on human rights and to eliminate human rights as a policy consideration. Secretary of State Haig informed the Senate Foreign Relations Committee that a campaign against terrorism would replace human rights as the cornerstone of U.S. foreign policy. The United States would defend human rights, he stated elsewhere, primarily by resisting the Soviet Union and would not try bilaterally to encourage better human rights conditions in other countries: "There are limits to what we can and should do to transform other cultures, customs, and institutions,"[5] he said, implying that human rights concern was, at best, a form of arrogance and intervention. But by late 1981, it was recognized as poor public relations to inveigh against human rights policy per se. That that approach could not succeed was evident when Ernest Lefever was nominated to be assistant secretary of state for human rights and humanitarian affairs. A neoconservative activist, Lefever expressed his intention to use the post to reverse or at least to circumvent the human rights legislation that Congress had developed under Carter, and the Foreign Relations Committee rejected his nomination. With the subsequent appointment of Elliott Abrams as assistant secretary, the administration took a new tack: It would include issues of human rights in its agenda, but human rights as defined by its own priorities, without reference to other, widely accepted measurements.

The shift became necessary because, in the words of an October 1981 confidential memo to the secretary of state, "Congressional belief that we have no consistent human rights policy threatens to disrupt important foreign policy initiatives."[6] The memo suggested that for policy purposes "human rights" could be limited to political and individual liberties, excluding social, cultural, and economic issues that help to make up the internationally accepted definition of human rights. The new approach could emphasize a broadly defined threat of terrorism, linked to revolutions and the Soviet Union, as the principal threat to basic rights; it could, indeed, be useful as a vehicle for demonstrating "that the difference between East and West is the crucial political distinction of our times."[7]

The State Department's Bureau of Human Rights was to wage what the memo called "a battle of ideas,"[8] in which the administration's arsenal would consist largely of a new definition of the issues. Projecting its message that human rights and Western values go hand in hand, the bureau would seek to move away from the term "human rights" and use instead less freighted, more colloquial terms such as "individual rights," narrowing the focus of concern. The memo made clear that the primary target was still to be the Soviet Union, inasmuch as the central issue would be framed in terms of "our" commitment to individual freedom and expression versus "their" emphasis on state authority.

This was not what Congress had intended in 1975 when it first passed a ban on aid to governments engaging in a "consistent pattern of gross and systematic violations of internationally recognized human rights." The emphasis then was on ending aid to, and morally disassociating the United States from, a range of nations in both East and West. And the substance of this provision in the Foreign Assistance Act derives from the term "internationally recognized." U.S. law was developed in the context of thirty years of international human rights law based on the Universal Declaration of Human Rights of 1948. It can be persuasively argued that this wording of U.S. law binds us to observe international covenants and treaties on human rights even when these have not been expressly ratified by the United States (see Chapter 2). At the very least it binds the United States to the definition of human rights contained in those documents.

The Reagan administration, however, could not pursue its foreign policy and respect these precedents at the same time. As a former State Department adviser has observed in *Foreign Policy:* "If the definitional priorities of the Foreign Assistance Act were allowed to stand, Marxist governments with repressive but by no means murderous human rights records, such as Poland or Czechoslovakia, would show up as no worse than nominal democracies, such as South Korea or the Philippines; and Nicaragua's Sandinistas would certainly compare favorably with the murderous regimes of Guatemala or El Salvador."[9]

To obscure this contradiction the State Department charged that the law should not be applied simplistically, that realism required supporting a government for "progress" toward respect for human rights even if actual conditions remained poor. This argument could be stretched to find a basis in the law—the Foreign Assistance Act provides that human rights policy "promote and encourage increased respect for human rights and fundamental freedoms"—but in practice it was used to justify rewarding governments that clearly had no interest in protecting such rights and freedoms: in Latin America, the likes of Paraguay, which has endured the rule of a single dictator since 1954, and elsewhere such appalling regimes as that of Turkey, where conditions of political imprisonment are among the worst on earth. Having decided to depart from the terms of the law, the administration also chose to disregard its universal force.

The administration further refined its new approach as it entered a third phase of policymaking toward the end of 1982, following the president's June speech to the British Parliament, in which he called for efforts "to foster the infrastructure of democracy." Asking the question "Must freedom wither—in a quiet, deadening accommodation with totalitarian evil?" [10] and linking current forms of dictatorship to the Soviet Union exclusively, the president stated that resistance, even armed resistance, was in some cases justified. As Senator Christopher Dodd would later observe, the administration had come to define a "new sort of human rights conditions [which] would be the overthrow or changing of Communist governments . . ." [11] as a means of supporting democracy—aggression in the name of human rights. Thus human rights were invoked to justify the October 1983 invasion of Grenada and the covert-overt war against Nicaragua. No longer did the rhetoric of human rights withdraw into demurs about the "limits to what we can and should do." The administration had by now fully committed itself to a double standard.

Under such logic, the U.S. devotion to democracy was not inconsistent with CIA meddling in the Salvadoran elections of 1982 and 1984. Support for democracy was cited to explain why the administration favored multilateral loans to military regimes in Chile, Argentina, and Uruguay. It was used to justify militarizing Honduras, offering unwanted military aid to the new democratic government of Argentina, and failing to speak out on abuses of personal, political, and civil rights by friendly governments generally. To criticize the human rights record of a friendly government—no matter how justified—was seen by the administration as positively encouraging leftist advances in the hemisphere. As Deputy Assistant Secretary of State James Michel would put it, human rights violations by an ally government "serve the common enemy" [12]—rather than criticize it was better to ignore them.

The Human Rights Bureau

In October 1981, the confidential memo's author took for granted that "we will have to speak honestly about our friends' human rights violations. . . . There is no escaping this without destroying the credibility of our policy."[13] Elliott Abrams, who became assistant secretary for human rights, seemed capable of maintaining that credibility. A former aide to Democratic Senators Daniel Patrick Moynihan and Henry Jackson, and familiar with human rights issues from another State Department post in the Reagan administration, Abrams seemed to be equipped for the job and, even more important after the Lefever debacle, was seen as an independent in the Republican ranks, capable of bucking the State Department tide if necessary to promote an autonomous agenda for human rights.

To his credit, Abrams has effectively addressed individual cases of human rights abuse when these have been brought to his attention by nongovernmental groups. With respect to Chile, his objections have prevented the administration from certifying human rights progress and renewing bilateral aid, although he might not have prevailed on this issue without strong congressional backing. His department has obviously put great effort into the annual State Department *Country Reports on Human Rights Practices* (initiated by Congress under the Ford administration and developed further by Carter's human rights secretary, Patricia Derian). Although Americas Watch and other human rights organizations have criticized the contents of the reports in numerous instances, we recognize that under his stewardship, they have reflected effort and thought and have taken on a quality of institutional permanence. Within these limits, the Human Rights Bureau has fulfilled its mandate. Overall, however, the bureau has failed to develop a meaningful human rights policy and indeed has tended to distort and politicize the substance of human rights.

The bureau's agenda on human rights is set out in the introductions to its *Country Reports*. Under the Reagan administration these documents have emphasized some aspects of political rights—as suggested in the 1981 memo—on which all other human rights are deemed dependent. "Political participation," states the introduction for 1982, "is not only an important right in itself, but also the best guarantee that other rights will be observed."[14] The 1983 *Country Reports* raises political rights to a category in itself, on the theory that "political rights tend to determine behavior in many other categories."[15] While the short-term goal is described as improving human rights conditions in various countries, the long-range goal is said to be the "development of democratic governments, which are the surest safeguard of human rights."[16]

Thus the administration developed a two-tiered concept of human rights, such that some rights mean more than others. Democracy, moreover, is treated in its narrowest sense only, defined primarily as a system of periodic, competitive elections—a definition without standing in international human rights instruments. International law suggests no reason why the holding of elections per se should be placed on a higher plane of importance than the rights that elections are intended to protect and enhance—be those the right not to be assassinated, the right not to be abducted and not to "disappear," the right not to be tortured, or any of a host of other rights basic to civilized humanity. (For further discussion of this issue, see Chapter 2.) In practice, elections in much of the world do not necessarily guarantee a democratic society or many basic human rights. But the administration's logic insists on defining the prerequisites for human rights primarily in terms of Western-style democratic forms —not always the same as democratic control—rather than in terms of actual conditions of life. At the same time, this logic can emphasize East/West differences rather than question the performances of allies.

From such a framework has emerged a dubious concept, the "transition to democracy," that situation in which a nondemocratic and unpopular government that abuses its citizens systematically is said to be on the road to elections. Linked to the notion of rewards for "progress," this concept has been liberally applied by Assistant Secretary Abrams and other officials in defense of the "friendly" governments of El Salvador, Chile, Guatemala, and Uruguay in this hemisphere—as well as Turkey, South Korea, and other gross violators of human rights elsewhere—on grounds that they deserve U.S. support for their efforts to move toward the formalities of political participation. In such instances, the administration tends to downplay ongoing abuses, atrocities, and outrages while emphasizing the possibility of formal democracy, or, as in El Salvador, claiming that democracy has been achieved. On an even more tentative plane, these governments' very friendliness toward the United States and their antagonism to the Soviet Union and/or domestic left-wing constituencies are held up as evidence of their preference for democracy over totalitarianism, whatever actual conditions under these governments may be.

As Abrams has explained, "We think that people who are friends of the United States should get some points for that." [17] The language of "democracy" developed by the bureau attempts to give friends the points; it is narrowly conceived and selectively applied, a geopolitical instrument like any other aspect of State Department policymaking.

Abrams himself has contributed to the political tone of human rights discussion by using provocative language to defend "friends" and excoriate their critics. Often he has abandoned facts for personalities and innuendo as his weapons in the "battle of ideas." He has dismissed as "guerrilla sympathizers" the Guatemalan refugees who have told of army massacres; in 1983, he called the continued functioning of far-right Salvadoran death squads the fault of the left "because they like to see Salvadoran society divided." [18] In various *Country Reports* his department has slurred the motives of Latin American human rights organizations, and he has referred to American journalists and religious and secular human rights organizations as "simply yesterday's peace activists in a somewhat more decorous garb." [19] His predecessor he has bullied with equal zeal: In response to her criticism of Reagan's policy toward Argentina under the military, Abrams publicly called Patricia Derian's views "romantic, sentimental, and silly." [20]

This style of argument-by-invective has gone far to create tensions between the administration and human rights advocates both in Congress and in nongovernmental groups. It has also helped lock the assistant secretary into extreme positions as an apologist for the administration. In his published rebuttal to Patricia Derian on Argentina, for example, Abrams went so far as to claim, in support of his indignation, that "we refused to certify Argentina's human rights progress until the inauguration of the democratically elected Alfonsin government" in December 1983.[21] A response from Congressman Michael Barnes, chairman of a subcommittee of the House Foreign Affairs Committee, pointed out that the statement was "a simple falsehood. . . . It was Congress that refused"[22] to countenance certification, despite strong administration pressure.

The bureau's lack of an independent agenda is nowhere more chillingly evident than in its recommendation for a policy to end torture. At hearings before a subcommittee of the House Foreign Affairs Committee in May 1984, Abrams argued that legislation that prohibits aid to train foreign police forces—Section 660 of the Foreign Assistance Act—should be repealed "if the effect of 660 were to block efforts at improving human rights performance. . . . To inculcate in police and security forces more professional standards of conduct is one way, I think, of improving rights performance. . . . "[23]

It need hardly be noted that Latin America's most professional police and armed forces—those of Argentina, Chile, Colombia, Brazil, and comparatively in Central America, Guatemala—have all been, or currently are, engaged in terrible abuses of human rights including torture. In the cases of Chile and Argentina, they have engaged in sophisticated torture—indeed, have utilized torture in a scientific way. In the cases of Colombia, Guatemala, and Chile, these forces are the products of long-term U.S. investments of military aid and counterinsurgency training. The Abrams line of thinking recalls the U.S. Public Safety Program, that civic-action police training program for Latin Americans in the 1960s, which became so identified with brutal interrogation methods—that is, torture—that Congress dissolved it in 1974.

On the other hand, it has been shown repeatedly that where direction from the top prohibits human rights abuse, such abuse declines and often ends, whether or not the police and armed forces are highly professional. In El Salvador at the end of 1983, after Vice President Bush warned military leaders that U.S. aid would stop unless death squads were curbed, death squad killings fell off sharply. In Argentina, under the current democratic government, arbitrary detentions, intimidation, and other violations of human rights, which had been common even in late 1983, when it took office, have virtually ceased. Ending human rights abuse, in other words, is largely a matter of political will. The administration's aid policies, strongly supported by the Human Rights Bureau, refuse to acknowledge this.

U.S. Human Rights Legislation

The administration's aid policy has repeatedly defied the Foreign Assistance Act's legal prohibition on aid to gross violators of human rights, in Latin America and elsewhere. It has also ignored, vetoed, and circumvented other human rights legislation, some of it country-specific and some of it general. The legislation has effectively been stripped of all force whenever its application would have conflicted with overall policy objectives.[24] A few examples:

Section 701 of the International Financial Institutions Act of 1977 requires United States representatives to six multilateral development banks not to support assistance to countries whose governments engage in "a consistent pattern of gross violations of internationally recognized human rights." Gross violations specifically include "torture or cruel, inhuman, or degrading treatment or punishment, prolonged detention without charges, or other flagrant denials of life, liberty, and the security of the person." Beginning in July 1981, the Reagan administration has reversed prior U.S. policy by supporting multilateral bank loans to Uruguay, Chile, El Salvador, Guatemala, Argentina (during the period of military rule), and Paraguay, all countries with consistent records of grave human rights violations. Multilateral loans to these countries between July 1981 and September 1984, virtually all with U.S. support, totaled over $3.94 billion.[25]

Despite the clear mandate of Section 701, Assistant Secretary Abrams told a subcommittee of the House Banking Committee in June 1983 that he did not consider the legislation binding in any sense. "I think [Section] 701 does not call for a decision pattern. It calls for us to try to decide among the various means of influencing human rights conditions in a variety of countries. We have to choose when and where to use tools, including these votes . . . " he said.

In the past seven years, Congress has passed a series of country-specific laws requiring the president to certify compliance with certain conditions before aid can be given to Argentina, Chile, El Salvador, Nicaragua, and Haiti. Of these laws, Section 728 of the Foreign Assistance Act, titled "Human Rights Certification of El Salvador," has received the most attention. Adopted in December 1981 and in effect for two years, the law required, as a precondition to continued aid to El Salvador, that the president certify every 180 days that the government of El Salvador was:

- making a "concerted and significant effort" to comply with internationally recognized human rights;

- achieving "substantial control" over all elements of its armed forces in order to end torture and murder by those forces;

- making "continued progress" in land reform and other economic programs;

- committed to holding free elections and demonstrating "good-faith efforts" to begin discussions with "all major political groups in El Salvador";

- making "good-faith efforts" to investigate and prosecute the cases of Americans who had been killed in El Salvador.

The administration routinely certified that these conditions had been satisfied, despite overwhelming evidence to the contrary. (See Chapter 2 for discussion of the legal mechanism of certification.) In 1982 and 1983, when the law was in effect, the administration thereby succeeded in sending $117.4 million in military aid to the Salvadoran government. In November 1983, moreover, President Reagan pocket-vetoed a law that would have continued certification into 1984—an action that an appeals court later found unconstitutional. In the following year, $196.5 million more in military aid went to El Salvador, although gross violations of human rights continued without early prospect for change.

Human Rights Reporting

Starting with the El Salvador certifications, much of human rights debate since 1982, and much of the administration's self-defense against criticism on human rights, especially in Central America, have centered on disputes over the facts. This in turn has led to controversy over the methods used to gather and interpret human rights data. The administration's attitude on this question has been one of its least constructive and most confrontational.

Beyond the loose characterizations made by Assistant Secretary Abrams, the State Department, in *Country Reports* and other formal ways, has tried to dismiss the documented findings of independent human rights monitors who embarrass U.S. allies as less than serious, describing their data as mere allegations even when abuses are obvious and relatively well known. In countries where friendly armed forces are violating human rights, the U.S. embassy avoids contact with domestic human rights monitors, sending a signal to local powers that these groups enjoy no concern of the United States.

In some especially delicate cases, an embassy and the State Department have sought to discredit local human rights groups directly, attacking their findings and impugning their motives. The prime example has been human rights groups in El Salvador, in particular the legal aid/human rights monitoring office of the archdiocese of San Salvador, which, for over two years, has had to defend itself against not only the hostility of the security forces but that of the United States as well.[26]

By contrast, the Bureau of Human Rights has functioned as promotional agent and appointments secretary for the U.S. visits of anti-Sandinista rebel representatives, whom it presents as neutral sources on human rights in Nicaragua. The double standard is similarly evident with regard to international bodies and their research. On Guatemala, for example, the 1983 *Country Reports* made much of the upbeat conclusions (later repudiated by the U.N. Human Rights Commission) prepared by a U.N. Rapporteur (Special Observer) while playing down the critical findings of investigators from the OAS.

The State Department's lack of credence for many human rights monitors is not balanced by equivalent independent research of its own. For its *Country Reports* and general positions the department relies most heavily on local U.S. embassies, which have neither the staff nor the time nor the contact with local people that are essential for serious investigation. They typically rely upon a pool of contacts predominantly in or close to the government and armed forces and upon the press, which may be censored, "advised" what to print, or censoring itself for fear of punishment.

Embassy staff, who may have many other duties, rarely conduct on-site human rights inspections, especially in zones outside of capital cities that may be difficult to reach and, in situations of internal conflict, are very likely to be dangerous. Even in the case of a reported large massacre with policy implications, their examination of the evidence may be cursory at best, as in regard to the so-called Mozote massacre, named for one of nine Salvadoran hamlets where the army—including a U.S.-trained battalion—murdered at least seven hundred peasants in December 1981. Embassy staff sent to investigate, one month after the fact, could not approach the area on foot because of combat; instead they flew over in a helicopter, and on that basis they decided that no massacre had taken place.

Assistant Secretary of State Thomas Enders then told a congressional committee that the embassy had "found no evidence"[27] of civilian deaths, without revealing the limits of its efforts. And this takes abstraction from reality one step farther, for the final issue is less an embassy's failure to produce reliable human rights material on its own, than the way its superiors deal with that state of affairs. It would be unrealistic to demand of embassies that they investigate with the thoroughness of a full-time human rights organization, or that they cease to be a political arm of the U.S. government, identified with and guided by its policies.

But the State Department has been thoroughly cynical in its use of embassy information. Where convenient, it has ignored or contradicted embassy findings—for example, when it has accused Nicaragua of systematic torture and of anti-Semitism, though the embassy in Managua had found no evidence to support those accusations, or when it has misrepresented embassy findings in El Salvador. (See sections in Chapter 4 on El Salvador and Nicaragua.) On the other hand, where embassy positions better reflect U.S. strategic interests than the findings of specialized human rights groups, the administration argues for the superiority of embassy research in spite of its weak methodology and limited scope.

It is no coincidence that such manipulation of fact—and of public perception—has taken place primarily in regard to countries of strategic or political-image importance to this administration. The effort to present its own investigations of these countries as superior to those of local and international human rights groups is part and parcel of the "battle of ideas"—the battle to persuade a public generally "soft" on human rights that the political and military hard line is justified and that groups who present a different picture are working from political bias. Rather than proving its points with clear evidence, the administration has relied instead on the credibility attached to office and has thrown that weight, full force, against the reputations of those whose own credibility—in some cases considerable—depends on reliable research and the appearance, as well as the fact, of nonpartisanship.

In September 1982, for example, during a period of massive political killings in Guatemala and of delicate U.S.-Guatemalan rapprochement, the State Department decided to set its embassy's credibility against that of Amnesty International. The human rights organization had recently published a report based on official as well as nonofficial sources finding that the Guatemalan government of General Efrain Rios Montt was condoning mass killings in rural areas, as previous governments had done. In a letter to an executive of Amnesty International, Assistant Secretary Enders stated that the organization's reporting "appears to contrast greatly" with embassy information and that the Rios Montt government had "made significant progress" on human rights. The letter contended that a town called Covadonga, which AI had named as the site of extrajudicial executions, "doesn't appear on any map available to the embassy," a careful phrase that implied that the deaths, like the town, had been fabricated. An appendix to the letter disputed seven specific incidents of deaths reported by AI on which the embassy had "sharply contrasting" data.[28]

The embassy's map apparently was incomplete: Covadonga does exist and was known to personnel of U.S. AID; it would appear that the embassy had failed to consult anyone truly knowledgeable about the country. In addition, the seven incidents, when examined, were not subject to any significant dispute: In four of them, embassy accounts (based primarily on newspaper stories) tended to confirm Amnesty's conclusions, although AI's information was the more detailed; in two more, Amnesty attributed the killings to neither side in the conflict—and therefore took no position for the State Department to legitimately contest. (In the seventh incident, AI blamed the army, based on eyewitness testimony.)

Why this fight had been picked where none was warranted became evident when the embassy in Guatemala circulated the letter to the local press as if it were a public document rather than private correspondence. The embassy treated the critique of Amnesty as an official handout, citing it to explain why the administration would not be dissuaded from its support of Rios Montt and his "significant progress" on human rights. An October 1982 Americas Watch delegation to Guatemala found "this use of the letter unconscionable in light of the risks run by human rights investigators in a political climate like Guatemala's" and called it evidence that, for the State Department, "the bringer of bad news becomes . . . part of the enemy, to be discredited if possible." [29]

If more proof of malice were needed, the State Department would offer it two months later with the preparation of a paper titled "Guatemala: Human Rights Analysis." Intended for public circulation, this shoddy document purported to examine the sources and reports of Amnesty, the Washington Office on Latin America (an organization supported by several Protestant churches), and two smaller groups concerned solely with Guatemala. Its principal conclusion, contained in its opening paragraph, was that "a concerted disinformation campaign . . . by groups supporting the left-wing insurgency in Guatemala . . . has enlisted the support" of the groups under study. The alleged campaign's purpose was to deny U.S. weapons to the Guatemalan army by accusing it of human rights abuses, and the document implicitly questioned the investigators' "allegiance" while admitting that, in fact, "the Guatemalan army has indeed committed some atrocities."

With regard to all the groups, it was riddled with unsupported and misleading assumptions on methodology and sources, and it repeated a false charge made in the Enders letter, that Amnesty International had refused an official Guatemalan invitation to visit and investigate (Amnesty had received no such invitation, though it had communicated an interest in one). Shown to human rights advocates who pointed out its myriad errors, the paper was not released to the press as planned, because it was potentially more embarrassing to its authors than to its targets.*

---

* The *Washington Post*, however, did obtain a copy and published excerpts.

Amnesty International can withstand such pressure, but small local groups in Latin America, already functioning with little money and less security, are much more vulnerable. The State Department's hostile stance has a chilling effect on independent human rights research not only in El Salvador and Guatemala but also, by their example, throughout the hemisphere. To equate the publication of facts embarrassing to a government with an attempt to overthrow or replace that government, as the State Department has done repeatedly in El Salvador and occasionally in other countries such as Chile,* is not only deliberately misleading and unjust to the groups in question but also an attempt to censor the debate on human rights where it is most necessary—to intimidate, and thus to silence, those who labor in the harshest conditions and thereby perform the most essential service.

Democracy and Double Standards

The administration's taste for military ties and East-West rhetoric often obscures the fact that in Latin America there are democracies that truly deserve support but whose problems are not susceptible to rhetoric or military hardware. Argentina, now under civilian rule, is one such country, where economic needs are paramount and the administration prefers to peddle arms. In Colombia the case is more complex but no less appropriate: In 1984 the popular president, Belisario Betancur, arrived at limited-term cease-fire agreements with guerrillas, whose activity for many years had given the army a rationale, or pretext, for violence

* The 1983 *Country Report* on Chile contained this sentence on p. 504: "The Chilean Commission for Human Rights . . . openly devotes its efforts not only to human rights issues but to bringing about major changes in the nature of the Government." The commission has protested this characterization of its monitoring work to the Bureau of Human Rights, and its representatives have pointed out that even its relations with the Chilean military government are based on a better understanding of its function and methodology than this sentence suggests to be the case with the United States. The commission is one of the most respected human rights organizations in Latin America.

against civilians. Colombia was offered the possibility of
peace, and Latin America was offered a model of negotiation. Rather than treat this development as the landmark it
was, the State Department said only, "We hope that these
agreements will contribute to the rule of law in Colombia."
Rather than give Colombia the economic aid it has so badly
needed to develop the basis for peace, on the other hand,
this administration has multiplied U.S. aid to the armed
forces, even when their abuses were widespread and their
hostility to Betancur was manifest.

While the administration has been supporting, aiding, and
apologizing for Latin American allies who violate human
rights, it has spared no effort to criticize and undermine the
Sandinista regime in Nicaragua, to which it is hostile, although human rights conditions there have been far from
the worst in the hemisphere and have even shown some
signs of genuine improvement. Its attitude toward human
rights monitors in Nicaragua is friendly; its promotion of
anti-Sandinista spokespersons claiming to be human rights
monitors has been notable. Its program of assistance to the
contras seeking to overthrow the Nicaraguan government
contrasts sharply with its portrayal of the Salvadoran, Guatemalan, or Colombian guerrillas as terrorists and its casual
use of words such as "terrorism" to describe opposition
movements elsewhere. The Nicaraguan elections of 1984
were dismissed as a fraud even before the registration period
began.

So consistent is this double standard that it can be fairly
said the Reagan administration has no true human rights
policy. It has, rather, what the October 1981 memo warned
against: "something we tack on to our foreign policy,"[30] a
rhetoric of convenience. But if, as officials argue, the test is
effectiveness, it is worth examining what pursuit of the double standard adds up to in Latin America.

If the measure is cooperation for economic betterment,
this administration's record is controversial; it has essentially
abandoned the pursuit of economic improvements through
social investment—cutting back on basic-needs economic
aid, promoting a market approach and internal austerity pro-

grams—while favoring support for the military and for national-security arguments to explain and overcome social unrest. If the measure, on the other hand, is promotion of U.S. strategic goals, the results must be seen as mixed, especially in Central America, where victory has been elusive, but also less obviously in the ill will that has been sown among popular movements and leaders in much of the hemisphere. When Raul Alfonsin prepared for his inauguration as Argentina's first civilian president in seven years, he made no special gestures to current U.S. officials but invited Patricia Derian, assistant secretary of state for human rights for the Carter administration, to be his guest. He apparently did not recall the previous administration's policy as "romantic" or "silly"; nor would many other Argentines.

If, finally, the measure is the promotion of democratic rule —even in the administration's narrow understanding of the term—it has less of a track record than it claims, and not all of it good. Consider the introduction to the 1983 *Country Reports*, which points to an "accelerated"[31] process of democratization in Latin America since Reagan's advent, credited in part to U.S. policies of encouragement and example. "Between 1976 and 1980," it states, "only one Latin American nation, Ecuador, elected a civilian president to replace the military. Since 1980, however, nine . . . have either held free elections, or declared their intention of doing so. . . . "[32] The year 1980, of course, was still during the Carter administration, though this wording tries to claim it for Reagan. And leaving aside any dispute about the "freedom" of elections in El Salvador and elsewhere, the statement deliberately misleads by mixing apples with oranges: The landmark Dominican election of 1978 is excluded from the first period because it was civilian-to-civilian, while in the second period, "intention" counts as accomplishment.

An examination of the nine countries deemed to have been helped toward elections by this administration is more instructive. They are listed as Argentina, Bolivia, Brazil, El Salvador, Guatemala, Honduras, Panama, Peru, and Uruguay. But with the exception of El Salvador, the administration cannot honestly take credit for elections in these countries. The Honduran, Brazilian, Peruvian, and Bolivian processes toward elections got under way before the change of administrations and must be linked to Carter if to any U.S. leader. The 1981 Honduran elections were, in fact, one of the Carter administration's success stories, so much so that the new administration did not replace Carter's well-respected ambassador there until after the vote. As for Bolivia, this administration was initially so hostile to the elected left-of-center president, Hernan Siles Zuazo, that to his 1982 inauguration they refused to send anyone even as senior as an assistant secretary of state.

Guatemala remained under extremely brutal military rule, such that even its inclusion in the list showed contempt for the truth. Argentina's return to democracy had resulted more from defeat in the Falklands/Malvinas war, and the nation's economic problems, and public outrage over human rights abuses, than from the Reagan administration's policy toward the military regime, which was one of consistent support and apology. The U.S. role in Uruguay has been first to give support to military hard-liners, then when elections were imminent, to promote one candidate at the expense of others. And in the elections of two other countries, El Salvador and Panama, there has been illegal interference by agencies using U.S. funds to support candidates —not a fact to be proud of.*

In sum, the Reagan administration has used the considerable tools at its command to render human rights a marginal concern in U.S.-Latin America relations. U.S. prestige, economic power, military aid, decades of predominant influence in the hemisphere, and the executive branch's mandate

---

* As noted previously, CIA funds have reportedly been spent to "aid" the Salvadoran elections of 1982 and 1984, in the latter instance to undermine a candidate, Roberto D'Aubuisson, whose victory would have imperiled congressional support for aid to the Salvadoran military. In Panama's 1984 presidential elections, a candidate received $20,000 from the AFL-CIO, which in turn had received the funds from the newly established National Endowment for Democracy. On learning of the interference, Congress sharply reduced 1985 appropriations to the endowment, which was to have been the fountainhead of promoting democracy, projected in President Reagan's London speech.

to direct the making of foreign policy—all have been combined to pursue the Santa Fe document's version of ethical realism. In practice this has meant that allies of an all-too-often abusive kind are helped, promoted, and misrepresented, while their critics are accused of abetting the enemy, and neutrality is not allowed.

The administration has manipulated U.S. public concern for human rights with a certain skill, always identifying its perspective with a tradition of democratic values of which that public is proud. That its manipulation has served to confuse the issues for Americans is only one effect and perhaps the least damaging; the offensive it has launched to distort the nature of human rights—and the integrity of human rights advocates—has also had a profound indirect impact on human rights in the most controversial countries, where the armed forces and other agents of abuse take U.S. signals to mean no target is off limits, no number of deaths will diminish U.S. support.

There have been exceptions, of course—Vice President Bush's warning the Salvadoran military to stop the death squads; the noncertifications of Chile and, for a decent interval, Argentina. Not only are these few and far between, however; they are also mainly the result of public and congressional pressure, and amount to concessions offered in exchange for a minimum of credibility.

This administration is at home with confrontation, often resorting to it, rarely condemning it. Dialogue, on the other hand, is not its way, either with protesters in Latin America or with its own critics at home. The long-term solution, the program for reform, have little appeal compared with the "Third World War" and all that such a phrase implies of victories, decisions, quick solutions. To the extent that human rights have been a factor in policy toward Latin America, they have served as weapon in a "battle of ideas" within that larger war. In wars, of course, there are always casualties; it has often been said that truth is the first.

2

THE LAW AND
LAWLESSNESS

Not until after World War II
was it widely accepted that the way governments deal with
their own citizens is a matter of legitimate concern to citizens and governments elsewhere. The idea gained support
at that time because of what the Nazis had done to Jews,
leftists, and others in lands they controlled and because it
became apparent that how a government acts inside its own
borders may ultimately affect world peace. Accordingly, the
United Nations Charter, adopted in 1945, provided that "the
United Nations shall promote universal respect for, and ob-
servance of, human rights and fundamental freedoms for all
without distinction as to race, sex, language, or religion."[1]
This, Article 55, was the foundation of international law
seeking to protect human rights. Further to establish the
responsibility of governments to promote respect for human
rights by other governments, the U.N. Charter provided that
"all members pledge themselves to take joint and separate
action in cooperation with the Organization for the achievement of the purposes set forth in Article 55."[2]

The international community has since adopted a considerable number of agreements that define what is meant by

"human rights and fundamental freedoms."* These are "binding"—as international law—on those governments that have signed and, where appropriate, ratified them. More important, since there is, as yet, little international machinery to enforce this body of law, the agreements have established a series of internationally accepted norms, or standards, against which governments' practices can be measured.

Although the laws carry no penalty, a government that systematically and intransigently violates these standards may be embarrassed by international criticism, diplomatically isolated at the U.N. on human rights grounds—as Chile, El Salvador, and Guatemala have been—or, like South Africa, may become a political pariah.

History and Basic Principles

The Universal Declaration of Human Rights—though not precisely an agreement among nations, in the sense that it was adopted by the United Nations but not presented to member nations for signature and ratification—is perhaps the single most important source of international norms on human rights. Like England's Magna Carta, the English Bill of Rights in 1689, the American Declaration of Independence, and the French Declaration of the Rights of Man, the historical circumstances of its adoption are the main source of its significance. It was proclaimed in 1948 at a time of great hope for the development of a world community that would come to abide by its principles, and it has come to symbolize that spirit of hope. No nation voted against it,

* These include the Convention on the Prevention and Punishment of Genocide (1948); the Convention Relating to the Status of Refugees (1951); the Standard Minimum Rules for the Treatment of Prisoners (1955); the International Convention on the Elimination of All Forms of Racial Discrimination (1955); the International Covenant on Economic, Social, and Cultural Rights (1966); the International Covenant on Civil and Political Rights (1966); The European Convention on Human Rights (1953); the American Convention on Human Rights (1969); the Helsinki accords (1975); and the African Charter on Human and People's Rights (1981).

although there were abstentions from the Soviet bloc countries, South Africa, and Saudi Arabia.

Some of the principles that the Universal Declaration proclaims internationally are analogous to those embodied in the United States Constitution: the right to live; the right to equal protection of the laws; a prohibition on slavery; a prohibition on torture or cruel punishments; a prohibition against arbitrary arrest, detention, or exile; the right to a fair trial and the right to be presumed innocent until proven guilty; a right to privacy; freedom of expression and assembly; freedom of religion; and a right to take part in government through periodic elections. In addition, the Universal Declaration proclaims a series of social and economic rights that are not recognized in the U.S. Constitution, including a right to an education and a "right to a standard of living adequate for health and well-being."

Some of the principles of the Universal Declaration enjoy more widespread acceptance than others. Though the United States, in the person of Eleanor Roosevelt, helped to draft the Universal Declaration, and voted for it, the United States has never accepted that economic questions, such as employment and standard of living, should be considered legal rights. Many countries, including the Soviet Union, reject the political rights to which the United States is committed, such as freedom of expression and periodic elections, but consider that people should enjoy economic rights. Rights to personal security, on the other hand, such as the right to live and the right not to be tortured, are universally accepted; that is, virtually every government, whatever its practices, professes to respect these rights.

Although specific enforcement mechanisms have not been created, the universal acceptance of certain principles has legal significance in another sense. These principles are part of what is considered "customary international law." Just as the common law of England developed over centuries before England had a legislature, so customary international law has developed in the absence of a world legislature. It is accepted by the domestic courts of many nations, including the courts of the United States. As the Supreme Court of the United States has held, "where there is no treaty, and no controlling executive or legislative act or judicial decision, resort must be had to the customs and usages of civilized nations."[3] Citing that language, a United States court of appeals decided in 1980 that a former Paraguayan police officer who had immigrated to the United States could be sued in the courts of the United States for torturing someone to death in Paraguay because various international agreements and declarations had become part of customary international law and "official torture is now prohibited by the law of nations."[4]

Long before it was widely accepted that the way governments treat their own people is of international concern, international law was regulating the conduct of wars, to limit their ferocity. Rules to govern warfare are discussed in ancient texts of several civilizations, East and West, and some of these helped to shape the thinking of a seventeenth-century Dutch lawyer, Hugo Grotius, who wrote a magisterial three-volume work, *On the Law of War and Peace*. Grotius's writings are the starting points for the development of the modern laws of war.

A number of international agreements setting standards for the conduct of wars were adopted in the nineteenth century and in the early twentieth.* These applied only to conflicts between two or more governments that had signed such agreements. The "laws or customs of war," under which the Nazi defendants at Nuremberg were convicted, had been established by these agreements.

In essence, the laws of war had provided that belligerents are justified in using any amount of force that is necessary to subdue the enemy. This is known as the principle of military necessity. On the other hand, belligerents may not deliberately use any amount of force that is not necessary for the purpose of war—such as violence against civilians taking no part in hostilities, against the sick, the wounded, against belligerents who have laid down their arms to surrender, or

---

* These include the Geneva conventions of 1864 and 1929 and the Hague conventions of 1899 and 1907.

against prisoners of war. This is known as the principle of humanity.

At Nuremberg, the Nazis were also tried for crimes against peace for waging aggressive warfare, and for crimes against humanity. The concept of crimes against humanity was new and was intended to cover crimes that were entirely independent of the war and that no conception of military necessity could sustain.

It was objected at the time and also later that, whatever authority an international tribunal might have to try the Nazis for violating the laws of war that had been previously adopted by international agreement, the tribunal lacked authority to put anyone on trial for crimes that had never previously been established by international agreement and, thereby, made subject to international jurisdiction. In response, it was argued—and accepted by the tribunal at Nuremberg—that there is a principle of universal jurisdiction against those who commit crimes against humanity. This is similar to a principle in traditional international law, under which a pirate is considered *hostis humani generis*: The pirate commits his crime on the high seas and, therefore, outside the territory covered by the laws of any particular country, but he is considered "the enemy of all alike" and may be judged by all. Similarly, it is argued, those who commit crimes against humanity are the enemy of all, and all have the right and, indeed, the responsibility to judge them.

In our time, the controversy over jurisdiction to try crimes against humanity has been echoed in Argentina. Before yielding power in December 1983, the Argentine armed forces purported to apply amnesty to themselves for crimes committed during the "dirty war" against subversion of the 1970s, in an effort to deprive the successor civilian government of jurisdiction to place those responsible on trial. (See the section on Argentina in Chapter Three.) The National Commission on Disappeared Persons, which was established by President Alfonsin soon after he took office, issued a report documenting the disappearance and murder of some nine thousand persons and describing these cases—pursued in a coordinated, systematic campaign—as "crimes against

prevent the executive branch from repeating such policies. At the same time, adoption of these laws reflected the view held by many in Congress that the human rights issue could be used effectively to distinguish the United States and some of its allies from the Soviet Union and countries aligned with it. The coalescence of those seeking to distance the United States from governments such as those in South Vietnam and Chile and those seeking to provide the United States with an advantage in competition with the Soviet bloc—the two groups overlapped somewhat—provided a majority, and an important series of laws became binding on the United States specifically.

These measures required that various forms of U.S. assistance should be denied to governments that "engage in a consistent practice of gross violations of internationally recognized human rights." Accordingly, even though the United States itself has not ratified the international agreements in which these rights are enumerated, the law of the United States acknowledges that these rights are "internationally recognized" and requires that U.S. foreign policy be conditioned accordingly. This language appears, among other places, in the laws prohibiting security assistance to abusive governments;[7] denying them economic assistance;[8] and denying U.S. support for multilateral development bank loans to them.[9]

Some of the laws spell out what is meant by "gross violations of internationally recognized human rights." These include, according to the law regulating economic assistance, "torture or cruel, inhuman, or degrading treatment or punishment, prolonged detention without charges, causing the disappearance of persons by the abduction or clandestine detention of those persons, or other flagrant denial of the right to life, liberty, and the security of the person."[10]

Recognizing that general prohibitions might not be sufficiently respected by the executive branch, and in an effort to modify particular abuses in certain countries, Congress since 1981 has also adopted a series of what are known as "country-specific" laws conditioning U.S. assistance on human rights performance. Typically, these require that the president certify that certain conditions have been met, such as an end to death squad activity, or that a government has accounted for the disappeared, or that prisoners held without charges have been released or tried. Assistance is withheld unless and until there is such a certification.

The certification itself is a document presented to Congress, which explains the president's reasons for offering U.S. assistance to the government in question. Congress has no authority to challenge a certification as such, but—as with any other aid proposal—it may cut the requested funds from the foreign assistance legislation. In practice, it has never done this; any political battles over a certification have been fought before certification was made, in the interests of avoiding major voting battles over foreign aid. Yet an unwarranted certification can realistically be fought only in Congress, because enforcement of human rights laws through litigation has not been possible; Americans cannot demonstrate that they themselves are directly affected to the extent necessary to give them the requisite legal standing to sue. Moreover, even if the problem of standing could be overcome, the courts would be reluctant to rule on such matters because of the traditional deference they give to the executive branch on matters involving foreign policy. This has allowed the Reagan administration to get away with its disregard of these laws, yet that has not made them entirely useless. The certification law regarding El Salvador[11] is a case in point.

Because El Salvador has been of utmost political importance to the Reagan administration, it was always a foregone conclusion that the president would certify. Yet the disregard of the law in that act has forced the Reagan administration to modify its policies in areas that are less significant to it. Accordingly, the administration did not certify Argentina while the generals held power and, at this writing, has not yet certified Chile as eligible for military assistance. The laws establishing certification of compliance with human rights conditions as a prerequisite for military assistance to these two countries[12] were enacted at the same time as the law dealing with certification of El Salvador. The Reagan administration had made plain its interest in ending the U.S. arms embargo against Argentina and Chile and, at least in the case of Argentina under the generals, repeatedly announced its plans to certify. Ultimately, however, it did not do so until the day President Alfonsin took office, and it has not yet done so in the case of Chile because the administration feared this would offend some members of Congress, damaging its efforts to maintain congressional support for military assistance to El Salvador.

Even in the case of El Salvador itself, the certification law has had some effect. To try to enhance the credibility of its periodic certifications, the Reagan administration put pressure on the Salvadoran government to end certain kinds of abuses. When the Reagan administration decided to rid itself of the certification requirement by a pocket veto of its extension in November 1983,* it found that it had to couple this with a demonstration that it was securing an improvement of the human rights situation in El Salvador in other ways. The fact that this was the moment the administration chose to acknowledge, at last, the links between the Salvadoran death squads and the security forces, and to launch a campaign to reduce death squad killings (see the section on El Salvador in Chapter 4), probably was not coincidental.

The Reagan administration has evaded the certification requirements on El Salvador largely by arguing that the country is democratic and that promoting democratic government is the best way to secure protection of human rights. Whether or not this is valid in theory, democratic government—at the least in the sense of periodic elections to which the Reagan administration attaches particular significance—does not occupy a central place in either international or U.S. law concerned with human rights. The emphasis in both international and domestic law is on the rights of the person against arbitrary deprivation of life or

---

* The U.S. Court of Appeals for the District of Columbia subsequently ruled the pocket veto in this case to be unconstitutional.

liberty and against maltreatment.* United States laws that apply to our relations with countries worldwide are silent on the subject of electoral democracy. The question is dealt with only in certain country-specific laws, such as those dealing with U.S. aid to El Salvador, Haiti, Nicaragua, and Pakistan.

Internal War and Human Rights

The Reagan administration's policy has been out of step with both international and domestic law on human rights in another respect as well: its denunciation of certain human rights groups for monitoring abuses of rights by governments only—that is, for not also publishing reports on abuses by antigovernment groups. (The Reagan administration has been selective in criticizing human rights groups; it has attempted to discredit a Salvadoran group for only monitoring governmental abuses but has had only praise for a Nicaraguan group that followed a similar practice.) Leaving aside for the moment the Geneva conventions, international agreements on human rights apply only to governments. U.S. laws, too, apply only to governments. Abuses by those not connected to governments are considered common crimes. International and domestic human rights laws rest on the assumption that, while governments can be trusted

---

* International law of worldwide application does attempt to protect the freedoms to speak, assemble, and publish that are essential if democratic elections are to take place. On the other hand, international law permits the suspension of these rights in time of public emergency that threatens the life of the nation to the extent required by the emergency.[13] Personal security rights, such as those seeking to protect individuals from arbitrary deprivation of life or torture, may never be suspended.[14] Domestic U.S. human rights law (with the exception of certain country-specific laws) is silent about freedom of expression, conditioning U.S. assistance on the way other countries respect personal security. As is obvious, of course, such violations of personal security as murder and torture are generally practiced by governments as a way of punishing those who express views that governments find obnoxious. In that respect, the inviolability of certain rights of personal security under international law and under U.S. law seeking to promote compliance with international law represents an attempt to protect freedom of expression. Yet it is not expression itself that is absolutely protected, only the right not to be subjected to gross abuses in reprisal for expression.

to try to prosecute those committing common crimes, they cannot be trusted to prosecute themselves for their own crimes. Accordingly, these must be dealt with by setting international standards, monitoring abuses, and taking into account the crimes of a government in the conduct of intergovernmental relations.

Following World War II, when numerous wars were being fought by indigenous peoples seeking to free themselves from colonial powers, the laws of war were also made applicable to "the case of armed conflict not of an international character occurring in the territory of one of the High Contracting Parties." This language, which appears in Article 3 in each of the four Geneva conventions of 1949 * (accordingly known as "Common Article 3"), has become a crucial part of the international system for the protection of human rights because many of the most serious abuses of our time take place during civil wars or armed conflicts within a nation. Moreover, virtually every country in the world has signed and ratified the Geneva conventions, making them, at least on paper, almost universally binding.

The Geneva conventions do apply to both sides in certain kinds of conflicts. As defined in Protocol II (adopted in 1977), conflicts covered are those that "take place in the territory of a High Contracting Party between its armed forces and dissident armed forces or other organized armed groups which, under responsible command, exercise such control over a part of its territory as to enable them to carry out sustained and concerted military operations and to implement this Protocol." [15] In effect, this language helps to define when an opposition force in an internal conflict is considered "belligerent" under international law. The protocol goes on to specify that it does "not apply to situations of internal disturbances and tensions, such as riots, isolated and sporadic acts of violence and other acts of a similar nature, as not being armed conflicts." [16]

From the standpoint of those trying to monitor human

* The four conventions deal, respectively, with the treatment of the wounded and sick in the field; the wounded and sick shipwrecked at sea; prisoners of war; and the protection of civilians in times of war.

rights internationally, the distinction between organized armed conflict and sporadic violence makes a great deal of sense. Where belligerent groups control territory and carry out sustained operations, the enforcement of domestic law is not an effective way of punishing abuses. Accordingly, the same devices used to deter abuses by governments—that is, monitoring abuses, measuring them against international norms, and thereby embarrassing those responsible—are the only effective means of curbing such abuses. Belligerent groups conducting sustained operations, such as the FMLN in El Salvador or the *contras* combatting the government of Nicaragua, typically seek international recognition and support and, therefore, denunciations of their abuses of human rights may have a significant effect on their practices. Moreover, the requirements in the protocol that it should apply only in situations where such groups are "under responsible command" makes it clear that it is meant to deal with cases in which there is a leadership that could be affected by denunciations. In contrast, it would be fruitless for those concerned with international human rights to monitor abuses committed during riots or sporadic acts of violence. There is no leadership with control that would be embarrassed by denunciations; international support for rioters or small groups of terrorists is either not a factor, or it would not be affected by denunciations by human rights groups; and governments that control the territory in which such violence takes place can be trusted to make every effort to punish those involved. Moreover, groups monitoring human rights should avoid elevating rioters and terrorists to the status of belligerents recognized in international law.

In the case of El Salvador in particular, the United States has tended to ignore the requirements of the Geneva conventions in attempting to justify the conduct of the Salvadoran armed forces. The conventions prohibit attacks on the civilian population and prohibit acts or threats of violence intended to spread terror among civilians. They assert that civilians are entitled to protection "unless and for such time as they take a direct part in hostilities."[17] In contrast, the Department of State has, at least at times, justified attacks on civilians on the ground that they are *masas*—civilian supporters of the guerrillas and therefore "something other than innocent civilian bystanders."[18]

Other provisions of the Geneva conventions that have been repeatedly violated in El Salvador have been those forbidding mistreatment of prisoners of war[19] and those involving provision of medical care for the sick and wounded without distinction.[20] The State Department has claimed not to know how the Salvadoran army treats its prisoners, and it has excused the armed forces' attacks on doctors. One such case involved Dr. Angel Ibarra, medical director of the camps for displaced persons operated by the Lutheran Church in El Salvador. Dr. Ibarra was abducted by the National Police on April 26, 1983, and, after a period in which he could not be located, he was eventually found in the custody of the National Police, who had severely tortured him.

When a representative of Americas Watch called a high official of the State Department's Human Rights Bureau to inquire about the Ibarra case, the official asserted, "I hear they got him dead to rights." Asked what this meant, the official said that Ibarra had been caught giving medical treatment to guerrillas. Asked if he was aware of the provisions of the Geneva conventions dealing with medical care, the official responded, "I'm not a lawyer. I don't know anything about that."[21]

Protocol II additionally requires, "The displacement of the civilian population shall not be ordered for reasons related to the conflict unless the security of the civilians involved or imperative military reasons so demand."[22] The Reagan administration has raised no protest against gross violations of this provision by its allies, such as the massive relocations of hundreds of thousands that have been carried out by the armed forces in Guatemala in 1982–84. These were related to that nation's internal conflict, in the sense that they were intended to establish effective systems of long-term official control, but they were not dictated either by concern for the security of the civilians involved or by imperative military reasons. While failing to speak out on these events, the Reagan administration has been unrelenting in its attacks on the forced relocation of a much smaller number of Indians by the Nicaraguan government, even though the latter reloca- tion apparently was dictated by imperative military reasons when border attacks by the *contras* began to mount.

Disregard for the Geneva conventions and protocols, as well as domestic U.S. law, was also evident in a manual prepared by the Central Intelligence Agency for use by the *contras*. The manual, titled "Psychological Operations in Guerrilla Warfare," came to light in October 1984. It advises the *contras* "to neutralize carefully selected and planned tar- gets such as court judges, *mesta** judges, police and State Security officials, CDS [local Sandinista organizations] chiefs, etc."[23] The manual goes on to make it clear that "neutralize" means kill by advising the *contras* "to gather together the population affected, so that they will be present, take part in the act" and to insure that "the person who will replace the target should be chosen carefully."[24] In addition, the manual advises the *contras* how to justify the need "to fire on a citizen who was trying to leave the town or city in which the guerrillas are carrying out armed propaganda or political proselytism";[25] use "professional criminals . . . to carry out specific jobs";[26] and infiltrate peaceful demonstra- tions with men who "should be equipped with weapons (knives, razors, chains, clubs, bludgeons) and should march slightly behind the innocent and gullible participants."[27] All of these recommendations, and many more, demonstrate contempt for the laws of war which are binding on the United States and which seek to protect civilians taking no active part in hostilities.

Domestic U.S. law was violated in the call that appears in the manual to the *contras* to "overthrow" and "replace" the Sandinista government. The Boland Amendment, which be- came part of U.S. law in December 1982, prohibits the use of U.S. funds to overthrow the government of Nicaragua or to provoke a military exchange between Nicaragua and Hon-

---

* *Mesta:* a word used in Nicaragua to mean local officials who are roughly comparable to justices of the peace.

duras. In adopting the Boland Amendment, Congress took the Reagan administration at its word: that U.S. support for the *contras* was intended to disrupt the flow of arms from Nicaragua to the Salvadoran guerrillas. The manual never mentions the matter of arms shipments.

Preparation and distribution of the manual also violated President Reagan's own executive order prohibiting the C.I.A. from taking part in assassinations or requesting others to engage in assassinations. A similar prohibition on assassinations had been ordered by President Reagan's predecessor, President Carter, and by his predecessor, President Ford, who acted after the U.S. Senate Select Committee to Study Government Operations with Respect to Intelligence—known as the Church Committee—issued a report in 1975 documenting C.I.A. efforts to assassinate the leaders of several foreign governments.

The revelation of the contents of the manual was dramatic evidence that, in its conduct of the war against Nicaragua, the C.I.A. had reverted to the lawlessness that characterized many of its operations for two and a half decades prior to the Church Committee investigation.

If anything, the contempt for law that is reflected in the manual was exceeded by William J. Casey, director of Central Intelligence, in an October 25, 1984, letter attempting to defend the publication of the manual. The letter, which was sent to the members of the House and Senate Intelligence committees after the manual came to light, approvingly quotes a passage from the manual which justifies the practices it recommends on the ground that, "while not desirable, [they are] necessary because the final objective of the insurrection is a free and democratic society where acts of force are not necessary."[28] In other words, the end justifies any means at all, and certainly nothing so trivial as law—U.S. or international—should be a constraint.

The Basis of Policy

There is, of course, room for a great deal of debate about how best to go about promoting human rights in other coun-

tries, and about the place that human rights should have in
the formulation of U.S. foreign policy, especially in relation
to such other national interests as security and trade. When
it comes to the law, however, the scope of debate should
narrow and should be restricted only to what is meant by the
law. From time to time, the Reagan administration has attempted to justify its violations of laws by quarreling with
human rights advocates over the meaning of the laws. Yet
some of its interpretations are so ludicrous that it is difficult
to take them seriously.

It is impossible to take seriously an argument for the support of loans to Chile, where torture has been practiced systematically for more than a decade, when U.S. law prohibits
such loans to a government that engages in a consistent
practice of gross violations of human rights. It is impossible
to take seriously an argument for redefining trucks and jeeps
sold to Guatemala as something other than "security assistance." It is impossible to take seriously an argument for
repeated certification that El Salvador was achieving control
over all elements of its armed forces to end torture and murder by those forces when those forces were torturing and
murdering thousands. It is impossible to take seriously an
argument for indiscriminate attacks on civilians that rests on
labeling those civilians *masas*.

Possibly the most disturbing a⋅   ⋅he Reagan administration's attitude toward in⋅ ⋅⋅⋅⋅⋅⋅⋅⋅⋅ and domestic laws
concerning human rights is that the laws themselves are
considered of no great moment. If the laws mattered, it
hardly seems possible, for example, that a high official responsible for promoting human rights would be ignorant of
the commitment to respect medical neutrality of the United
States and El Salvador as parties to the Geneva conventions.
It seems even more unlikely that it would be considered
appropriate to respond, when the applicability of the conventions was pointed out, in a manner that suggests that
these are technicalities where only lawyers are concerned.
Such trivialization of the law does long-lasting damage to
efforts to protect human rights through the rule of law.

3

"TRANSITIONS" TO DEMOCRACY: THE SOUTHERN CONE
Chile
Uruguay
Argentina

In the 1970s, three distinct but similar military governments brought to the Southern Cone a new model of dictatorship. The regimes of Chile, Uruguay, and Argentina, all three overthrowing democratic governments, combined systematic official violence and legal manipulation with monetarist economic policies intended to reverse years of reform. The economic model held down wages, broke unions, and encouraged the "free" flow of imports such that domestic business soon could not compete, while the denial of political freedoms was coupled with mass arrests, torture, and disappearances.

The politico-economic model was applied on the basis of an ideology, the doctrine of national security. Its proponents were contemptuous of liberal democracy, which they regarded as failing to control the spread of anti-Christian, communistic values. Pioneered in Brazil with the coup of 1964, the national security state found dogmatic expression in the Southern Cone, although each country's history, social problems, and armed forces would create a slightly different version.

The Reagan administration inherited these governments. It also inherited a U.S. policy that had criticized them while actively promoting and identifying itself with the cause of human rights. Finally, it inherited a set of human rights laws drafted in response to the suffering in Chile, Uruguay, and Argentina, and designed to prevent the United States, through its aid programs, from being allied with repression.

The new administration dismantled the Carter policy almost immediately. Through goodwill visits, aid decisions, and public statements of support and exculpation, the Reagan administration embraced the armed forces of the Southern Cone and abandoned their victims. One of its arguments for the reversal was that U.S. warmth toward the dictators would encourage political flexibility and a return to democracy. What it did, in fact, was work against the popular pressure for change.

Conditions in these three countries offer three scenarios for the transition from institutionalized dictatorship to democratic rule. Chile's process, the most controlled, promises no democracy worth the name and is being challenged in regular mass protests. In Uruguay the military's design for "transition" gave way to negotiation and a limited election in November 1984, potentially opening the way to full democratic participation. Argentina's armed forces, militarily defeated by Britain in 1983, surrendered to the weight of their failures and are being judged for their abuses.

The Reagan administration, too, is being judged. At the inauguration of Argentina's new civilian president, in December 1983, U.S. Vice President Bush was booed loudly by the crowd. By contrast, the following year the Argentines gave former President Carter a hero's welcome as officials acknowledged the country's debt to him. The Reagan administration's close alliances with the region's armed forces have reversed the goodwill felt toward the United States under Carter. However democracy returns in the Southern Cone, its leaders and supporters are bound to question U.S. motives, for the administration is now identified with precisely what civilian movements for change and human rights have struggled, and suffered, to overcome.

CHILE

In early 1981, when the new administration was sweeping away the Carter legacy on human rights, Jeane Kirkpatrick was interviewed on that subject and was asked whether the old policy hadn't, in fact, led to improvements at least in Argentina and Chile. She replied, bluntly as usual:

> To think that such improvements were the result of our policy is a good example of the arrogance of power, of a colossal overestimation of our influence. In both of these countries, as well as in Brazil and other Latin American countries, there is a long tradition of swings between military dictatorship and constitutionalism. It is this and not our policy that explains the current movement in these countries toward a return to government by law.[1]

According to the Reagan administration's highest-ranking Latin American expert, Chile has a "long tradition of swings between military dictatorship and constitutionalism." This pendulum version of history explains why an American human rights policy cannot encourage improvements: By implication, military dictatorships like that of Augusto Pinochet in Chile are like the seasons, and any interference in their cyclical, almost preordained existence would be presumptuous. Mrs. Kirkpatrick would also have it that Chile is moving toward "government by law," a phrase that suggests increasing respect for human rights but in Chile's case means nothing of the sort.

The analysis is not only Kirkpatrick's. It has been elaborated, for example, by Deputy Assistant Secretary of State James Michel, who used it in an extensive April 1984 speech on Chile to explain that the United States has supported a transition to democracy but that there are dangers in unrestrained pluralism. Chile's political development, he said, has been "a pendular process"—a process "aggravated by the permeability of Chilean society to foreign ideas and ideologies." In Michel's view, current conditions should be understood as "a historical predicament" rather than one created by particular persons or actions.[2]

This argument strains to avoid the questions of how Pinochet came to power and how he remains there. In fact, the military regime that took power in 1973 was, for Chile, not a repetition but something quite new: a national security state, with a systematic program for dismantling democratic institutions. Neither inevitable nor an act of God, the military takeover was made possible by three years of U.S. encouragement and by pervasive U.S. interference in Chile's economic and political life—a program of destabilization that became one of the chief political scandals of the 1970s. Although often given the label of pariah state, the regime led by General Pinochet has remained afloat, economically and diplomatically, thanks in large part to private and public American support, which even in the Carter years did not quite evaporate. As to government by law, the "protected democracy" due to mature in 1997 bears little resemblance to the democracy for which Chile had been so respected and the destruction of which was the military's first concern.

A country of currently eleven million people, Chile had been one of the region's most stable constitutional democracies. In some 150 years it had experienced only one brief period of dictatorship—under Colonel Carlos Ibanez, from 1927 to 1931—and since 1932 the armed forces had not interfered in civilian politics. This is not to say that Chile did not go through earlier uncertain periods, or that the military had never intervened; from 1827 to 1932 there were ten coups, and in 1891 the armed forces overthrew the great reformist president, Jose Manuel Balmaceda. But the military's tenure was always brief, the purpose of intervention generally being to broker civilian disputes rather than to shift power out of civilian hands. Even in its most contentious periods—as Michel acknowledged—Chilean history is placid compared with much of South America.

At the same time, in Chile as throughout Latin America, there have long been social inequities leading to sharp differences of political views. Though Chile developed a relatively influential middle class, its extremes of rich and poor were also important. By 1968, for example, the richest 2 percent of the population received 45.9 percent of the income, while the poorest 28.3 percent received under 5 percent of it[3]— and this after Chile had been a principal client of the Alliance for Progress. The success of Chilean democracy lay in its ability to contain ideological and social conflict with relatively few and minor breakdowns. Elections were essentially honest, and citizens could express their preferences through political parties, trade unions, student bodies, and grassroots organizations that represented the entire spectrum. For two decades prior to the coup the Marxist parties had functioned freely; perhaps because pluralism was possible, Chile lacked the guerrilla tradition of a Guatemala or a Colombia.*

The 1970 election of a Socialist, Dr. Salvador Allende, as president did not interrupt this continuum but rather was very much part of it. Chilean leftist parties, including radical Catholics, social-democrats, and Marxists (later Socialist and Communist), had been forming coalitions to compete in elections since 1938, when a Popular Front candidate won the presidency. Leading such coalitions and proposing radical structural changes within a legal framework, Allende had made a strong showing in 1958 and had increased his percentage of the vote in 1964, although in the latter election the United States covertly spent at least $4 million (one reliable source says over $20 million) to oppose and discredit him.[4] He won with a plurality in 1970 on a platform of change by democratic means—again, despite CIA disinformation campaigns, massive support to his opponents, and a U.S. attempt to block him from taking office. Most important, his administration observed the democratic forms and rights outlined in the 1925 Constitution, even when faced

* Marxist parties had existed since 1912, and had participated in electoral politics since 1920, but in later years there were periods of intolerance: the Communist Party was outlawed during the Ibanez regime and again in 1948 under a "law for the permanent defense of democracy," which was abrogated in 1958.

with provocations later found to have been CIA-financed and -directed at the behest of the Nixon White House.

A CIA Intelligence Memorandum issued in 1970 concluded that Allende's victory posed no danger to the military balance of power or regional peace and that the United States had no vital interests in Chile. Former aides to Henry Kissinger have pointed out that it was Allende's very commitment to democratic processes that made him seem dangerous to the Nixon White House; he posed a genuine alternative to traditional American allies in the region.[5]

As Allende had represented a new kind of democratic government for Chile, so Pinochet replaced him with a new kind of military rule, one intended to leave a lasting mark. Inverting the Chilean legal tradition, the regime has created what it terms "protected democracy" or "authoritarian democracy," a complete coercive system where legalism covers for official violence. The Chilean experiment in social transformation has been more systematic than in any other military regime in the hemisphere, with the possible exception of Uruguay, and human rights violations in Chile over the years reflect this.

The basis for the transformation may have been historical —so strong a civil tradition would require a strong antidote —but its thrust was ideological: the concept of national security that defines liberal democracy as an exhausted system, political parties as divisive, and free speech as permissive of what the regime's first decree called "alien principles." The state governed by the doctrine of national security is the state in which all institutions—courts, educational system, political organizations, media, labor unions—work for the goals of the military government, and in which the military has an explicit mission against internal critics rather than external enemies.* Thus, Chile has completed more than eleven years under states of emergency that legally presuppose internal threats to order, while new definitions of the "threat"

---

* Chile does have long-standing disputes with its neighbors. For example, its claim to the Beagle Channel (resolved in 1984) in recent years brought it close to war with Argentina. This does not alter the thrust of perceptions of the military's role as transformer of society, however

are constantly developed. Collaboration in this process has brought about the thorough corruption of national institutions, such that only the Church has emerged untainted.

The armed forces themselves are a casualty of this corruption. Once regarded as among Latin America's most professional military establishments—led by such respected constitutionalists as General Rene Schneider (murdered by kidnappers backed by the CIA in 1970) and General Carlos Prats (murdered in exile by the regime in 1974)—the Chilean armed forces have been personally corrupted by new wealth, favoritism, and their extraordinary status in the society, while Pinochet has enriched himself and his family in a style unprecedented for a Chilean official.

The pattern of control in Chile since 1973 can be divided roughly into three stages. The regime has consistently relied on force, but there have also been modulations of tone or tactic. The initial program was an open assault upon the sector of the population that had supported Allende, including assassinations abroad and mass detentions and summary executions at home. One-fourth of the organized work force was blacklisted.* Thousands of critics were expelled or fled. This was the period of political earth-scorching.

Three years into the regime most major adversaries were dead, in exile, or disappeared, and all democratic organizations were banned, suspended, or transformed. Torture had become sophisticated, as had the subtler forms of coercion that are products of experience and time. This second stage coincided with the launching and apparent early success of the junta's monetarist economic policies, overseen by the so-called Chicago Boys. The model's strategy was in part the reversal of reforms that had been integral to the Chilean system since even before Allende—land reform, trade union freedom, social services, and the like—and in part an "opening" to foreign investment and imports. The "free market" model developed in Chile was later used, to varying degrees,

* Of a total unionized labor force of slightly over 1 million, United Nations investigators reported that by 1975 some 300,000 had been dismissed for political reasons. (See second footnote, page 55.)

by the military regimes of Argentina and Uruguay. Massive
foreign bank loans supported this policy, and during the resulting "boom" period, 1977 to 1980, the regime was able to
consolidate. This period included a self-amnesty law and a
new labor code as well as efforts to improve the government's
image abroad. The regime began its transition to a "new
institutionality," a process that culminated in the Constitution of 1980.

In 1981 Chile began its projected sixteen-year "transition
to democracy." Based on new constitutional provisions, opposition was defined as terrorist, and Chile was declared to
have returned to a "state of law." But the regime's economic
failures were by now in evidence; the foreign debt had become, per capita, the highest in Latin America, bankruptcies
multiplied, and high unemployment went still higher. By
1983, building from a base in the banned political parties and
labor unions, a national protest movement emerged.

The protest took many forms, primarily monthly days of
school and work absenteeism, when Chileans would bang
together their empty pots and pans to symbolize hunger, and
when tens of thousands would gather at peaceful rallies,
often to be attacked by the police. The protest movement
came to be led by political fronts with divergent constituencies—principally one of the center and one of the left. But
they agreed on the basic demand for democracy—that is, a
new constitution, Pinochet's immediate removal, and open,
early congressional elections. The government responded in
1983 with a mixture of minor political concessions and extreme force. When protests continued, it offered some economic relief but politically abandoned the appearance of
conciliation and returned in 1984 to a simple hard line.

At each stage the regime has broken new ground in the
practice of abuse in Chile; it has explored both psychological
and physical cruelty, and it has refined the shell game of
legal definitions to a degree unusual anywhere. It has reversed thirty-five years of economic development, deliberately traumatizing the nation to benefit an elite. In short,
the Pinochet government has done what it considered necessary to replace one system with another, to take Chile into

new political territory and prevent its returning to the old. To deny these realities, as representatives of the Reagan administration have done, distorts not only the past decade in Chile but also the truth of Pinochet's plan for its future "democracy."

Legalism and the "Transition to Democracy"

Well before 1981 and the new Constitution's being brought into force, the regime was laying a basis for "protected democracy." Indeed, the four-man military junta, with Pinochet as president-by-decree, began altering the fundamental laws of Chile almost immediately, making clear that its design was not only to hold power but also to reshape the state so its rule would be "legitimate," even "democratic."

The myth of an internal war served to justify states of exception suspending basic personal, political, and social rights. Chile has completed over eleven years under supposedly temporary states of exception: a state of siege from September 11, 1973, renewed at three-month intervals until March 11, 1978; a state of emergency renewed every six months since then, with a brief interruption from August 1983 to March 1984. As of March 11, 1981 (the day the new Constitution was promulgated), another state of exception has been in force: the state of "risk of disturbance to internal order," renewable and legally capable of lasting until 1989. In November 1984, the state of siege was reimposed. At no time has any international or Chilean human rights investigator found any of these measures justified.

In April 1978 the government announced a transition to "new institutionality." As part of this design, and a concession to international pressure, the junta decreed an amnesty for all those who "as principals or accessories, committed criminal offenses" under the state of siege between the coup (September 11, 1973) and March 10, 1978, with certain exceptions. Hundreds of political prisoners were released as a result. In the manner of such laws, however, the amnesty pardoned the perpetrators of violence as well as their victims —closing the book on cases filed by the relatives of missing and murdered detainees. The amnesty law has since been cited in a number of disappearance cases as reason for the courts' inability to go forward.

This was only one of many legal tools that the junta developed whereby ordinary courts could deal with political crime according to the military's wishes. The amnesty decree appeared shortly after the state of siege was replaced by a state of emergency; under the latter, wartime military tribunals— or *consejos de guerra*, which handled political cases summarily under the state of siege—had ceased to function. In compensation, the junta decreed an antiterrorism law in April 1979 that made punishable "an attack on the social order, morality, persons, or property." The penalties for mere possession of arms, "illicit association," and a variety of other acts were increased. The law furthermore confounded the most basic assumption of criminal law: As the minister of justice explained, "[I]t will no longer be for the judge to prove guilt in order to convict but for the accused person to prove his innocence."[6] With this law in place, Chile's court system could be counted upon to collaborate.

The suborning of the courts did not start in 1979, however. Pressure on the judiciary at the start of the regime included transfers and removal of judges for political reasons. There has been consistent harassment of lawyers defending political detainees. In addition, the courts have tied their own hands, failing to protect human rights even in areas in which they maintained jurisdiction and power to investigate. Writs of *amparo*, similar to *habeas corpus*, have been filed regularly by the relatives of detainees, but the courts either have rejected them out of hand, or else have addressed them so slowly that no protection is offered during the initial incommunicado detention period, when most violent abuses occur.

Faced with cases of major political and constitutional weight, the courts have shown a willingness to accept virtually any abuse as "legal." In a well-known 1982 case involving eight human rights monitors accused of political activity, the judge's ruling accepted the existence of secret prisons and the validity of confessions extracted in such places. In

1984, the Chilean Supreme Court itself upheld the government's right to exile its critics without a hearing. In both cases, the rulings were based on Transitory Article 24, one of twenty-nine transitory articles of the new Constitution that expanded presidential powers during the "transition." Transitory Article 24 was brought into force by Pinochet on March 11, 1981, the same day the new Constitution was promulgated. It stipulates that where acts of violence against public order occur, "or should there be a risk of disturbance to internal order," the president may declare a state of exception, renewable every six months. Under this provision, persons may be held in their homes or places other than jails for up to twenty days; rights of assembly and free information may be restricted; political opponents of the regime may be expelled or excluded from Chile; and persons may be banished, summarily, for three months of internal exile.

This, added to the state of emergency has legalized measures of unprecedented scope and severity in the guise of resisting not an actual threat but a "risk of disturbance." The U.N.'s Special Rapporteur on the Situation of Human Rights in Chile observed in 1981, "The simultaneous existence of two states of emergency restricts individual rights in the same way as would the state of siege . . . and judicial protection is virtually nonexistent, since judges have no means of verifying the merits of measures imposed by the authorities."[7]

With the 1981 promulgation of its new Constitution, Chile was officially proclaimed to have returned to a "state of law." But less than a week after the Constitution went into effect, the government promulgated a new decree-law that reestablished the wartime military courts to deal with persons accused of attacking or killing any high official, general, or one of several other types of public figure—including any member of the armed forces or police—if the action was due to that person's official position. The investigation of charges is made summarily by a special military prosecutor, the results kept secret from the defense, and the period for presenting evidence before the court (sumario) is a mere forty-eight hours. The tribunals may order the death penalty, and there is no appeal. Their existence is unconstitutional, for the country is not at war. Indeed, the three specific prerequisites for wartime tribunals laid out in the decree itself are all absent in Chile today. But the law's effect is to reinforce the myth of internal armed conflict.

Despite the battery of legal instruments already at hand, the government continues to redefine crimes of political orientation or of dissent. In May 1984, for example, it approved a new antiterrorism law that would apply to alleged acts deemed terrorist even in intent—that is, "committed in order to create disruption or serious fear in the population." The law is a legal anomaly in that it does not specify what actions constitute crimes. Essentially aimed at political association, it makes all members (or presumed members) of a so-called terrorist organization guilty of an act allegedly carried out (or planned, or conceived) by one member. As the Church's human rights office has emphasized, the law is designed to maintain a climate of fear, since extrajudicial accusations and even suspicion can be grounds for arrest.

Legalism as façade and psychological instrument has found its highest expression in the 1980 Constitution's design of government. Pinochet was given an eight-year presidential term (1981–89), with expanded powers under the twenty-nine transitory articles. The junta was defined as the legislative "branch." As such it would select a president (not excluding Pinochet) for the 1989–97 term, * during which term a partly elected, partly appointed Congress would make some of the nation's laws, while the president would make others. Over half of Chile's citizenry would not be eligible as candidates for Congress: To stand as candidate, one must have completed both primary and secondary school. In 1997 would occur direct presidential elections, under guidelines not yet made into law. The presidency and Congress could be contested only by authorized parties—under provisions

---

* The junta's candidate would be submitted for popular approval by plebiscite; see following material for the limitations involved in such a procedure.

also not yet made into law. These two rather central elements have been held, as it were, in reserve.

The transitory articles are to remain in effect until 1989, thus allowing the president to impose new states of exception and controlling a wide range of activities from public gatherings to free exchange of information. And once it arrives, the new democracy is to deal with the fact of a historically strong left-wing constituency in Chile, especially its Marxist elements, by the Constitution's Article 8, a permanent ban on activity "intended to propagate" concepts "of a totalitarian character or based on class warfare." Persons "intending" to spread such concepts are to be ineligible for numerous positions in public life and media for a period of ten years—each time so found.

The Constitution's only claim to legitimacy is its approval by popular vote in a March 1980 plebiscite. Like an earlier plebiscite called to reject international human rights criticism, the 1980 vote was controversial at best—not because of allegations of vote fraud, but because of an atmosphere of intimidation that was both current and cumulative. For objecting to the proposed charter, the then president of the Christian Democratic Party was expelled. A combination of official violence against political figures, confusion as to the contents of the proposal, general intimidation, and an absence of open debate clearly influenced the outcome. Human rights observers emphasize this precedent when anticipating the conditions likely to surround a 1989 plebiscite on the junta's choice for president, with free and fair debate prevented by Transitory Article 24 and/or other constitutional provisions—and organized dissent discouraged by more than a decade of extreme, systematic repression.

Violent Deprivation of Rights

According to the junta's Declaration of Principles, "Never again must a naïve democracy allow within its midst organized groups acting under the guise of misunderstood pluralism . . ." Thus the regime dismantled democratic and participatory institutions and forbade free assembly as it went about extracting a human price for the "naïveté" of the past. Within two weeks of the coup, Congress and the central labor federation (CUT) had been dissolved and a "political recess" declared along with the state of siege. Political activity as such was therefore illegal, as it remains today. Within a month the parties of the Popular Unity coalition, Allende's supporters, had been outlawed. By six months later all other parties and political entities were suspended. Universities and the information media were immediately placed under military control—a control that has since been modified but not fully removed.

At the same time, the armed forces and police (carabineros) unleashed a violence entirely new to Chile and exceptional even in the history of the region. In one year between 5,000 and 30,000 Chileans were murdered for their beliefs and associations.[8] By two years after the coup, over 40,000 had been politically detained for periods longer than twenty-four hours[9]—some for weeks or months—and some 140,000 more were held briefly, for intimidation purposes.[10]

The years 1975–79 saw a flood of Chilean leaders, workers, intellectuals, and their families disperse around the globe—about 37,000 of them formally exiled and more than four times that number forced to flee blacklisting and harassment, or to accompany a close relative.[11] Exile thus directly affects about 1 in every 55 Chileans, not counting the relatives left behind, who also suffer. During this early period, too, Chileans "disappeared" after detention by DINA, the newly formed and virtually autonomous secret police that was another innovation of this regime. The incidence of disappearance was not so frequent in Chile as elsewhere: Some 640 cases have been fully documented, and the total number is estimated at 1,600 to 2,500 by 1978, when the practice effectively ended.[12] This did not reflect a lack of official zeal, however, for disappearance in Chile was a supplementary measure; with so many organized and outspoken Chileans murdered, it served to target and remove the most important, articulate, and energetic who remained. Although eight mass graves and some identifiable bodies have been discovered, the government has given no accounting of the disappeared.*

While the junta set about dismantling the democratic process and eliminating the legitimate leadership, it did not wish to leave a vacuum. At the universities there were government-recognized, limited-participation student federations. In the labor sector, government-chosen union officials and an officialist confederation functioned in the place of freely elected representatives. This effort to create replacement institutions and leaders is one more aspect of the façade of legalism to which the regime has clung so steadily. It was essential that, if something were destroyed, it be replaced with the government's version of its correct counterpart, to show that Chile was still a "participatory" society.

Thus, as the new Constitution would impose a new political structure, so new labor decrees, culminating in the 1979 Labor Code, replaced a half century of union-building with the junta's version of responsible labor activity. Disbanded and harassed, the labor unions were in no position to protect the approximately three hundred thousand workers—one-fourth of the unionized work force—dismissed for political reasons in the regime's first two years.[13] The Labor Code codified this helplessness, permitting collective bargaining only for some workers and only on a company-by-company basis, as well as giving employers the right to hire strikebreakers. By 1984 the unionized labor force had shrunk by 70 percent—a key factor in political control of the population, for not only had organized labor opposed the coup, but also the junta's economic policies had pushed real wages below 1970 levels and unemployment to over 30 percent.† Under

* During 1984, especially after national protests resumed in September, human rights organizations noted a series of temporary disappearances (long, unacknowledged detentions ending in release). Their concern increased further in October, when the body of a man arrested one month earlier but not acknowledged as a detainee appeared floating in a river. He had been tortured to death and partially dismembered.
† The official figure for unemployment in 1984 was 15 percent, but Church studies—and even the progovernment newspaper La Tercera—had reported figures in excess of 30%, including some half-million temporary workers paid well below the minimum wage by government programs for unskilled labor.

these conditions, labor's leadership in the early months of the national protest movement, starting in May 1983, represented an enormous effort of will.

In the early years only the Church could safely perform the task of defending political prisoners, taking testimony, recording and publicizing the vast extent of suffering. To carry out this work it established the Vicariate of Solidarity for legal aid and to shelter groups such as the relatives of the disappeared, one of the earliest and most courageous examples of human rights advocacy in Chile. Later the Chilean Commission for Human Rights (CCDH) and other groups and coalitions formed to monitor and publicize abuses. In 1980 the archbishop of Santiago was threatened with death. In 1981, CCDH's president was expelled, and eight human rights advocates were arrested on charges of political activity. Threats and harassment have continued, including ongoing violent intimidation of Church lawyers, the May 1984 summary expulsion of a CCDH administrator, and the order in November 1984 that forbade the head of the Vicariate of Solidarity to return to Chile from abroad.

In most categories the physical violation of rights abated somewhat after 1977 while the regime codified its control. But since 1981 violent abuses have again increased. The new Constitution has legalized several summary penalties, under Transitory Article 24. In addition, when confronted with organized nationwide opposition in 1983 and 1984, the regime has further hardened its hand.

Restrictions on the press have increased since 1981, beginning with Transitory Article 24. It regulates specifically new publications, but the definition has been stretched when convenient. Loath to impose formal prior censorship, the Interior Ministry instead "advised" editors and media managers as to admissible news, or confiscated issues of magazines considered too bold. In 1984, however, the regime censored three oppositionist magazines and a newspaper and

---

In the junta's version of the free market, bankruptcy became so widespread that by 1983 many professionals were applying to these programs, earning barely enough for a family's tea and bread.

forbade two radio stations to broadcast news. It also promulgated a new law prohibiting reporting that "causes or could cause" damage to the reputation of a public official, even if the reports are provably true. That March, a newspaper publisher and activist who planned to release documents on Pinochet's self-enrichment in office was attacked and severely beaten by a group of "unknowns" (a euphemism for secret-police agents), and in April a magazine editor was jailed for an editorial that called for a new government. When the state of siege was reimposed, virtually all opposition print media were suspended from publication and the rest of the media were forbidden to carry national political news.

Individual detentions doubled from 1982 to 1983; group detentions at public gatherings—mainly the days of monthly national protest—increased tenfold in 1983.[14] In 1984, though protests subsided for several months, arrests continued high, and when national protests resumed on September 4, over 1,500 were arrested. Among the now common forms of control, as well, are mass detentions not only at public gatherings, as in the past, but also preemptively, to ensure "public order"—often carried out at night in military occupations of poor urban neighborhoods, or *poblaciones*. Typically, on one night in May 1983, six such neighborhoods of Santiago were occupied by combined forces of CNI (the secret-police replacement of DINA*), civil police detectives called *Investigaciones*, regular police, and elements of the army and air force. CCDH reported that in the area called La Victoria the action lasted over fifteen hours; as eight thousand people were taken to a soccer field for a review of their documents, the rest of the area's twenty-one thousand residents were ordered to remain in their houses. The pre-

---

* CNI was established in 1977 after DINA became a political liability to the regime: Its chief and two other officials had been indicted by a U.S. grand jury for ordering the 1976 Washington, D.C., assassination of exile leader and former cabinet minister Orlando Letelier. Another DINA agent had helped arrange the murder. Replacing DINA was a cosmetic gesture only, for the new agency conducts itself much as did the old—making arbitrary arrests, maintaining secret detention centers, and carrying out sophisticated tortures.

text for these raids is a search for arms and/or criminals—an antiterrorist and antidelinquency campaign—but known criminals in La Victoria were not detained with the others. More to the point was the fact that just three days earlier, May 11, had been a day of national protest in which these communities had been active.

In 1984 the raids continued so systematically that, for the first time, the Church's human rights office presented a writ of *amparo* to cover an entire sector of Santiago. The frequent overnight arrests of male heads of households, abusive in themselves, were also preventing breadwinners from reaching jobs on time the next morning—thus directly contributing to loss of work in areas where hunger is now commonplace and unemployment may exceed 50 percent.

Despite the abundance of coercive laws and a compliant court system, prosecution for political crimes is relatively rare. For example, during the 1981–83 period some 5,900 persons were individually arrested, according to the Church figures, and of these a yearly average of 67 percent were released without being charged. At the end of 1983, Chile had 131 political prisoners, as compared to some 32,700 arrested individually and en masse during the year (including only partial statistics by CCDH on arrests during occupations of *poblaciones*). But those who are prosecuted and convicted face continual abuse: They are not recognized as political prisoners, they lack medical assistance, they are scattered in prisons around the country to make communication difficult, and they are treated with special hostility. Their repeated hunger strikes for recognition of their status have been to no avail.

Transitory Article 24 legalized administrative expulsion from Chile and internal exile, or *relegacion*. Chile is the only Latin American country to use the latter penalty. Internal exile—by administrative decision for three months, or by court sentence for a period of years*—is typically a term of extreme deprivation and loneliness in a remote, economi-

---

* The state of siege reimposed in November permits *relegacion* for an unlimited period.

cally depressed area of the far North or South, with the *relegado* reporting daily to the local police and supporting himself or herself as best as possible. The penalty is typically used against poorer men whose absence means near-starvation for their families—local and national labor union activists, leaders of the federation of Mapuche Indians, underemployed youths—but leftist political party leaders and human rights monitors have also been punished in this way. Most spend their term in small towns; some, in 1983 and 1984, were sent to a prison camp in the North where even the limited freedoms of the normal *relegado* are not possible.

In the first few weeks after the state of siege was reimposed in November 1984, some 650 people were sent into *relegacion*, more than 500 of them to the northern concentration camp at Pisagua—set in the desert, contained by barbed wire —where the government claimed to be sending "delinquents" for "rehabilitation." The government subsequently decreed that the camp at Pisagua would no longer be considered a place of *relegacion* but instead a prison, and that its inmates would therefore be subject to detention not only for the normal three-month term of internal banishment but for as long as the state of siege itself lasted. Since the state of siege was renewable indefinitely, the sentences thus became open-ended.

Internal banishment has been used more often in the regime's later years; the reverse is true of exile, which was frequently employed before 1978 and has been used seldom, though to great effect, since. Recent victims of this practice include Father Ignacio Gutierrez, who was prevented from returning to Chile from a trip abroad; he was head of the Vicariate of Solidarity at the time, and his absence from Chile deprived the human rights movement of an eloquent voice against the state of siege. Soon to follow him into exile was an American priest, Father Denis O'Mara, who in December 1984 was expelled for handing out holiday cards that called for a "New Year without torture."

Exile became an issue of widespread public concern in Chile in 1982; in 1983, as a concession in the face of protests, the regime issued several lists of external exiles permitted to return. Of a total of some 3,000 names listed, however, over 1,000 were those of people already living in Chile, or who had never been exiles, or who were dead.[15] As a few important figures returned and demands grew for an opening to all of the up to 200,000 exiles, the regime canceled the lists; even those named would have to reapply for entry. In 1984 the policy hardened further, as a list of some 4,900 exiles was issued to airlines in September with the order not to accept them as passengers to Chile. And with Transitory Article 24 in place, Chileans inside cannot count on being able to remain there: In July 1984, in an important political case, the Chilean Supreme Court upheld the government's authority to use the provision to expel its critics without trial and for an indefinite period.

As serious as any of these features of Transitory Article 24 is its extension of the legal incommunicado detention period to twenty days, a virtual license to "temporary disappearance" and torture. According to the National Commission Against Torture, a coalition of Chilean human rights organizations, virtually all persons detained individually by CNI and many detained by other security forces are tortured.

As documented by Chilean groups, U.N. investigators, Amnesty International, and others, this regime has used torture systematically on political detainees since it took power, experimenting until the secret police have acquired a scientific level of sophistication. CCDH reports that CNI interrogators "rely on an arsenal of technical instruments . . . [and on] personnel trained for torture who use the technical support of doctors and assistants like television cameramen, photographers and makeup artists."[16] Torturers play interchangeable roles to disorient the prisoner; some specialize in one or another torture technique. Video cameras record the victims' post-torture "confessions." And the function of doctors—or what seem to be qualified doctors—in this context is to keep victims alive for further torture, to advise the interrogators as to prisoners' limits of endurance, and to administer nontherapeutic drugs. Occasionally the experts slip up, however, as in two deaths by torture in October 1984.

Standard methods of physical torture include electric shock to face and genitals, beatings, burnings, near asphyxiations, the maintenance of the prisoner in forced positions, and rape. In addition, during 1983 and 1984 Chilean human rights monitors noted that the CNI increasingly concentrated on psychological torture—repeated sexual humiliation, the forced witnessing of another's torture, threats against spouses and children, the videotaping of prisoners "confessing" after torture—with the evident aim of creating a lasting self-disgust and fear. This sort of torture is applied not merely to punish but also to cripple.

A related development, profoundly important to the society's scale of accepted values, is that torture is no longer the specialized, hidden province of the security elite, a sufficient source of shame to be kept secret. Since late 1982, the police and the *Investigaciones* have begun to use torture as well—on political detainees, whom they increasingly arrest, and on nonpolitical suspects—the youth picked up for loitering after dark, the slum dweller whose documents are not in order. Police interrogators use electric prods, employ disorientation techniques, force prisoners to stand for hours—all methods borrowed from the CNI. CCDH analysts report that a detainee feels lucky if he or she is tortured "only" by the comparatively unsophisticated police. Thus the unthinkable becomes mundane.

Torture complaints filed in court over the years—a fraction of actual cases—number many hundreds, but none has prospered. The despair and outrage to which this situation reduces even an indirect victim is evident in the case of Sebastian Acevedo. In November 1983, this middle-aged Concepcion accountant, on learning that his son and daughter were in CNI hands, proceeded to the city's main square and, in a plea for his children's release and for national repudiation of torture, set himself aflame and died.

Political Murder

Like Acevedo's, the deaths of other Chileans are becoming an index of the increasingly desperate situation: In recent

years the Chilean government has resumed the practice of
political murder. Between May 11, 1983 (the first formal day
of national protest) and May 1984, the Church's Vicariate of
Solidarity documented a hundred political killings, part of
what it has called "the culture of death." In 1983 as a whole
the victims whose cases reached CCDH numbered ninety
three; in the first five months of 1984, thirty three were killed
and forty more wounded by bullets or explosions in what
CCDH termed "frustrated murders." The causes ranged
from police attacking unarmed persons engaged in petty
crime, to beating persons erecting barricades during a protest, to planting a bomb in an activist's house, to extreme
punishment of a prisoner in custody, to supposed armed
"confrontations" between security forces and oppositionists.

The latter type of case provides the authorities with public-
ity on a so-called terrorist threat that serves to rationalize the
enormous scope of security operations and the maintenance
of the state of "risk of disturbance." The reimposition of the
state of siege in November 1984 was also explained as an
antiterrorist measure. But according to a 1984 report by the
Vicariate of Solidarity, the vast majority of "confrontations"
are simply assassinations by security personnel, many timed
to precede the days of national protest, most of them witnessed. For example:

> Authorities announced that on May 17, 1984, a woman
> "terrorist" had been blown up while setting a bomb at the
> base of an electrical tower in outer Santiago. After she was
> identified, however, her husband came forward, under
> Church protection, and stated that he and she had been
> detained together on May 16 by unidentified men who
> beat them both so severely that he lost consciousness. He
> awoke once at the base of the electrical pylon, and seeing
> his wife being beaten, blacked out again. When he re-
> gained consciousness, he was in another ravine nearby,
> and a bomb had been set with the fuse burning next to
> him. He escaped, but could not find his wife. The CCDH
> designated her case a political execution.[17]

On the night of July 2, 1984, in Santiago, two people in a car were surrounded by police and machine-gunned. One victim was a regional representative of the human rights/ advocacy organization CODEPU (Committee for the Defense of the People's Rights) and leader of a dissident organization of young professionals. Openly taking credit for the deaths, CNI described the incident as a "confrontation." But numerous witnesses contradicted that story. Two other people were killed in the same manner the same night, also witnessed.[18]

A leftist "brigade" has taken credit for scattered acts of sabotage and other incidents of tactical violence. But according to CCDH and the Vicariate of Solidarity, no terrorist campaign exists, nor even anything approaching such a campaign. An official study by *Investigaciones*, Chile's equivalent of the FBI, supports this conclusion. Based on Interpol and Chilean official figures, the study compared the incidence of terrorism in Chile with that in nineteen other countries of varying sizes and political makeups for the period January 1980 through September 1984. Its findings appeared, surprisingly, in the progovernment newspaper *La Segunda* in mid-November 1984 and indicated that there were no attacks on diplomatic posts in Chile (as compared to ten in Italy, nine in France); three attacks on military posts (as compared to fourteen in Spain); and in almost four years, 30 deaths from what the regime considered political attacks by oppositionists (compared with over 600 in Colombia).* That is, terrorism in Chile was essentially nonexistent during precisely the period when the regime was claiming to need, and was imposing, new antiterrorism laws.

The government's rhetoric on this issue is perhaps best portrayed by a document it presented in June 1984 to the U.N. Human Rights Commission. The document purports

---

* The study did not include sabotage, which Interpol does not classify as terrorism.

to list all incidents of sabotage and terrorist attacks on persons (resulting in wounds or deaths) from December 1983
through May 1984. But consider the six civilian deaths listed
for March 1984: All, according to testimony filed by relatives
and witnesses with CCDH, were murdered by government
forces. They include a fifteen-year-old boy detained by police while helping to construct a street barricade, and beaten
to death; they also include a fifteen-year-old girl shot by police while standing outside her house on the day of a protest.[19] The list even includes several persons wounded by
bullets "due to a protest," suggesting that armed violence
during protests is generated by demonstrators and not, as
has consistently been true, by the security forces.

The military regime has invoked a terrorist, or armed,
threat since its earliest days. The coup itself and subsequent
executions were explained as the necessary response to an
alleged Allende plan to take over the country with an armed
political militia—a fabrication the junta called "Plan Z." *
The antiterrorism law of 1979 and its more sweeping successor of 1984 follow the same logic to justify the same methods.
And as has become typical of a regime that so cares about
legalities, "terrorism" is defined in the 1984 law so as to exclude acts by entities of the state. Thus it may be terrorism
to know a political prisoner but, in an official capacity, not
so to shoot a child.

The U.S. Policy

The story of the military regime is inseparable from the story
of U.S.-Chilean relations. Extensive covert CIA operations
against Allende laid at the U.S. door a significant responsibility for the rupture of Chilean democracy; what the Nixon

---

* "Plan Z" was set forth in *The White Book of the Change of Government in
Chile,* a disinformation document published soon after the coup to justify
Allende's overthrow. According to the Senate committee that uncovered
the U.S. destabilization of Allende, the document was written by CIA collaborators.

and Ford administrations did later identified the U.S. fully with the dictatorship. After a hiatus during the Carter years, that identification has been largely revived under the Reagan administration, which calls its warmth toward Pinochet a form of support for democracy.

The Nixon and Ford administrations offered covert political assistance to the junta, through close CIA contact, and also gave unprecedented economic support: Debt renegotiations suddenly sped forward, and by September 1976 Chile had been granted and loaned $350.5 million in bilateral economic aid, making it the largest U.S. aid recipient in Latin America. On the other hand, concern over Chile was a prime impetus for human rights legislation developed after 1974, as Congress cut off first military, then economic bilateral aid, and a succession of events added to the public debate. In 1975 and 1976, the findings of Senator Church's special investigative committee on CIA activities revealed the covert strategy against Allende. During the presidential campaign of 1976, human rights and specifically Chile emerged as a talking point. Then in September 1976, the Washington, D.C., assassination of Orlando Letelier, former Chilean ambassador to the United States and defense minister for Allende, took the debate several steps farther; the U.S. government became responsible for investigating the murder.

Carter administration policy toward Chile involved public criticism of the junta's human rights record—for example, votes in favor of yearly U.N. resolutions condemning the junta on human rights grounds—and a limited opening to the Chilean opposition. The newly established Bureau of Human Rights and Humanitarian Affairs in the State Department met with relatives of the missing, responded to individual and mass arrests, and sought to dissociate the administration from regimes such as Chile's, which survived through violence against their own people. Other parts of the administration, however, sought a *modus vivendi* with the junta in pursuit of other elements of policy. Thus, when human rights pressure contributed to "reforms" in

Chile (the cosmetic dissolution of DINA, the amnesty decree), the State Department tended to greet these adjustments as evidence of progress without confronting their lack of real content. Taken as a whole, the Carter administration could neither live with the junta nor live without it.

As human rights conditions worsened in Chile after 1980, the U.S. posture became more friendly in all respects, including various forms of aid. One of the Reagan administration's earliest foreign policy moves was to lift a set of Carter sanctions imposed due to the Letelier case: a ban on "pipeline" military aid, a commitment to halt all Export-Import Bank lending, and a symbolic decrease in military contacts. These restrictions were to have remained in place until Chile extradicted the former chief of DINA and two subordinates indicted by a U.S. grand jury. In lifting them—and with such alacrity, after one month in office—the new administration signaled its tolerance of the Chilean refusal to honor its extradition treaty.

A few months later the decision was made to reverse the U.S. voting pattern on loans to Chile in international financial institutions. Under a human rights amendment,[20] the United States has been required to vote against multilateral loans to human rights violators since 1976, and the Carter administration had done so with regard to Chile and several other countries. Since July 1981, the Reagan administration has helped Chile to receive about $1 billion from multilateral lenders—while the Chilean economy has shown less and less basis for confidence. Administration spokesmen have explained this shift as a means of supporting Chile's transition to democracy. Beyond the cynicism of that approach, the language of the law is clear. The decision to redefine Chile as a country free of gross human rights violations betrayed contempt for the meaning and force of the legislation and for Congress.

These policy shifts, moreover, took place in the context of 1981 and 1982 visits to Chile by eager goodwill ambassadors such as Jeane Kirkpatrick, who refused to meet with the president of the Chilean Commission on Human Rights,* but who expressed the administration's "desire to fully normalize our relations with Chile"; and a then deputy assistant secretary of state, Everett Briggs, who in July 1982 expressed the administration's hope for resuming military aid to Chile. During 1983, while the Chilean government was sweeping up thousands at the protests and in night raids, $194 million worth of direct U.S. economic aid was earmarked (unilaterally, by the executive branch) for Chile, and an international insurance agreement was revived through OPIC.

These myriad small and large gestures, a pattern of friendship quite consistent with Reagan policy elsewhere in the hemisphere, stand in contrast to legislation that requires that three human rights conditions be met and certified if full bilateral aid to Chile—economic and military—is to resume. This certification requirement, effective since December 1981 and imposed by Congress precisely because of the evident administration rush to make up, covers the general human rights situation and demands cooperation of Chilean authorities in the Letelier case. To its credit, the administration has honored the certification law: Although from time to time there has been pressure within the State Department to certify Chile, the Human Rights Bureau, backed by influential congressmen, has successfully argued against it. In the haze of administration goodwill toward Pinochet, this adherence to the letter of the law is a welcome point of light.

Unfortunately, it is not enough to counter the impression made by the pattern of aid and reinforced by the embassy in Santiago. Ambassador James Theberge, a Latin America scholar posted in Chile since 1982, maintained virtually no contact with Chilean human rights groups and less with vic-

* Jaime Castillo, the CCDH president, was expelled from Chile just days after Mrs. Kirkpatrick's visit, and it is hard to avoid the conclusion that her militant lack of interest in meeting the distinguished lawyer—the embassy had arranged an appointment, but she canceled it—may have removed what little protection he had left at the time.

tims of abuse.* In this he was quite unlike Carter's emissary George Landau, whose close relations with human rights monitors made for quick response in numerous prisoner cases and balanced the U.S. image in Chile. Ambassador Theberge's contacts with even centrist leaders were known to be minimal. And while he made occasional statements about supporting democracy—raising hopes in 1983 that he and his government considered the protests representative— this actually appears to have meant little, for he left unclear whose version of democracy was meant. Absent any real criticism of the "protected" variety, or any real encouragement to proponents of political and individual rights and legal changes, human rights organizations perceived him as thoroughly identified with the regime. This identification was reinforced on the eleventh anniversary of the coup (September 11, 1984), when ambassadors of the Common Market countries boycotted the "celebration" ceremonies, while Theberge was conspicuously present.

If more evidence were needed, the *Country Reports* on Chilean human rights conditions prepared by his staff have reflected an increasingly greater effort to play down the negative—producing such bloopers as "Chileans are free to leave their country" (report for 1981); "the pace of improvements has slowed" (1982); and "freedom of speech in private discussions is the norm in Chile" (1983). The 1982 report consistently sought to compare conditions favorably to the 1973–77 period of earth-scorching violence, rather than to admit that, relative to 1980 and 1981, repression was intensifying. The 1983 report featured the theme of "terrorism" cast solely in the government's terms—a gross distortion of the real source and design of terror in Chile during a year of massive reprisals against the unarmed population.

The official violence of 1983 did prompt some State Department comments, primarily referring to individual cases

---

* In December 1984 the State Department announced the replacement or shifting of several U.S. ambassadors in Latin America, including Mr. Theberge. Others who will be mentioned in this book were Thomas Pickering (El Salvador), John Negroponte (Honduras), and Lewis Tambs (Colombia).

and ranging from mild to moderately concerned. Significantly more energy was devoted to promoting talks between what Deputy Assistant Secretary Michel, the main spokesperson on this issue, has called "moderates on all sides," including the government. (The chief government "moderate" referred to here was the interior minister, who gained his early political experience as a Nazi Party militant.) After an attempt at such talks failed in October 1983, Michel continued to speak of a so-called dialogue as the best available path to progress, a way of bringing together the centrist opposition and those in the government presumably open to early elections.

The opposition's problem with this proposal was that to enter discussions on early elections presupposed basing talks on the 1980 Constitution, an illegitimate instrument, and left open the possibility of Pinochet's remaining as president while a new, limited Congress functioned beneath him; for the idea was not to change the *content* of the Constitution's so-called transition to democracy, but only to shorten the timetable. Thus the dialogue's premise ignored the opposition's chief demand: that Pinochet resign and permit a pluralistic constitutional order to be established.

By 1984 Pinochet had made clear that he would not consider even early elections. He had also upset the so-called dialogue with a surge of repression that temporarily stifled protests. In retrospect the chimera of talks had been a boon to Pinochet, softening his image as he toughened his response. Whether the administration understood this at the time is debatable, but tactically the "dialogue" would have split the opposition, and evidently this was part of its appeal.

The administration stuck to this logic even after the state of siege was reimposed, and as earlier, the overall effect of its actions was to convey a preference for Pinochet over any broadly united opposition. During 1984, while calling for an early transition to democracy, the administration voted for over $400 million in loans to Chile from the World Bank and IDB. As the state of siege took hold, the administration criticized "violence from the left" as vigorously as official repression. In December, when the United Nations passed its yearly condemnation of Pinochet on human rights grounds, taking note of the state of siege, the United States was the only Western democracy to vote "no."

The message of these and other actions was that, for all its sins, the Pinochet government deserved to be considered a legitimate player in negotiations and transition. Significant parts of the opposition did not enjoy the same U.S. tolerance. In January 1985, when visiting congressmen asked that the embassy in Santiago arrange a meeting with the Democratic Popular Movement (MDP), the leftist opposition front, the embassy flatly refused. At the same time, it became known that Ambassador Theberge had written to the Inter-American Foundation, a U.S.-funded, semiautonomous development institution, demanding that it withdraw its grants to five Chilean research centers, including three connected to the Christian Democratic Party. The range of political acceptability, as defined by such actions, appeared narrow indeed.

What the administration had in mind for Chile is essentially what it has had in mind for El Salvador: as Michel has said, to "institutionalize a durable consensus of the center"[21] through alliance with the right and exclusion of the left. In a 1984 speech Michel outlined the reasoning at some length. It assumes that Allende was the starting point of current problems and that the aim of policy must be "to avoid a repetition of the trauma Chile has experienced since 1970" when Allende was elected, not just since 1973, when traditional democracy was overthrown and eviscerated. The problem thus is not seen as rooted in the violent deprivation of rights and pluralism and the imposition of coercive laws, but in a democratic system that—though it kept Chile stable —permitted an Allende victory. The coup, in other words, was Chilean democracy's fault.

Where Jeane Kirkpatrick saw a historical pendulum, Michel attributes to the military a high and noble purpose, "what it perceives as a historical obligation to reestablish democracy." Its vehicle, of course, is the transition, whose repressive nature Michel neglects to mention. To the extent that the military's human rights abuses are noted as negative, it is because "they are self-defeating and serve only the common enemy." Under its detached language, therefore, the Reagan administration's position is not so different from Pinochet's. The perception of Chilean history and traditional democracy is the same. The view of military guiltlessness—even of military mission—is the same. And, for both, human rights are a matter of expediency.

URUGUAY

From the early 1900s to the late 1960s Uruguay was a stable democracy in a continent plagued by political turbulence and social unrest. Uruguay's democratic institutions took hold early in the century, under the leadership of President Jose Batlle y Ordoñez (1903–7, 1911–15), when the state began playing a paramount role in promoting social justice and welfare. Batlle achieved a broad national consensus around the politics of redistribution, which fostered class harmony and was to shape Uruguay's political development.

The system historically was dominated by two political parties, the Colorados (Reds), linked to the liberal urban middle and working classes, and the Blancos (Whites) or National Party, tied to conservative rural agrarian interests. For the past eighteen years, however, both parties have become increasingly divided along conservative-liberal lines. In both parties the conservative wings predominated through the 1971 elections, but since the 1973 coup, while the Colorado Party has moved farther to the right, the Blancos have become more reformist and liberal.

From the early 1900s to the late 1940s, the policies of national consensus designed by Batlle brought both political stability and economic prosperity. By the early 1950s, Uruguay had the highest per capita income, as well as the lowest illiteracy, infant mortality, and birth rates in Latin America. Its advanced social welfare policies also helped to avoid the extremes of wealth and poverty so prevalent in the region. However, after the Korean War, international demand and prices for Uruguay's traditional exports—wool, beef, and hides—began a steady decline, while its public sector expenditures and employment continued to increase. Chronic deficits in its trade balance in the 1960s consumed Uruguay's vast gold and foreign exchange reserves. Inflation—182 percent from 1967 to 1968—steadily eroded the high living standards of the urban working and middle classes.

So spectacular was the country's economic decline that its gross domestic product in 1967 was lower than in 1957. Real wages fell 24 percent in the private sector and 40 percent in the public sector during this same decade. When by 1967 the state could no longer finance its welfare programs, the country's social peace and political stability began to disintegrate. Labor unrest erupted in frequent and often violent public and private sector strikes supported by increasingly radicalized segments of the middle class and intelligentsia. The country's two traditional parties, both internally fragmented, seemed powerless to deal with the worsening crisis. Even the Communist Party's control of the labor movement was challenged by various far-left revolutionary groups.

The general climate became more uncertain in 1967 with the emergence of the Movement of National Liberation ("Tupamaros"), a Marxist revolutionary organization whose principal leaders had been members of Uruguay's Marxist Socialist Party. For the next three years, the Tupamaros staged a series of robberies and abductions, some of which resulted in well-publicized exposures of corrupt politicians and businessmen. In 1970, however, their tactics became increasingly violent, consisting of bombings, armed attacks against government agents, and assassinations. What little support they may have enjoyed with the people, particularly the left, quickly evaporated. As evidence of that fact, the most influential parties of the left formed a coalition called Frente Amplio (Broad Front), which participated in the 1971 general elections. The Broad Front won only 18.3 percent of the vote, with the remainder almost equally divided between the two traditional parties.

When its inexperienced police failed to wipe out the Tupamaros, Uruguay's civilian government entrusted its military with the task and placed the police under direct military control. For the first time the chiefs of the armed forces formed a joint command, in December 1971, to carry out the antiterrorist campaign. As a supporting measure, the government proclaimed a "state of internal war" in April 1972, and at the request of the executive branch, the Congress enacted various measures that suspended rights guaranteed in the 1967 Constitution. Among these was the "law of national security," which suspends certain basic rights of persons charged with "subversive activities" and gives military courts jurisdiction over civilians charged with security offenses. This law remained in effect through the elections of November 1984 and was expected to be an issue for the new civilian government.

Since the early 1900s Uruguay, with no conscription, had maintained only token armed forces, and they had never intervened in the country's political affairs. A military officer in Uruguay, in contrast to his Argentine or Brazilian counterpart, was neither prestigious nor well paid. Poorly educated and utterly unskilled in statecraft, Uruguay's generals nonetheless were ardent believers in the doctrine of national security.

In the Name of National Security

The national security doctrine, popularized in the late 1960s in Latin America, postulates the division of the world into two opposing blocs: the Christian West and the Communist East; the defenders of the West having a duty to wage "permanent war" against ever-present Communist subversion. This is the "Third World War" against internal subversion, whose victory must be assured through the use of any means or tactics.[1] Uruguay's generals saw the Tupamaros as the embodiment of Communist subversion. But they viewed this terrorist group as merely one symptom of a pervasive malignancy threatening the nation—liberal democracy, whose permissiveness had enabled communism to infiltrate and subvert Uruguay's social, cultural, educational, and moral fabric. Thus, despite the fact that by their own admission they had completely destroyed the Tupamaros by early 1973 —the group's leaders were dead or in prison, its organization dismantled—the armed forces demanded and received from the president a greater role in political decisionmaking through the creation of the National Security Council. This clearly indicated that their struggle against internal subversion was not over.

Rather than permitting the restoration of suspended rights after the Tupamaros' defeat, the military forced President Juan Maria Bordaberry to decree on June 1, 1973, an indefinite suspension of basic constitutional rights without congressional approval. Four weeks later, Bordaberry, with the army's backing, illegally dissolved the elected Congress and transferred legislative powers to a newly created Council of State, whose members he named. Uruguay's military regime effectively began on this date, June 27, 1973, for thereafter, the armed forces were in control. The military's removal of Bordaberry in June 1976 merely formalized this control. The June 1973 coup was not a response to a violent guerrilla threat, which the military had crushed some six months earlier; it was, rather, the beginning of the armed forces' crusade in the name of national security and order. This campaign came to define as "subversive" anyone who peacefully opposed or who simply did not share the military's goals or methods.

Unlike the other military regimes in the Americas, Uruguay has not had any single military ruler. Civilian "provisional" presidents provided a façade for the actual power, which resided in a committee of twenty-six generals and admirals and, in particular, in the fourteen generals of the army.

The institutional character of the regime, one of its trademarks, grew out of the need to maintain the fragile unity of the armed forces and a desire to prevent the emergence of strong figures. This government's approach to social control was, not surprisingly, formal and systematic.

Through a series of so-called institutional acts, the military transformed and took control of the country's three branches of government and entire administrative apparatus, including all state-owned public services, municipal councils, and the education system. Institutional Act No. 2 created the Council of the Nation, composed of the thirty-five members of the Council of State and the twenty-six officers of the armed forces' high command. The Council of the Nation appointed the country's president, the members of the Council of State, and all other important governmental authorities, and the military had effective veto power, since a two-thirds majority was needed for all council decisions. Under Institutional Act No. 8, the civilian judiciary similarly lost its independence. Basic rights were further denied by the executive branch's arbitrary use of the prompt security measures, a constitutional grant of emergency powers in case of domestic turmoil. *

Thus, the military institutionalized a state of exception in Uruguay for over ten years. For this and for the gross violations of human rights that have occurred, Uruguay has been criticized by the Inter-American Commission on Human Rights (IACHR) of the OAS, by the OAS General Assembly, by the International Labor Organisation and the United Nations Human Rights Commission and Human Rights Committee, as well as by reliable private groups, such as Amnesty International.

Prisons and Prisoners

During this period, Uruguay has had one of the highest ratios of prisoners to population in the world, ranging from a high of around six thousand in 1975 to eight hundred in early 1984. Amnesty International has estimated that between 1973 and 1979, one in every five hundred Uruguayans was imprisoned for political reasons and one in every fifty was detained for interrogation. A series of mass arrests since 1979 has more than maintained the latter ratio.

In addition, since 1974, over a hundred Uruguayan citizens, including nine children and pregnant women, have disappeared both within and outside Uruguay. Eyewitness testimonies confirm that ninety-three Uruguayans, many of whom were under the official protection of the U.N. High Commissioner for Refugees, were abducted in Argentina by Uruguayan government operatives and subsequently trans-

* Under Article 168 of Uruguay's 1967 Constitution, the Executive may "take prompt security measures in grave and unforeseen cases of external attack or domestic turmoil," but in cases of administrative detention must report the reasons for that detention within twenty-four hours to the legislature, which has absolute discretion to order the detainee freed. The 1973 coup destroyed the independence of the legislative branch and thus removed all protection against arbitrary exercise of these exceptional measures.

ferred to Uruguay in flagrant violation of international conventions to which both Uruguay and Argentina are parties.
Since 1970, more than five hundred thousand Uruguayans
have left the country for political or economic reasons.

The brutal treatment accorded to political prisoners has
been a major focus of the concern of international human
rights organizations. Since 1973, nearly a hundred political
prisoners have died either in custody or shortly after their
release. Reports on conditions at Libertad (men's prison) and
Punta del Rieles (women's prison) indicate that adequate
medical care has been systematically denied to political prisoners; hospitalization has been seriously delayed, even in
severe cases, and once provided has been inadequate. A
leaked confidential report of an International Red Cross
committee visit to Uruguay in early 1980 confirmed that
"Libertad has the reputation of bringing about the physical
and moral breakdown of the inmates" and that the military
jailers were "in search of every possible means of hurting the
prisoners."

The report also stated that physical violence against prisoners was no longer necessary in most cases, because "the
purpose of detention is a *sui generis* 'rehabilitation' process
methodically directed to the destruction of the inmates' per-
sonality."[2] Nonetheless, as standard practice, convicted political prisoners, as well as suspected subversives and
detainees of both sexes, have been savagely tortured by the
police, the military, and other government agents. In a 1978
report on Uruguay,[3] the IACHR catalogued various methods
of such torture, including blows to all parts of the body, the
application of electric current to the genitals and other parts
of the body, *el pau de arara* ("the parrot perch"—the hanging
of the victim by his or her hands and knees from a horizontal
bar), "the submarine" (dunkings in a tank of water, often
mixed with vomit, urine, and blood, until the victim nears
asphyxia), and forcing prisoners to sit straddling iron or
wooden bars that cut into the groin (*caballete*). Among the
psychological methods of torture are verbal threats and
abuse, simulated executions, forcing detainees to witness the

torture of others (either directly or by means of tape record-ings), threats of the torture of spouses or children, humilia-tion, and techniques of sensory disorientation.

Evidence gathered by international human rights groups and the detailed testimonies of released prisoners and ex-members of Uruguay's armed forces* establish that torture ordinarily occurred in a large number of barracks belonging to the different branches of Uruguay's armed forces and to police intelligence. In June 1980 the International Commis-sion of Jurists (ICJ) stated:

> Torture methods have been refined. It is applied today in a more selective and "scientific" manner. Army and police torturers are assisted by physicians whose task it is to su-pervise the condition of the victim undergoing question-ing. Not even prisoners who have stood trial and are serving a sentence are exempted from this aberrant prac-tice.[4]

Of the thousands who have been arbitrarily detained and frequently held incommunicado without *habeas corpus* pro-tection or adequate counsel,† at least fifty-eight hundred to date have been tried and sentenced under Uruguay's military justice system. As of December 1975 the jurisdiction of mil-itary courts was extended to prosecute persons under the law of national security whatever the date of the offense. This

* Hugo Walter Garcia Rivas, Daniel Rey Piuma, Victor Paulo Laborde Baf-fico, and Rodolfo Gonzalez Diaz are all former members of Uruguay's armed forces who have sought refuge in Europe during the past several years and have offered detailed testimony on torture in Uruguay.

† The writ of *habeas corpus* and the basic guarantee against arbitrary arrest, set forth in Articles 17 and 7, respectively, of the 1967 Constitution, were totally denied in virtually every case of a person held under either the na-tional security law or the prompt security measures. In addition, civilian defense attorneys willing to defend these political prisoners lived in fear and became the object of official hostility and repression merely for representing these clients. Many of these attorneys have been jailed and/or forced into exile, with the result that by late 1984, in the great majority of cases, pris-oners were relegated to having military officers, who most often are not lawyers, as their advocates. These officers, in turn, were directly responsible to the same authority whose goal was to secure convictions in every case.

retroactively permitted military courts to try civilians for offenses committed *prior* to the April 1972 declaration of the "state of internal war" and prior to the passage of the law of national security.

It is important to note that the gradual decline in the political prisoner population over the years did not result from an "amnesty" or any improvement in the administration of military justice. Rather, the great majority of political prisoners released by 1984 had served, in full, an average six-year sentence for such vaguely defined crimes as "insulting the morale of the armed forces," for distribution of political materials, and for other nonviolent activity. In addition, more than seventy prisoners had been held in detention after having served their sentences, and other prisoners who had completed their sentences remained in custody facing new trials for security offenses allegedly committed during their incarceration.[5]

Political Rights

Uruguay's military government also imposed some of the severest restrictions in the hemisphere on the free flow of information by the media. Between 1973 and 1982, the government permanently closed twenty-eight newspapers and magazines. In 1983 it shut down nine other newspapers and a radio station. The banned publications covered the full spectrum of political-economic thought in Uruguay; even Church publications have been censored or closed. Those publications that continued to operate did so either under censorship or self-censorship, for whenever opposition papers criticized the government, they routinely were closed, at times for several months. On various occasions their editors and/or reporters were detained or arrested, or forced into exile.* After August 2, 1983, media coverage of all political activities was prohibited, and between December 1983

* A report by the Committee to Protect Journalists and the PEN American Center states that several hundred journalists were forced to flee Uruguay between 1973 and 1983 and that at least fifteen reporters had been imprisoned in those ten years.[6]

and February 1984, political party and trade union weeklies were subject to prior censorship.

"Illicit association" and "political association" were two of the regime's most flexible charges. On June 27, 1973, the day of the coup, the government dissolved and declared as "illicit associations" five major student groups. Shortly thereafter it dissolved the National Workers' Convention (CNT), the country's largest labor organization, and other unions on the same pretext. The leaders of these unions and student groups, and many of their members, were later singled out for particularly harsh treatment by the government. For example, the measure dissolving the CNT made the mere fact of membership in or support of this constitutionally sanctioned organization a punishable crime *retroactively*, and several thousand trade unionists later faced penalties of up to thirty years' imprisonment as a result.

In May 1981 the government issued the Vocational Association Act, which permitted only private sector employees to organize unions and only within a company, not on an industrywide or national basis. This measure did not recognize the right to strike, or collective work contracts or union dues. An *ad hoc* confederation of 150 trade unions, the Inter-Union Workers' Plenary (PIT), was declared illegal and dissolved by the government in January 1984 for having organized the country's first nationwide strike since the coup.

One way the government prohibited the right of assembly for "political" purposes was to require prior authorization. (Assembly under the law meant a gathering of *two or more* persons.) A communiqué issued by Montevideo's police listed as activities requiring prior authorization "public events, assemblies (of social, cultural, professional sports, and cooperative institutions, businesses, mutual medical aid societies, etc., even in certain cases of religious organizations when they go beyond the mere exercise of worship on their own premises), elections, benefits, conferences, cultural and artistic events, tributes (to living or dead persons, to be held on sites [or at] cemeteries, monuments, etc.), processions, including sports parades, scientific, technical, and other congresses . . ."[7] Further, representative organizations were required to obtain the government's approval of all candidates for their officers and committees.

"Limited Democracy"

The 1973 coup ended not only the country's parliamentary democracy, but also all civilian political activity. On that day, the executive branch dissolved and declared as "illicit associations" the left-of-center political parties * and banned the small Christian Democratic Party and right-wing Civic Union. The country's two traditional parties, the Blancos and Colorados, were declared "in recess"—a euphemism for total prohibition on political party activity.

In June 1976, Institutional Act No. 1 suspended indefinitely the general elections scheduled for that November. Three months later, Institutional Act No. 4 prohibited for a period of fifteen years—that is, until 1991—all political activities by, among others, the following classes of persons: all directors of the political parties; legislators elected in the 1966 and 1971 elections; all candidates of Marxist or pro-Marxist parties, or of parties electorally associated with these, who ran for offices in the 1966 and 1971 elections; and all individuals tried for political crimes under the national security law. Thus the military planned to clear away the country's former, legitimate leadership and impose a new model of government: "limited democracy."

The military's *cronograma*, or timetable, for moving to "limited democracy" called for a November 1980 plebiscite on a draft constitution, and a one-candidate presidential election in 1981. The draft constitution, made public less than a month before the plebiscite, ensured the military's

---

* These included all parties forming the Frente Amplio, the broad leftist coalition that won 18.3 percent of the vote in 1971—these being the Communist Party, the smaller Socialist Party, and other less important Marxist parties, such as the Group of Unifying Action, the 26 of March Movement, and the Workers' Revolutionary Party. In addition, several left-wing parties and groups not participating in the Frente Amplio were also banned.

control over future civilian governments by giving the armed forces direct responsibility "to take all measures needed for national security." Through the National Security Council the military high command would share with an elected president broad authority to declare three different kinds of national emergency, all of which would permit the suspension or restriction of constitutional guarantees and the arrest of "suspected subversives." The national legislature's authority to lift the state of emergency, provided in the 1967 Constitution, was drastically curtailed in the draft constitution. On the other hand, the use of military courts to try civilians, prohibited by the 1967 Constitution, was expressly mandated by the proposed one in cases of subversive crimes.

The Turning Point

The government spent approximately $20 million in a saturation media campaign urging a "yes" vote on the new constitution, seeing the plebiscite as a device for improving its international image and legitimizing its rule. Television and other media ran continuous advertisements recalling the murders, bombings, and kidnappings carried out by the Tupamaros, suggesting that a "no" vote would mean their resurgence. On November 13, the nation's air force commander told the newspaper *El Dia* that only "terrorists, Marxists, and all those who do not love their country will vote no." Other prominent military officials took a subtler tack, publicly stating that a "no" vote would represent a desire to maintain the status quo without elections.

At the same time, Uruguay's civilian political leaders, emerging from the forced inactivity of eight years, portrayed the plebiscite as a referendum on the military government itself. The government tried to control free public debate on the proposal in numerous ways—temporarily lifting some restrictions on political meetings and the press only with the publication of the proposed constitution twenty-nine days before the plebiscite, arresting politicians who called for a "no" vote, and cracking down on opposition media. Nonetheless, on November 30, 1980, Uruguay's voters rejected the proposed constitution by an impressive margin of 58 to 42 percent.

The stunned and humiliated government now reassessed its prospects. Ignoring a minority in the armed forces who favored dialogue with the political parties, the government renewed its ban on all political activity, reimposed media censorship, and set about developing a new plan. In August 1981, with Institutional Act No. 11, it proposed to restore civilian government on an arbitrarily slower timetable—elections in November 1984 and the installation of the new government six months later. Similarly, its new law on electoral participation imposed arbitrary limits to the political process. That law ended the "recess" on the traditional Colorados and Blancos and the right-wing Civic Union, but it retained the "proscribed" status on all left-of-center parties and stipulated that proscribed persons and former members of illegal parties were ineligible for membership in the sanctioned parties.

The latter restriction made it impossible for many Uruguayans to participate in internal delegate elections of the Blancos and Colorados in November 1982 and thus to influence the choice of presidential candidates at party congresses in March 1983. Nonetheless, taking advantage of the limited opening available, the participating parties met and committed themselves to open the process fully as soon as possible.

Pressure and Counterpressure

The military's plan comprised another restriction, however. Its proposal, as the basis of negotiations with the political parties, provided that the 1984 elections would be conditioned on public approval of a draft constitution similar to the one rejected in the 1980 plebiscite.[8] Representatives of the armed forces and political parties met seven times in mid-1983 without reaching any agreement on the military's draft constitution or the parties' demands. In early August, after the parties broke off negotiations, the government banned indefinitely all public political activity, imposed strict censorship on the press, and decreed a new institutional act providing severe sanctions for those found to engage in politics.*

Despite these measures, during the remainder of 1983 there were numerous nonviolent protests. And popular frustration welled to the surface in early 1984, when a general strike, the first since 1973, brought the country to a standstill on January 18. Called to support democratic elections, amnesty for political prisoners, increases in the minimum wage, and other economic and political reforms, the strike was organized by an *ad hoc* confederation of 150 trade unions, the Inter-Union Workers' Plenary (PIT), which was immediately declared illegal by the government. Argentina's return to democracy also had a profound effect. While it further divided the hard-liners and moderates within Uruguay's armed forces, it gave renewed confidence to civilian politicians to demand publicly a prompt return to democracy in Uruguay. The Blancos and Colorados called for the deproscription of all persons, participation by all political parties in national elections, unconditional return of all exiles, and an amnesty for all political prisoners. Responding to these demands and international pressure, the government released two of its most famous political prisoners, General Liber Seregni, presidential candidate in 1971 of the Frente Amplio, and Jose Luis Massera, a distinguished mathematician and former legislator.

Informal negotiations took place through most of 1984, but the situation remained volatile. Underscoring the arbitrariness of military rule and the uncertainty surrounding the transition to democracy were the June arrests of Wilson Ferreira Aldunate and his son, Juan Raul, as they returned from nine years of forced exile. Ferreira had been the leading vote-getter in the 1971 elections. Although proscribed from all political activity since 1976, he nonetheless was chosen overwhelmingly as the Blanco Party's presidential candidate for the November 1984 elections. Thousands of Uruguayans participated in peaceful demonstrations and

---

* Loss of political rights for two to fifteen years by executive fiat not subject to judicial review.

work stoppages demanding his release, and the Blanco Party initially voted to break off transition talks with the military and to boycott the November elections unless Ferreira was released. When Ferreira renounced his candidacy, however, calling on the party to participate in the elections, the Blancos nominated a journalist, Alberto Zumaran, as a stand-in candidate.

Realizing that Ferreira's aborted candidacy could only enhance the electoral chances of his opportunistic civilian political rivals, the military cleverly exploited the differences between the two traditional parties. The government on July 17 legalized the Socialist and Christian Democratic parties, both banned since 1973 and coalition partners in the Frente Amplio. This move was calculated not so much to broaden voter choice in the November elections as it was to draw votes away from the Blanco Party and to shield the Colorado Party from voter backlash for dealing alone with the military. On August 3, the Colorados, the partially reconstituted Frente Amplio, and Civic Union signed an agreement with the armed forces on terms for the return to civilian government. The agreement, incorporated in a new institutional act, formally scheduled presidential and congressional elections for November 25, 1984, and set March 1, 1985, for the inauguration of a civilian government. The Blanco Party publicly rejected the accord.

The military's shrewd efforts to bolster the Colorado Party's presidential candidate, Julio Maria Sanguinetti, paid off. With Ferreira and Seregni out of the race, and over 400,000 Uruguayan exiles unable to vote, Sanguinetti won the election with his party receiving 38.6 percent of the total vote, against the Blancos' 32.8 percent and the Frente Amplio's 20.4 percent. A few days after the election, the military released Ferreira.

In contrast to the Argentine military, Uruguay's armed forces could anticipate relinquishing power with their unity intact and thus, would be in a strong position to influence a new civilian government's policies, particularly should the issue of their accountability for human rights abuses arise.

The View from the United States

From 1977 to 1979, Uruguay was a relatively high priority on the Carter administration's human rights agenda. The new administration quickly broke with the Nixon-Ford policy of maintaining friendly relations with Uruguay's military government, despite the fact that 1973–77 had been the high-water mark of repression and that after 1977 the regime was consolidating. The administration took little risk in publicly distancing itself from the armed forces' excesses; Uruguay was strategically unimportant to the United States, had little direct U.S. foreign investment, and was an insignificant trading partner. Nonetheless, the Carter administration's public criticism of the military government was matched by its actions. It requested no new military assistance or sales to Uruguay, instructed the U.S. directors of international financial institutions to oppose loans to the country, and successfully blocked Uruguay's bid to hold the 1979 OAS General Assembly meeting in Montevideo.

Carter also sent to Uruguay a new ambassador, who opened the embassy to opposition leaders and relatives of political prisoners and of disappeared persons. Although bilateral relations between the United States and Uruguay suffered as a result, the Carter administration was widely perceived as trying to alleviate human rights conditions and edging the military toward a more rapid redemocratization.

The Reagan administration arrived claiming to support redemocratization in the Southern Cone countries—and Uruguay's case would have seemed an easy place to demonstrate such a commitment, even for a State Department that has tended to view U.S. choices in the area as between "authoritarianism" and "totalitarianism." The results of the 1980 plebiscite demonstrated that Uruguay's people and political parties were opposed to "limited democracy" and that the country's democratic political leaders still enjoyed the people's loyalty. In addition, none of the national security concerns that shape the administration's policies elsewhere in the region have been present in Uruguay. No left-wing guerrilla or terrorist activities have occurred in the country for over eleven years, and the left has posed no real electoral threat in the democratization process. Only the military's intransigence has blocked an immediate return to civilian democracy. When President Reagan took office, Uruguay was seen throughout the hemisphere as an easy test case of the sincerity of his commitment to democracy and the effectiveness of "quiet" diplomacy.

But apparently even this test was too difficult, for the administration again and again signaled its support for the military government. In July 1981, it began by claiming "significant improvements" in human rights conditions in Uruguay and, without consulting Congress, reversed previous policy by voting for a $50 million World Bank loan to Uruguay.* Given the findings of the OAS Human Rights Commission and human rights groups that had detected no meaningful improvements in the human rights situation during 1980 and the first half of 1981, the shift was seen by many in Congress as a direct violation of Section 701 of the International Financial Institutions Act, which requires that the United States oppose multilateral bank loans to governments guilty of gross violations of internationally recognized human rights.†

Shortly thereafter, again deliberately circumventing human rights legislation, the State Department moved to resume the sale of weapons to Uruguay. Rather than make a direct sale, the administration arranged for South Korea to sell Uruguay howitzers, air defense guns, and ammunition made in Korea under technical data packages previously sold to Korea by the United States. The sale was a quid pro quo for Uruguay's agreement to contribute troops to the Sinai

---

* On July 1, 1981, the U.S. Treasury Department notified Congress that in addition to Uruguay, the administration would no longer oppose multilateral bank loans to Argentina, Chile, Paraguay, and South Korea.
† See letter signed by forty-nine members of Congress to Treasury Secretary Regan protesting the administration's decision to vote for multilateral bank loans to Chile, Argentina, Paraguay, Uruguay, and South Korea, printed in hearings "Human Rights and U.S. Policy in the Multilateral Development Banks" before the Subcommittee on International Development Institutions and Finance of the House Committee on Banking, Finance, and Urban Affairs, 97th Congress, 1st session (1981), pp. 478–81.

multinational force but was publicly explained as a response to "significantly" improved human rights conditions. With congressional attention diverted to the human rights and military situation in Central America, opponents of the sale simply could not muster the votes to block it. In this sense, the promotion of human rights in Uruguay became an indirect victim of the Reagan administration's policies in Central America. The sale was viewed within Uruguay as U.S. support in particular for the hard-liners in the armed forces high command who advocated a return to limited democracy in which they would institutionalize their presence. In the aftermath of the hard-liners' defeat in the 1980 plebiscite, the sale seriously undercut the negotiating strength of civilian leaders seeking concessions from the military and weakened moderates in the armed forces who were pressing for a broader dialogue.

Having successfully changed policy on military sales and multilateral bank loans to Uruguay, the Reagan administration then decided to remove the restrictions imposed by Congress in 1977 on military assistance to that country. It requested $50,000 in military training (IMET) aid to Uruguay for fiscal year 1983, a gesture not financially significant, but symbolically very much so. The justification for this newest policy shift was, not surprisingly, the need to show U.S. support for the military government's improved human rights record.

But in August 1983, when Uruguay's government banned all political party activity and imposed new censorship in response to the break-off of dialogue with opposition leaders, the Reagan administration did not reduce, much less withdraw, its IMET request. Rather, it sent a reprogramming notice to Congress nearly doubling IMET aid from $50,000 to $90,000. The State Department's sole comment on the August crackdown expressed no regret, annoyance, or disapproval of the government's actions but merely "concern" that these actions might "constitute potential obstacles for democracy." Soon after, the administration requested an additional $100,000 in IMET for fiscal year 1984.

This narrow and unresponsive U.S. position has been

reinforced since 1981 by periodic visits of Reagan administration representatives, such as Jeane Kirkpatrick and retired General Vernon Walters, who have publicly lauded the military government as a steadfast friend and ally of the United States. The conduct of the new U.S. ambassador, a Reagan political appointee, has been particularly partisan. Shortly after his arrival, Ambassador Thomas Aranda effectively shut the embassy to government opponents and victims of human rights abuses and their families. Further, every one of the *Country Reports* on Uruguay prepared since 1981 by the U.S. State Department, based on information from the U.S. embassy in Montevideo, has consistently attempted to ignore, whitewash, or downplay the severity of the human rights situation in Uruguay. Reports tend to accept as fact the Uruguayan government's assertions, while discounting or labeling as "allegations" disputed information from private bodies. In particular, the department has tried to sidestep, by frequent references to the military's so-called progress in the democratization process, any discussion of continuing government repression.

The Reagan administration's attitude toward Uruguay's most popular opposition leader, Wilson Ferreira Aldunate, also contradicts its expressed commitment to fair elections and the restoration of genuine democracy. When Ferreira visited the United States in 1983, he was received by members of Congress from both parties, but no State Department official directly involved with inter-American or Uruguayan affairs would agree to see him. On the other hand, the U.S. government last fall brought the Colorado Party's presidential nominee, Julio Maria Sanguinetti, to Washington, where he met with key State Department officials and, when he returned to Uruguay, he began holding publicized meetings with the U.S. ambassador. Although Ferreira's 1984 arrest brought immediate protests from most European and Latin American democracies, the Reagan administration's belated response was to express the expectation that Ferreira and his son "will be processed expeditiously with all the guarantees of due process of law" and the hope that "this incident does not jeopardize" the return to civilian government.

Apart from knowing that the charges against Ferreira were political and fabricated to keep him out of the country, the State Department also knew that he would be tried not by civilian courts but by a military tribunal whose very procedures the department has criticized for denying defendants basic fair trial guarantees.* If a democratic leader of Ferreira's stature were tried for political crimes by a "totalitarian" government, one wonders whether the State Department would implicitly endorse that government's actions, as it has in Uruguay's case. The department's response did little to dispel the view, widely shared in Washington and Montevideo, that the Reagan administration favored Sanguinetti's election. In fact, on September 1, 1984, the Blanco Party lodged a protest with the U.S. embassy over statements made by the U.S. ambassador that were interpreted as blatant U.S. support for the Colorado Party candidate.†

Sanguinetti's victory was greeted warmly by the State Department. Although flawed, Uruguay's November elections marked the first step toward an eventual restoration of civilian control. The new government, however, faces economic and social problems that would severely strain even the most stable democracy. At the end of 1984, inflation and unemployment were 17 percent and 15 percent respectively, and Uruguay's $5.3 billion foreign debt was particularly staggering given annual export earnings of only $1 billion. Demands upon the new government came from all quarters. Some 30,000 former public sector employees, fired by the military government for political reasons, demanded reinstatement and compensation. In addition, the new government was called upon to reassert civilian control over the armed forces, restore the rule of law, lift all political proscriptions, free the remaining political prisoners, and rebuild the entire education system.

---

* In its 1980 *Country Reports* on Uruguay, the State Department cited with approval the Inter-American Human Rights Commission's conclusion that "the military judicial system still does not guarantee due process."[9]
† "A few days ago, the U.S. ambassador said that in Uruguay there is a conflict between the people who want to return to democracy and those who put personal and party interests before the restoration of democracy."[10]

These problems make it unlikely that Uruguay can return to the kind of social welfare state that flourished until the early 1960s, or be free of the military's political influence. Indeed, whether genuine democracy eventually takes hold will require, at the least, that leaders of all key political parties reach a broad agreement on the country's direction for the immediate future.

Undoubtedly the new government will seek economic assistance from the Reagan administration which, its statements notwithstanding, did little to promote the return to democracy. In fact, there is no evidence that the Reagan administration has used "quiet" or any other kind of diplomacy to promote respect for human rights in Uruguay. Invoking, time and again, unsubstantiated improvement in the human rights situation and the need to support a traditionally "friendly" government, the administration sought to bolster the armed forces at the expense of the democratic opposition, conveniently ignoring the fact that, traditionally, Uruguay's friendly governments were democratic. Now the administration has another chance. If it is nearly as supportive of the new civilian government as it was of the discredited military regime, then it finally may do something to advance human rights in Uruguay.

ARGENTINA

The state terrorism imposed on the Argentine people by the military juntas between 1976 and 1983 soon became the testing ground of human rights as a component of U.S. foreign policy. The Carter administration, resisting pressures from within itself and from many other influential quarters, persistently condemned the Argentine armed forces for their practices of forced disappearances, torture, arbitrary arrest, and cold-blooded execution of prisoners. Conversely, conservative opinion in the United States used the example of Argentina to typify everything that was, in their view, wrong with a policy that alienated avowed friends of the United States who were doing the Western world a service by combating left-wing terrorism. Not surprisingly, some of the first major policy reversals implemented in this field by the Reagan administration were designed to show the Argentine military that now they were considered trusted and respected allies.

The Reagan administration's eagerness to please Argentina's despotic rulers reflected the Republicans' regard for Argentina as a source of influence in Latin America. More importantly, it reflected their persuasion that the armed forces are a permanent feature of Argentina's power structure, and the Republicans' desire that they remain such a powerful force in the future.

This view overlooked two other important aspects of that country's history: first, that overwhelming majorities of the Argentine population have repeatedly shown their preference for democracy and their rejection of militarism, and second, that despite their pro-Western rhetoric, the generals are unreliable partners. In 1982 they invaded the Falklands/ Malvinas Islands and were later humiliated in the war with Great Britain. In the aftermath, the military regime collapsed and democracy and human rights were finally restored to Argentina. The Reagan administration's early support for the generals has made the United States more unpopular than ever in a country that could be a valuable and democratic friend.

Independence and Nationalism

For geographical and economic reasons Argentina was, until after World War II, the Latin American country where U.S. influence was least important. By the turn of the century, Great Britain was not only the prime purchaser of Argentine beef and cereals but also the owner of the largest investments there, including an extended railroad network. Based on agricultural exports to Europe, the Argentine economy grew quickly after 1870, and between 1870 and 1930, cultural ties to Europe were equally strong as Argentina experienced a wave of immigration. More than 90 percent of the population today is of European stock, mostly Italian and Spanish.

Argentine landowners developed strong links with Britain and to a lesser extent with the rest of Europe. Simultaneously, they attempted to extend their influence over other Latin American countries and to compete in this sense with the increasing influence of the United States. In the early 1900s, the power of these landowners through the Conservative Party was challenged by more democratic and populist forces, the largest being the Union Civica Radical of Hipolito Yrigoyen, the party that returned to power in 1983 with the upset victory of Raul Alfonsin. The Radicals were nationalistic and therefore anti-British, and their attitude toward Latin America was one less of domination than of cooperation. With regard to the United States, on the other hand, they felt the same as the Conservatives, though for different reasons. The result was that Argentina and the United States took opposing positions on all important diplomatic initiatives in the first half of the century. Argentina opposed the creation of a regional League of Nations and succeeded in blocking the initiative. Most importantly, Argentina remained neutral in both world wars and to some extent convinced most other Latin American nations to adopt a neutral stance as well.

The U.S. response to this renegade nation was generally hostile. Argentine neutrality (in 1914 under Yrigoyen and in 1940 under a Conservative government) was repeatedly misrepresented as a pro-German stance. In 1946, the United

States attempted to exclude Argentina from the emerging United Nations. Secretary of State Cordell Hull and others in the Roosevelt administration said repeatedly that the threat of a third world war would come from the "pampas."[1]

A U.S. ambassador to Buenos Aires of the period, Spruille Braden, maintained this position so zealously that he even promoted an unseemly alliance among Conservatives, Radicals, Socialists, and Communists to defeat the emerging populist leader Colonel Juan Domingo Peron. Briefly jailed in October 1945, Peron emerged to organize a new party after his release, and using the slogan "Braden or Peron," he swept to victory in February 1946. Peronism, with its combination of nationalism and populism, brought together a broad social coalition, including some military elements, and became the dominant political movement in Argentina for over thirty-five years.

American liberals and conservatives alike have simplistically labeled Peronism as fascism. British diplomats of that time knew better; a Foreign Office record states: "The fundamental difficulty, as Sir David Kelly [British ambassador to Argentina] points out, is that the government of the United States is not as hostile to Colonel Peron as to Argentina herself, whatever her government, because thanks to her profitable links to Great Britain, she has the luxury of pursuing a comparatively independent policy vis-à-vis the dominant influence of the United States in the Western Hemisphere."[2]

British influence ended soon after World War II, in part because of Peron's nationalistic policies but largely due to the general demise of the British Empire. For a few years, Argentina prospered as a provider of food to Europe and embarked on an accelerated process of industrialization. Because this process was never quite completed, however, landowners remain even today an important economic force, and because their electoral power is insignificant, they influence policy and occasionally govern through their main ally, the armed forces. The fact that they are pro-Western and anti-Peronist has been enough to make the United

States consider the governments arising from military coups as generally "democratic."

Peron was ousted by one such coup in September 1955. Though there had been some diplomatic rapprochement with the Eisenhower administration in the final years of Peron, U.S. economic influence began only after that coup. Argentina joined the IMF and other international financial institutions. Large U.S. investments in industry began in the late 1950s, under President Frondizi. Another wave of U.S. investments occurred in the late 1960s, under the military regime of General Ongania.

Since 1955, Argentina has lived in a combination of economic stagnation and political instability. The country that had been ranked seventh in the world in economic power—predicted to become fourth in the world by 1960—has lost ground consistently to other nations, including several in Latin America. At the same time, the military has taken power in 1962, 1966, and 1976. The elections of 1958 and 1963 were flawed because Peronism was proscribed. When Peronism returned to power in 1973, internecine struggles made it first an inefficient term of office and later, after Peron's death in 1974, a bloodily repressive one.

The period of 1955–76 was not simply a succession of unstable civilian and military governments. Each time Argentines were able to vote, even under severe restrictions, they clearly supported human rights and antiauthoritarian policies. In economic and social terms, their choices always favored measures to protect local industry and promote growth with fair wages and welfare benefits. Conversely, with each coup and each time the military increased its influence over a civilian government, repression increased and, economically, the country was more open to multinational corporations. On the other hand, foreign policy remained relatively independent of the United States throughout those twenty years. Under Frondizi, Argentina abstained on the expulsion of Cuba from the OAS in 1962, and under Illia it refused to endorse the U.S. occupation of the Dominican Republic in 1965. In the early 1970s, under General Lanusse, Argentina began trading with the Soviet bloc, and under Peronism joined the nonaligned movement. During the military dictatorship of 1976–83, however, Argentine foreign policy became more schizophrenic and unpredictable.

The Military Regime, 1976–83

The Carter and Reagan administrations dealt with an Argentine government that in many ways was a radical departure from the past. On March 24, 1976, the three commanders-in-chief of the armed forces deposed acting President Isabel Peron, the leader's widow, and inaugurated a "process of national reorganization." General Jorge Videla was appointed president, but the three commanders (Videla for the army, Admiral Massera for the navy, and Brigadier Agosti for the air force) constituted a junta that retained the power not only to appoint the president but also to legislate in important areas and to amend the Constitution. In exercise of such extraordinary powers, the junta enacted extremely repressive legislation, establishing among other things the death penalty for political offenses, which is expressly prohibited in the Argentine constitution of 1852. Instead of deploying this arsenal of powers openly, however, the armed forces embarked on a deliberate and concerted effort to deal with a sector of the opposition by illegal means.

The coup had grown out of a polarization partly expressed in violence. In the late 1960s, the continued disregard for popular participation sparked a series of spontaneous upheavals in working-class districts of various cities. Very soon, large numbers of young people who were disenfranchised from the political process by the military government of that time embraced revolutionary leftist causes. Urban guerrilla movements mushroomed, growing not only in their capacity to engage in violent activity but also in the open support they received from significant sectors of working- and middle-class youth. By the early 1970s, when the military permitted a return to democracy, the influence of the armed groups was felt within the Peronist Party, where they soon encountered a violent right-wing opposition.

At the same time, however, the politics of change were not limited to terrorist activity. In fact, most working- and middle-class young people in the early 1970s joined trade unions, student federations, neighborhood committees and other forms of grass-roots organizations. After Peron died in 1974, these young activists were the main targets of death squads directed from the heart of the Peronist government and with the increasing participation of the military. Even before the March 1976 coup, the death squads claimed more than six hundred lives in a period of eighteen months, without having affected the activity of the guerrillas.

The principal reason given for the coup of March 1976 was to curb the "subversive threat." But what the generals called their "dirty war against subversion" was not directed exclusively against armed guerrillas. Lawyers, priests, relatives of the guerrillas, journalists, college professors, students—all became targets as long as they were seen as enemies of "Western and Christian civilization." The largest number of victims were rank-and-file workers and trade union leaders.

Direct persecution of opponents and critics was only the most visible effect of authoritarian rule. Censorship of news and of artistic expression, accompanied by incessant and boisterous government propaganda, made many middle-class Argentines react with fear and cynicism, attempting to ignore the crimes and corruption of the government or to dismiss criticism of them as part of an "anti-Argentine" campaign.

The economic team appointed by the military applied a "shock treatment" to Argentina's failing economy. They liberated prices and tightly controlled wages. They opened up the market to imports of all kinds and attracted financial capital with high yield and quick returns. As a consequence, the purchasing power of wages dropped in one year by 50 percent and remained at that level throughout the regime; most of local industry closed down or left the country; the standard of living of the middle class deteriorated sharply. In the final years of the dictatorship, the country found itself with an enormous foreign debt, with its industry in ruins, and with inflation soaring again. The only prosperous sectors were those that speculated in outrageous financial deals with foreign currency. Imposed with savage repression, the economic policy of the military regime had changed the economic structure of Argentine society, enriching a few and impoverishing most Argentines.

For all its anti-Communist and pro-Western rhetoric, however, the dictatorship's foreign policy was ambivalent. Trade with the Soviet Union was vastly expanded, to the point where the U.S.S.R. became Argentina's largest buyer of agricultural exports, and plans were made to allow Soviet investment in ambitious hydroelectrical programs. In the Western Hemisphere, meanwhile, Argentina exported its "war against subversion" by persecuting exiles abroad, by assisting in a repressive coup in Bolivia, and by sending advisers to Central America to help right-wing governments on intelligence matters and to train the U.S.-sponsored *contras* trying to overthrow the Sandinistas in Nicaragua.

By March 1976 there were already between three thousand and four thousand political prisoners in Argentina's jails. Within weeks of the coup, more than eighty-five hundred had been arrested and placed in prolonged administrative detention without trial, at the disposition of the executive branch (PEN) by virtue of the state of siege. As one of its first acts in office, the military suspended a constitutional provision called "right of option" that allowed state of siege detainees to choose to leave the country. That clause was later reinstated, but the government reserved for itself a veto power over applications for exile. As a result, hundreds of prisoners spent as many as eight years in prison, often after being declared innocent by the courts.

Most PEN detainees were brutally tortured, as were the majority of those who were eventually prosecuted by civilian or military courts. Torture consisted mostly of electric shock but also involved sexual abuse and rape of women prisoners, and beatings and psychological torment of all prisoners. Intimidated by the military, judges refused to investigate these charges and acquiesced in convictions and sentences that abused all notions of due process.

Perhaps the most distinctive feature of the Argentine dictatorship was its use of "disappearances": Between fifteen thousand and thirty thousand Argentines were arrested by security forces, taken to clandestine detention and torture centers, and their custody was never acknowledged. These actions were conducted pursuant to a deliberate plan ordered by the high command, and each "operation" was carefully checked and approved by regional military authorities.

In addition, both "legal" and "disappeared" prisoners were frequently murdered by their captors. Beginning in 1982, large common grave sites were found in many cemeteries, where corpses had been buried without identification. The great majority of the relatives of "disappeared" prisoners may never know the fate of their loved ones.

The Carter Period

In the same year that the military regime began, Jimmy Carter was campaigning for president of the United States and promising to make human rights a cornerstone of U.S. foreign policy. Early on, the Carter administration pointed to Argentina's as a regime whose violations of human rights were unacceptable no matter the degree to which its rulers shared Western goals. The executive branch first proposed a reduction of military aid to Argentina and other countries, specifically citing human rights violations as a reason. (Argentina rejected all aid in protest.) Beginning in January 1977 the administration voted against or abstained from twenty-three multilateral loans to Argentina. Patricia Derian, assistant secretary of state for human rights, traveled to Argentina and made strong representations to Videla about human rights, reinforcing the administration's concern. A high point of that concern came when Secretary of State Cyrus Vance paid an official visit to Argentina in November 1977 and submitted to the government a list of thousands of persons who were "disappeared" or in jail.

On a day-to-day basis, these efforts were assisted in Buenos Aires by F. Allen (Tex) Harris, a political officer at the embassy who became a full-time human rights officer. In two years, the embassy made more than twelve hundred representations to the Argentine government on cases of abuse. Harris also met frequently with relatives of the disappeared and with journalists, lawyers, and human rights activists. This attitude helped give the newly created human rights organizations a respectability that effectively protected them in their work.

The U.S. Congress went even farther than the administration. In September 1976, Congressman Don Fraser, chairman of the House Subcommittee on Human Rights, held hearings with Argentine victims of human rights violations. In 1978, Congress passed the Humphrey-Kennedy amendment to the Foreign Assistance Act, which prohibited all military sales, aid, loans, or training to Argentina because of that country's human rights record.

To counter the policy, the Argentine government engaged expensive public relations firms to lobby the U.S. press, the Congress, and the administration, and Argentine supporters of the regime were recruited to convince their contacts in the U.S. business community of the need to support the military. Many Wall Street banks, arms manufacturers, and other businesses enthusiastically lobbied for the lifting of sanctions.

The policy was not even unanimously supported within the Carter administration. Argentina's rulers were encouraged by the statements of Terence Todman, under secretary of state for inter-American affairs, in the course of a visit to Buenos Aires in August 1977, to the effect that human rights would not be an obstacle to improved relations with the United States. (Todman was later replaced.) Likewise, Carter's ambassador to Buenos Aires, Raul Castro, did little to support the efforts of the department and of his own staff, and he made frequent public statements in favor of the military government. And the Department of Commerce frequently objected to the imposition of conditions for trade with a relatively important partner.

The dictators, who had at first reacted in anger and disbelief at what they perceived as a betrayal by the United States, now hoped to weather the Carter years and to wait until relations "returned to normal." In 1978, they hosted the World Cup of soccer, using the opportunity to improve their image abroad and break their increasing isolation; their star guest was Henry Kissinger. At the same time, they continued to invest in the improvement of their image. One of the public relations firms hired for this purpose was Deaver and Hannaford, one of whose owners, Michael Deaver, later became a White House aide to President Reagan. The Center for Strategic and International Studies (CSIS) at Georgetown University offered a forum to Admiral Emilio Massera, right after he retired as commander-in-chief of the navy, to explain that the navy was not involved in disappearances. Roger Fontaine, CSIS's Latin America expert, became a Latin America specialist at the National Security Council with the advent of the Reagan administration. One of the dictatorship's most ardent supporters in Washington was General Gordon Sumner, who had been the chairman of the Inter-American Defense Board until 1977. As a spokesman for the American Security Council, he frequently defended the Argentine counterinsurgency strategy at congressional hearings. In 1981, he too became a Latin America specialist for the Reagan administration, first at the State Department and later at the National Security Council. Fontaine and Sumner were members of the Committee of Santa Fe, the group that wrote "A New Inter-American Policy for the Eighties," one of the most influential papers used by the Reagan transition team.

Reviving Relations

The new administration found in Argentina an excellent place to demonstrate its new tactic of patching up friendships broken over Carter's human rights policies. A first step was to embrace the regime publicly. After only two months in office, the new administration received President Roberto Viola as the third chief of state to be invited to Washington (after Jamaica's and South Korea's). General Viola, the junta's selection to replace General Videla, had been chief of staff and commander-in-chief of the army during the worst years of the repression.

As to policy, in February 1981, the administration issued an order to its representatives before international financial institutions to stop opposing loans to Argentina, Chile, Uruguay, and Paraguay based on human rights violations, in response to what Secretary Haig called "dramatic, dramatic improvements"[3] in human rights in all four countries. In Argentina at the time, there were still more than a thousand PEN prisoners held without charges; the government still refused to provide any accounting for the fate or whereabouts of the fifteen thousand to thirty thousand who had disappeared; and temporary disappearances, arbitrary arrests, and torture were still taking place.

In March 1981, as if testing the new waters, Argentine security forces raided the offices of a human rights organization and arrested its leaders. Administration officials exculpated the government, then gave credit to U.S. "quiet diplomacy" for the prisoners' release a week later. That same month, the administration moved to repeal Section 620(B) of the Foreign Assistance Act (the so-called Humphrey-Kennedy amendment) in order to resume military sales, loans, and training programs for Argentina, claiming that the government was moving toward elections and that the sanctions had not worked.[4]

Although Congress did repeal Section 620(B) in December 1981, it replaced that provision with a requirement that, before renewing military sales and assistance, the president certify improvement in human rights, in particular that the government of Argentina (1) had accounted for the fate and whereabouts of the disappeared and (2) had released or charged all PEN detainees. These conditions were uncertifiable, and the requirement under item (1) posed a seemingly insurmountable obstacle to the administration's plans. The Argentine military had not only refused to investigate disappearances or to disclose any information, but it had also moved to make future inquiries impossible, first in 1979, by allowing the courts to declare the presumptive death of persons listed as disappeared, and then by proposing a "self-amnesty" law for security forces. Nonetheless, the administration made clear that it was actively considering certification, and it might well have proceeded if some State Department officials had not argued that because of a border dispute, certifying Argentina without doing the same for Chile would be seen as an insult to Pinochet. At the same time, the Human Rights Bureau was reluctant to certify improvements in Chile in order to maintain a measure of credibility with Congress; after certifying that the human rights situation in El Salvador was good enough to merit continued military aid, the administration could not afford another controversial aid initiative.

This bureaucratic complication aside, "normal relations" with the Argentine military were pursued aggressively. The Argentine regime, for its part, viewed the possible renewal of arms sales as a "moral reparation" for unfair treatment by the Carter administration. During Viola's visit, in the course of several interviews with members of the U.S. Congress and of the executive branch, he argued that his forces had been unjustly accused of human rights violations for having successfully defeated a Marxist insurgency, a victory that— according to his argument—actually benefited all of the "free world." Although Argentina was not in urgent need of arms, the repeal of the Humphrey-Kennedy amendment was needed, then, as a correction of past wrongs.[5] With or without certifying, the Reagan White House showed, in word and in deed, that it was willing to allow the Argentines that moral victory.

Viola's visit in March 1981 was followed by a stream of visits to Argentina by high-ranking officers of the U.S. armed forces. Though the agendas of these meetings were never made public, the high visibility in Argentina of the meetings gave them enormous and no doubt intended value as "goodwill gestures" to the military rulers. Later in 1981, General Leopoldo Galtieri, then commander-in-chief of the army, visited the United States twice. In the course of the general's triumphant second visit to Washington, as president-designate, Defense Secretary Weinberger called Galtieri "magnificent."[6]

When he assumed the presidency in December 1981, Galtieri responded to these gestures of friendship with warm gestures of his own. His economic policy team was designed to continue favoring multinational banking interests. His minister of foreign relations, Nicanor Costa Mendez, announced that Argentina would abandon the pro-Third World position of the recent past and establish itself firmly "in the West." At the same time, Argentine clandestine participation in repression and covert operations in Central America was increased to assist the U.S. policy there.

By early 1982, the Argentine economy was showing alarming signs that "free market" prosperity—enjoyed mostly by speculators—was only a mirage. After several years' attempt to control it, the annual inflation rate shot up again to well over the 100 percent mark, and some of the more audacious banks were going under. As the image of economic success began to disintegrate, new forms of popular protest were beginning to be heard. The weekly demonstrations in front of the government house by the mothers of the disappeared, which had begun in pathetic isolation in 1978, were now supported by increasing numbers of young people. By 1982 eight human rights organizations, founded in the worst years of repression, had grown to enjoy considerable respect and support from most sectors of society. Although all labor activity continued to be forbidden, the trade unions began organizing strikes and demonstrations in demand for jobs, wage increases, and the release of imprisoned workers. Pushed by the demands of their rank and file, even the traditional political parties began addressing the regime in bolder and more sharply critical terms. Everybody, even Galtieri and his followers, agreed that it was time for democracy. But Galtieri, buoyed by what he perceived as his success with "the Americans," began making not-so-subtle hints at an electoral campaign, apparently thinking the tide was in his favor. His overconfidence, at least in part inspired by his friends in the Reagan administration, led Argentina to the greatest military disaster of her history.

On April 2, 1982, Argentina invaded and took over the Falkland Islands (or Malvinas, as they are known in Latin America), a British dependency but historically claimed by Argentina. After a month of failed negotiations, the British response was to take them back again, in a short but bloody war. At least two thousand young Argentine draftees were killed in battle—many of them abandoned by their officers to face the highly trained British troops by themselves. The defeat humiliated Argentina's proud military, and when the Argentine public learned of the treatment of draftees, its outrage further hastened the military's political decline.

President Reagan reacted to the invasion by deploring acts of war between "two friends" of the United States, and initially he attempted to mediate the dispute. When armed conflict became inevitable, the United States sided with Britain and provided her with important intelligence technology and some logistical support. The original attempt at mediation was prompted by Argentina's usefulness to our Central America policies, where its military was doing the dirty work of the United States. After that initial display of sympathy, the Reagan administration made no effort to examine the ultimate issue of sovereignty over the Falklands/Malvinas, and in fact undermined hemispheric support for the Argentine claim at the Organization of American States.

After the war, British opposition to certification became the prime obstacle to a renewal of arms sales to Argentina but by no means prevented the State Department and the Pentagon from "actively considering" it. To make up for its diplomatic "betrayal" during the war, the administration was seizing every opportunity to show goodwill toward the military regime, then headed by Generals Reynaldo Bignone as president and Cristino Nicolaides as commander-in-chief of the army.

By then, however, the generals had no political credibility and thus no immediate political future. They therefore embarked on a course to end the era of the "process of national reorganization" by permitting political activity and designing an electoral calendar. Bignone's presidency became little more than a caretaker government, except in one major aspect: His primary role was to see that the transition to democracy did not result in the army's losing its privileged position. In the process, the armed forces would not simply have to leave room in government for elected officials; they also risked losing their ability to apply pressure on the new government in important policy areas, as had been their role in most other democratic transitions of the recent past. More importantly, they risked losing the internal consistency and muscle they would need to step in and interrupt the democratic process in the future. No problem was more serious, in this regard, than the increasing demands for an accounting of the fate of the "disappeared," and in August 1982, to forestall further pressure, high officials of the Argentine government began announcing that they would issue a document explaining the "dirty war."

At this point, the Reagan administration had a choice: It could support the move toward democracy—at little or no diplomatic cost, even by staying silent and failing to certify as previously—or it could work to identify itself still further with a discredited and repressive regime on its way out. Consistent with its taste for military ties above all others, the administration chose the latter option. For example, in an apparent effort to lay the foundation for a certification, the State Department included an important exculpatory statement in the *Country Reports* for 1982. "[T]he Argentine government," it stated, ". . . is believed to have provided information to family members on the death and in some instances the location of the remains of the disappeared in about 1,450 cases."[7]

In the highly charged atmosphere of Argentina, even the military dared not make such an outrageous claim in public. Calculated to mislead, the phrase mixed apples and oranges. There were at least 1,450 persons who had died at the hands of the military, under a variety of circumstances: some resisting arrest, others executed upon their capture, still others executed after being taken away from prisons, and many in armed confrontations. In those cases, however, relatives knew of their deaths, so the victims were certainly not included in the list of the disappeared. A survey conducted by an Argentine human rights organization, the Center for Legal and Social Studies (CELS), and sponsored by Americas Watch, showed that the overwhelming majority of the relatives of the disappeared had not received any news about the fate of their loved ones and that only an insignificant percentage had received informal and unofficial reports, in most cases of questionable credibility.[8]

Even more revealing of the administration's priorities was its response to the "Final Document of the Military Junta on the Struggle Against Subversion and Terrorism." The self-justifying "Final Document" sought to deny that a policy had existed of holding detainees in clandestine centers and that many disappeared prisoners were summarily executed. And it paved the way for an announced amnesty for security agents to ensure their immunity from prosecution, by declaring that "the actions of the members of the armed forces in the conduct of the war were in the line of duty." When it appeared in April 1983, the "Final Document" was repudiated by all sectors of Argentine society and by, among others, the leaders of France, Spain, the Vatican, and the European Economic Community. In a letter to President Bignone, President Sandro Pertini of Italy said, "I have protested and I protest in the name of civil and human rights and in defence of the memory of the defenceless creatures who have been victims of horrendous death. All humanity should consider itself wounded and offended."[9]

In contrast, the United States first remained silent for two weeks, then issued a very weak statement, consisting, in its entirety, of the following:

We share the sense of disappointment others have expressed that an occasion has been lost to begin the resolution of this question. It is an issue which the Argentines themselves must resolve. We have consistently encouraged the authorities to provide as complete a report as possible on the fate of the disappeared.[10]

When the junta pushed through its self-amnesty law three weeks before the October 31 election, the Reagan administration had no comment.

The elections of October 31, 1983, were won by Raul Alfonsin of the Union Civica Radical. His surprise victory over the Peronists was largely credited to the fact that he had been able to show himself as the candidate least likely to compromise with the military, and the one who made the strongest and clearest promise to seek truth and justice on the human rights issue as well as on the matter of responsibility for the Malvinas fiasco and for the enormous corruption that was another feature of the dictatorship. Two days before Alfonsin's inauguration in December, the United States finally certified that human rights in Argentina had indeed improved to the point that it was now possible to resume military aid and sales.

While certification was certainly warranted, the tone of the certification document was not calculated to please the new government. It laid undue praise on the military for improving the human rights situation and for steering the country to a return to democratic rule, almost amounting to the kind of apology that the administration had so often made when the military still held power. Many in Argentina considered it an effort to shore up relations with the armed forces for the period of democratic government, when what was needed was public support for the new president and his programs—for democracy and all it could mean. Argentina found it ironic that the first action of the Reagan administration was to restore military aid to a country in such great need of all other kinds of political and economic support. The minister of foreign relations of the new government, Dante Caputo, stated that the certification was an internal matter of the United States and that the new Argentine administration placed very low priority on military acquisitions.

The Alfonsin Administration

Since December 1983, Argentines have finally enjoyed freedoms guaranteed in their Constitution. The new government took early measures to increase the penalty for torture, to void the "self-amnesty" law, to ratify the major international instruments on human rights, and to investigate the fate of the disappeared through a "blue ribbon" commission.

On September 20, 1984, this commission, headed by writer Ernesto Sabato, completed its work by delivering fifty thousand pages of evidence to President Alfonsin. In its summary of findings, the commission issued a strong condemnation of the methodology of disappearances as part of a deliberate, coordinated official policy that went far beyond any reasonable relationship with the need to curb violent political action.

The only outstanding human rights issue in Argentina in 1984 was how to deal with the abuses of the past. Alfonsin chose to have military courts investigate, prosecute, and punish those crimes. The human rights community, as well as the opposition parties, argued that civilian courts should have jurisdiction over them and that there should be no extraordinary excuses for those who could be found to have followed orders.

The extreme delicacy of the effort was repeatedly made evident. For example, less than a week after completion of the special commission's report, the Supreme Council of the Armed Forces, the military court empowered by the government to prosecute the crimes of the "dirty war," stunned Argentine public opinion with a statement finding "nothing objectionable" in the orders given by the high command in furtherance of the antisubversive campaign. The Supreme Council took this position in a report on its work requested by a federal court of appeals after months of council delay in pursuing the cases before it. Although not required to deal with the substance of the cases, that report went on to say that the commanders could, at worst, be found guilty of negligence for not controlling their subordinates. Besides engaging in an obvious prejudgment of the cases before it, the Supreme Council defiantly contradicted the substance of the Sabato report in many other ways.

Appelate jurisdiction over these cases rests with the federal court of appeals of Buenos Aires. Ultimately the decison to punish those guilty of human rights abuses lies with this court.

With conditions so changed in Argentina, the Reagan administration had many bridges to build, if it wished to do so. The administration appropriately took no position on the matter of prosecution of military leaders, since all Argentines agree that the issue of how to deal with abuses of the past is an internal one. For the same reason, no other government, international organization, or nongovernmental human rights institution has expressed an opinion in this matter.

The Alfonsin government undertook to improve relations with the United States without prejudice to its own initiatives on foreign policy, which are generally directed to strengthening Argentine involvement in the nonaligned movement. Also, in pursuit of U.S. cooperation in an area of central importance, the foreign debt, Foreign Minister Caputo toned down his critical statements about U.S. policies in Central America. A shipment of Argentine weapons to Honduras, presumably to be used by the *contras* against Nicaragua, was allowed to be delivered on the grounds that it had been committed earlier in 1983. Though the government stated that Argentine military personnel were no longer on duty as advisers in Central America, there were persistent rumors to the effect that these advisers had stayed on as CIA-sponsored mercenaries; the government refused to clarify the situation.

Unfortunately, the Reagan administration refused to play any part in the debt-rescheduling discussions, even though many in the foreign policy establishment, including Henry Kissinger, advocated an active stance such as the Argentines requested. On the other hand, in May 1984 the administration sent General Charles Gabriel, chief of staff of the air force, on an official visit to Argentina to promote the sale of U.S. arms.

The foreign policy of the Reagan administration with respect to Argentina falls well within the pattern of its attitude toward the Western Hemisphere generally. It is not uncomfortable with democratic regimes, but if possible it prefers a democratic government in which the armed forces retain considerable influence and are relatively free of civilian controls in broadly defined security areas. In the case of democratic Argentina, as in others, the administration maintains a two-track approach: a diplomatic channel to the civilian governments, and a separate, direct relationship between the Pentagon and the armed forces. This two-track relationship is particularly dangerous in Argentina because it contributes to the preservation of a military clique that has been the principal factor in Argentina's political instability and that constitutes an ever-present threat not only to the democratic process but also to the human rights of the Argentine people.

If the Reagan administration wishes to serve the long-term interests of the United States in Argentina, it should institute a policy that reinforces the Argentine people's support for stable and representative civilian institutions and a military with no other task than the protection of the nation's. borders. The future of Argentina will be difficult but is full of promise, and the Argentine people have expressed their desire for peace and democracy in no uncertain terms.

4

GEOPOLITICS AND HUMAN RIGHTS: CENTRAL AMERICA
El Salvador
Honduras
Nicaragua
Guatemala

Although the Nicaraguan revolution took place during the Carter administration, and by 1981 the United States had already begun to aid the Salvadoran armed forces, the Reagan administration is responsible for broadening U.S. commitment into a regional policy and for developing its geopolitical rationale. Such policies are as old as U.S. influence in the region; the contemporary version, however, combines geopolitical arguments with the claim that in U.S. policy lies the greatest guarantee of respect for human rights.

Accompanying the policy has been an explosion of human rights violations. The crisis in Central America is unprecedented even for a region long dominated by dictators and fraudently elected civilian governments, and no small part of the blame must go to the influx of U.S. arms, advisers, and diplomatic support to the armed forces of El Salvador, Honduras, Guatemala, and to the administration's proxies, the *contras* fighting the Nicaraguan government. The results have been the dislocation and extreme misery of over two million people, the murders of tens of thousands in El Salvador and Guatemala, the militarization of a country, Honduras, which itself is facing no guerrilla threat, and abuses in Nicaragua under pressure of a foreign-backed invasion.

The Reagan administration did not inherit a crisis in Central America; it inherited a challenge to U.S. vision and understanding of the roots of widespread protest. The causes of Central America's upheavals are structural; the administration's response has ignored all but their symptoms. El Salvador, Honduras, Nicaragua, and Guatemala are nations with much history in common whose development, or underdevelopment, has led inevitably to social schisms and to the reexamination of traditional beliefs and traditional governance. The Church is changing, expectations among the poor are changing, and to the extent that those in power refuse to change, they confront frustration in its many forms.

To the Reagan administration, "winning" in Central America, against the guerrillas of El Salvador and Guatemala, against the Sandinista government of Nicaragua, has become the most important aspect of hemispheric policy. In pursuing that course, the administration has circumvented both general and country-specific human rights laws of the United States, violated the charters of the U.N. and the OAS, and defied judgment by the International Court of Justice in The Hague. Yet the policy has failed to achieve a victory on any front. It is causing alarm among U.S. citizens and in Congress.

What the policy has failed to do in concrete terms, however, its architects have tried to do rhetorically, through a campaign to impugn the credibility of those who criticize violators of human rights and to convince the U.S. public and Congress that democracy is at hand. The agents of democracy, in this scenario, are the self-same armies and former agents of misrule whose repression for so long guaranteed the status quo. And if the scenario is true, then critics of these armies, those who prove that they are guilty of torture, massacres, indiscriminate aerial bombardment of civilians, systematic displacement of peasants from their lands, the murder of children—those who document these things are being unconstructive, even biased.

As a veteran journalist has pointed out in *Foreign Affairs*, "Central America has gone from being an ulcer that a new U.S. Administration thought it could lance and heal in a matter of months to a running sore that will plague the United States for years to come."[1] The United States is not the victim of these events, however. The victims are the noncombatants of the region, whose lives, if they still possess them, have been reduced to terror, displacement, and near starvation with the help of U.S. aid. The United States is a catalyst, even a controlling influence, and whatever the administration's motives or banner, the victims have found no sympathy in its shadow.

EL SALVADOR

More than 40,000 civilian noncombatants killed—murdered by government forces and "death squads" allied to them; another 3,000 disappeared; 750,000 or so (15 percent of the population) refugees beyond its borders; 500,000 or so (another 10 percent of the population) homeless or "displaced" within its borders. Those are a few of the more or less familiar statistics reflecting the consequences of political violence in El Salvador, the geographically tiniest country in the landmass of the Americas.

In a televised address to the American people on May 9, 1984, President Ronald Reagan attempted to explain the violence. "What we see in El Salvador," he said, "is an attempt to destabilize the entire region and eventually move chaos and anarchy toward the American border." The participants in this attempt and their purpose were clear to the president. What is going on, he said, is "a bold attempt by the Soviet Union, Cuba, and Nicaragua to install communism by force throughout the hemisphere." The violence that has taken so many lives, torn apart so many families, and driven so many people from their homes and from their country was attributed by the president to the guerrillas and to "a small, violent right wing as opposed to democracy as are the guerrillas but they are not part of the government. We," he added, "have consistently opposed both extremes, and so has the government of El Salvador."

"La Matanza" and After

Though President Reagan chose to see the violence in El Salvador as part of a worldwide struggle between forces allied with the United States and forces allied with the Soviet Union, it may also be seen as a contemporary phase of a struggle that has been under way during much of Salvadoran history. Land, which is scarce in El Salvador but capable of producing considerable riches, is at the heart of this historical struggle.

A century or so ago, rural police forces were established

in El Salvador to help wealthy coffee growers maintain control over the labor they required for their intensively cultivated crops. Working in close collaboration with special agrarian judges, the landowners and rural police forces imposed something close to slavery or serfdom on the landless laborers of El Salvador. Protest and unrest were dealt with harshly, and when a nationwide uprising took place in 1932, it was crushed with unrestrained savagery. In that episode, known as "La Matanza" (the massacre), some thirty thousand people were killed during a few weeks.

Two names from the period of La Matanza are still known: The military officer who overthrew a civilian government that had been elected in 1931 and who directed the forces that perpetrated the massacre was General Maximiliano Hernandez Martinez; the leader of El Salvador's small Communist Party that helped to stage the uprising was Agustin Farabundo Marti. One of the principal death squads operating in El Salvador in the past five years has perpetuated the general's name by calling itself the Maximiliano Hernandez Martinez Anti-Communist Brigade; the name of the Communist leader of the 1930s is known today because the guerrilla movement in El Salvador calls itself the Frente Farabundo Marti de Liberacion Nacional (FMLN).

For nearly half a century following La Matanza, memories of that event, combined with fear of the police forces that continued to serve El Salvador's wealthy landowners, sufficed to suppress rural unrest. During this period the police forces extended their control over rural life, as in the establishment in the late 1960s of ORDEN, which became an eighty-thousand-member paramilitary network that maintained effective surveillance over every village and hamlet in the country, summarily executing those even suspected of taking part in any protest.

A challenge to the control maintained by the landowners and their allies in the police forces and the army arose in 1972, when a reform coalition led by presidential candidate Jose Napoleon Duarte, a Christian Democrat, and vice-presidential candidate Guillermo Ungo, a social democrat, apparently prevailed in national elections. Engaging in obvious fraud, the armed forces deprived them of victory. Duarte was imprisoned, tortured, and sent into exile for seven years.

Another fraudulent election, in 1978, resulted in the inauguration of General Carlos Humberto Romero as president. Romero was overthrown in a military coup in October 1979 by reform-minded officers led by Colonel Adolfo Arnoldo Majano, who united on this occasion with more tradition-minded military officers led by Colonels Jose Guillermo Garcia and Jaime Abdul Gutierrez. A civilian-military junta was formed of which Guillermo Ungo and the Christian Democrats became members.

But the new government could not bring genuine progress. Popular demands for reform and human rights improvements—expressed in massive demonstrations and strikes—were suppressed by the armed forces with a brutality reminiscent of the period of La Matanza. Some members of the junta attempted to limit the violence but discovered that in practice the armed forces exercised unchecked authority. Guillermo Ungo resigned in January 1980; later in the year he became head of the newly established Democratic Revolutionary Front (FDR), a political opposition coalition that entered into an alliance with the guerrillas of the FMLN. Colonel Majano was forced out of the junta by Colonels Garcia and Gutierrez and sent into exile. In March 1980, the archbishop of San Salvador, Oscar Arnulfo Romero, who had been outspoken in condemning the abuses by the armed forces and paramilitary groups allied to them, was himself murdered. Jose Napoleon Duarte, however, joined the junta and, in December 1980, became its president— exercising little influence but providing the armed forces, which were slaughtering Salvadoran civilians by the tens of thousands in 1980 and 1981, with an effective public relations spokesman.

The Advent of the Reagan Administration

The election of Ronald Reagan as president of the United States in November 1980, and the sharp break his victory signaled from the policies espoused by the outgoing Carter administration, was greeted with rejoicing by wealthy Salvadoran landowners and their allies in the armed forces. The Carter administration had fitfully attempted to restrain human rights abuses, providing small amounts of military support and then occasionally pulling back in response to particularly gross abuses. Reagan directly repudiated the Carter human rights policy and seemed to promise military aid without restraints.

Expecting massive military aid for the Salvadoran armed forces, the FMLN launched in January 1981 a "final offensive" against the government before the new U.S. administration took office. The offensive failed, but the Salvadoran government's retaliation made this period between Ronald Reagan's election and his inauguration the bloodiest in El Salvador since La Matanza in 1932. Those murdered by the Salvadoran security forces included six top leaders of the FDR, who were kidnapped from a press conference and tortured and mutilated before they were killed. Less prominent Salvadorans were murdered by the thousands; in January 1981 alone, the legal aid office affiliated with the Roman Catholic archdiocese of San Salvador tabulated some 2,644 murders of civilian noncombatants by the Salvadoran armed forces and by paramilitary forces allied with them. In addition, the security forces and their allies murdered 7 North Americans during this period: 4 churchwomen, 2 labor advisers, and a free-lance journalist.

The slaughter, and especially the killings of the American citizens, helped to arouse U.S. congressional and public concern over human rights. After a while this forced the Reagan administration to reverse its professed position: Instead of repudiating human rights as a goal of U.S. foreign policy, it began to assert that its policies would foster them. However, it took up a new tactic by disputing its human rights critics on factual grounds, claiming that conditions were good or improving in countries that the United States was supporting on political or geopolitical grounds and that they were bad or deteriorating in countries opposed by the United States.

El Salvador was a key in making this policy work. By the time it took office, the Reagan administration had determined, in the words of its first secretary of state, Alexander Haig, to "draw the line" in El Salvador.[1] Up to then, no mention had been made of the civil war in El Salvador as a crucial East-West conflict. Yet the incoming Reagan administration, eager to overcome the anti-interventionist "Vietnam syndrome," determined to reassert American power after the humiliating hostage crisis in Iran, and intent on demonstrating U.S. hegemony over nearby countries as the Soviet Union was doing in Afghanistan, saw El Salvador as a convenient place to show that the United States could prevail. It is, after all, a very small country, and the war there seemed manageable. Accordingly, the more important it could be made to seem in East-West terms, the more significant a U.S. victory would appear.

Though Alexander Haig was the principal advocate of making the Salvadoran conflict a major focus of public attention, Haig himself had fueled the human rights controversy with his politically charged remarks about the murdered churchwomen.* The administration's effort to provide the Salvadoran armed forces with the aid it thought they needed seemed in jeopardy because of this controversy.†

Growing public interest in the human rights situation in El Salvador did influence legislation enacted by Congress in December 1981 that required the president to certify compliance with certain human rights conditions within thirty days

---

* "I would like to suggest to you that some of the investigations would lead one to believe that perhaps the vehicle that the nuns were riding in may have tried to run a roadblock or may have accidentally been perceived to have been doing so, and there may have been an exchange of gunfire. . . ." Haig told the House Committee on Foreign Affairs on March 18, 1981. There was not a word of truth to this. Similarly, there was no truth to the allegation by U.S. ambassador to the U.N. Jeane Kirkpatrick that the murdered churchwomen were "political activists on behalf of the Frente."[2]

† The Reagan administration succeeded in getting a good deal of the assistance to El Salvador that it sought. Military assistance went from $5.9 million in fiscal year 1980 to $35.5 million in 1981 to $82 million in 1982. During this same period, economic assistance went from $58.3 million in 1980 to $114 million in 1981 to $182.2 million in 1982.[3]

if U.S. military aid to El Salvador was to continue.* The law required further certifications by the president every 180 days thereafter as a prerequisite for continuing military aid.

Beginning January 28, 1982, President Reagan certified four times that the required conditions had been met, despite massive evidence that murder of civilians was a routine practice and policy of the Salvadoran armed forces and of paramilitary groups allied to them.[4] This ritual finally came to a halt in November 1983 when the president simply vetoed the legislation that would have extended the certification requirement.

The 1982 Elections

Though various certifications should have inspired disbelief —based as they were on data and arguments that bore only a tenuous relation to the conditions specified in the law— the administration's efforts to persuade Americans that its policies were fostering human rights were capped in March 1982, when elections were held in El Salvador for the Constituent Assembly. The elections were susceptible to reasonable criticism on many grounds—among them, the inability of the left to participate for fear their candidates would be murdered, as the six top leaders of the FDR had been murdered in November 1980; the inherent difficulties of holding an election while a guerrilla war is under way and a portion of the electorate cannot vote because it resides in guerrilla-held zones or conflict zones, or because it has been displaced; the restrictions on campaigning imposed by the violence; the elimination of the two newspapers critical of the government from the left, narrowing the range of opinion available to the electorate; the fraudulent 25 percent inflation of the vote totals;† and the decision of the armed forces

---

* For a description of the conditions for certification, see Chapter 1. For discussion of certification as a legal mechanism, see Chapter 2.

† *Estudios Centroamericanos,* a journal published by the Catholic University in El Salvador, had sparked a controversy when its April 1982 issue contained an article that calculated—on the basis of the number of polling places and the time needed to vote—that the vote totals were considerably

and the U.S. embassy to override the election results by installing as president someone who did not take part in the election, to prevent accession to that office by Major Roberto D'Aubuisson, leader of El Salvador's far right, who would have alienated public opinion in the United States. Nevertheless, the enduring image of the elections is of thousands of Salvadorans patiently waiting in line to cast their ballots. This scene, familiar to Americans from newspaper photos and television footage, seemed tangible evidence that the United States was indeed on the side of democracy in El Salvador and that the people of El Salvador were demonstrating support for their government—one incidentally compatible with Reagan policy.

Whatever their image, the 1982 elections for the Constituent Assembly had little effect on the exercise of power in El Salvador. The armed forces continued to dominate policy, and President Alvaro Magana—who had been selected for the post by the armed forces—served essentially as a public relations spokesman, just as Jose Napoleon Duarte had done during his tenure as president of the junta. Duarte's frequently expressed hope that the 1982 elections would legitimize a civilian government with authority to control the armed forces and end abuses of human rights was not realized. The armed forces remained in control, and systematic torture, kidnapping, and murder continued.

In this period of ostensible civilianization of the government of El Salvador, there were frequent pronouncements by President Magana and by the leadership of the armed forces purporting to respect human rights. These pronouncements were duly cited by the Reagan administration in the periodic certifications; in testimony by Reagan administration officials before Congress; and in various broadsides

---

inflated. This allegation was vigorously denied at the time by officials of the Reagan administration. Two years later, however, the president of El Salvador's Central Elections Council, Armando Rodriguez, conceded that more than a 25 percent inflation in the vote totals had taken place. "It's clear that there was fraud. We didn't denounce it because we didn't want to foul up the good results and the good image of the election" said Hugo Barrera, a leader of the Nationalist Republican Alliance (ARENA), the party of the far right.[5]

published by the administration. It appeared, however, that the main purpose of such pronouncements was to provide the administration with ammunition to use in its battle within the United States to maintain support for the Salvadoran armed forces. They had little to do with any facts.

"Progress" and Death

During 1982, Tutela Legal, the human rights office of the archdiocese of San Salvador, tabulated some 5,399 civilian deaths imputed to the army, the security forces, and paramilitary groups (death squads) allied to the security forces. Adding disappearances following abductions by such forces, and assuming that those who did not reappear were killed, the total number of political killings of civilian noncombatants by government forces and paramilitary groups allied to them during 1982 was over 6,000. This was "only" about half the number killed by those forces during the previous year, a sign of "progress," or "improvement" to the Reagan administration. Another way to look at the figures is that, in a country so tiny as El Salvador, it is astonishing that there were that many politically suspect persons still alive after the slaughter of tens of thousands in 1980 and 1981 and after hundreds of thousands had fled the country.

Though the extent of the killing meant that few sections of the Salvadoran population were spared, some groups appeared to be special targets. Local leaders of the Christian Democratic Party (PDC) were among the victims. In May 1982, for example, the PDC issued a statement accusing the armed forces and paramilitary groups of murdering nine party leaders, six party activists, and twenty-two peasant supporters during that month alone; in July 1982, Jose Napoleon Duarte (out of office since the March elections) charged that hundreds of PDC activists and mayors had been murdered (the time period was not specified); and in September 1982, the PDC denounced the murders of thirty-five Christian Democratic mayors, nine of whom had been killed in 1982.

The victimization of the Christian Democratic Party was, however, exceeded by the attacks on leaders of the FDR and on leaders of pro-FDR labor unions brave enough, or fool-hardy enough, to remain in the country. In a single two-week period, between October 8 and October 21, 1982, some seventeen such persons were kidnapped by groups of heavily armed men in civilian clothes. Six never reappeared; others eventually turned up in prison—after they had been severely tortured. Other such attacks on individuals associated with the FDR continued throughout the year, as they had during 1980 and 1981. Even so, the Reagan administration continued to denounce the FDR for its unwillingness to take part in elections, claiming that it was intent only on "shooting its way into power."

Human rights organizations, even those protected by the Catholic Church, also seemed to be special targets. Several members of their staffs were abducted by the security forces during 1982 and 1983 and never reappeared. In addition, employees of religious organizations providing humanitarian services to displaced persons were frequent victims of abductions, torture, and disappearance. Another important category of attacks focused on peasants who had been involved in land reform. On December 10, 1981, the centrist peasant organization, the Union Comunal Salvadorena (UCS), a group with close ties to the AFL-CIO, issued a report noting that at least ninety officials and promoters of *campesino* organizations had died in 1980 and 1981 "at the hands of the ex-landlords and their allies, who are often members of the local security forces,"[6] and that many beneficiaries of the "land to the tiller" program—an aspect of El Salvador's land reform that was supposed to benefit landless farm laborers—had also become murder victims. Such attacks continued in 1982 and 1983.

An episode that illustrates much about political violence against *campesinos* in El Salvador started at about six-thirty in the morning on February 22, 1983. Several truckloads of uniformed Salvadoran soldiers arrived at Las Hojas in the province of Sonsonate, a farming cooperative of Indians operated by the Asociacion Nacional de Indigenas Salvadorenos (ANIS). Masked members of the local civil defense unit guided the soldiers to selected huts; the soldiers then entered and dragged out the male occupants, including young boys and old men. Other soldiers seized young men walking through the canefields on their way to work.

Later that morning, family members and local authorities found eighteen corpses about a mile from Las Hojas in underbrush near the Cuyapa River. Their hands were tied behind their backs, and they had been shot in the head with high-powered weapons.

One of those who saw the bodies is Dr. Benjamin Cestoni, director of the Salvadoran government's Commission on Human Rights.[7] He says he visited the site with Cristobal Aleman, the labor representative on the commission, and that the commission submitted a report on the massacre at Las Hojas to President Magana on March 7, 1983. Cestoni's report mentioned the eighteen corpses initially found by family members from Las Hojas but made no reference to additional bodies found subsequently, of *campesinos* from neighboring communities. An official of the U.S. embassy in San Salvador who looked into the massacre in Las Hojas was one of those who informed Americas Watch that "more than seventy" persons were killed in the larger operation of which Las Hojas was a part.[8]

On February 23, 1983, General Jose Guillermo Garcia, then the Salvadoran minister of defense, publicly pledged that a full investigation would be conducted and that justice would be done for the Indian families victimized by the massacre.

The commander of the Salvadoran army garrison at Sonsonate and, accordingly, the individual directly responsible for the massacre at Las Hojas, is Colonel Elmer Gonzalez Araujo. At this writing a year and a half have elapsed since the massacre and since the Salvadoran government's own Commission on Human Rights filed a report on it with then President Magana, but as yet no disciplinary action has been taken against Colonel Gonzalez, and he remains in command of the garrison at Sonsonate. Of as many as two hundred soldiers who took part in the massacre, only one— a Captain Figueroa—was supposedly subjected to any disciplinary action. According to an official of the U.S. embassy in San Salvador, the captain was placed in administrative detention. Theoretically, that meant he was restricted to the army base where he was stationed. In practice, according to the U.S. embassy official, he was not restricted at all in his movements.[9]

It subsequently developed, moreover, that the captain was never detained but was promoted to head intelligence in the area. As the *New York Times* concluded, "It now appears the writing of the press release was as far as the arrest [of Captain Figueroa] went."[10] *

The massacre at Las Hojas grew out of a dispute over land and water rights between the members of the Indian farming cooperative and landowners in the region. It had nothing to do with East-West conflict, nor anything to do with the guerrilla war under way in El Salvador. Indeed, the Sonsonate area, in the western portion of El Salvador, has been largely untouched by the war. The army garrison at Sonsonate was performing a traditional function: murdering peasants who had managed to annoy El Salvador's well-to-do landowners. The army could not, as so often, accuse the victims of being subversives and thus rationalize the killing.

Because what happened at Las Hojas was reported in the *New York Times*, the *Washington Post*, and elsewhere outside El Salvador, there was unusual pressure in this case for criminal sanctions against the military officers responsible for the massacre. Even so, they appear to have gotten off scot-free. In that respect, the massacre at Las Hojas was typical.

In testimony before congressional committees and in other public pronouncements during 1982 and 1983, spokespeople for the Reagan administration frequently referred to disciplinary sanctions against members of the Salvadoran armed forces to support their contention that the government was acting to improve the human rights situation. One such assertion appeared in the Reagan administration's July

---

* As of December 1984, according to U.S. Ambassador to El Salvador Thomas Pickering, Colonel Gonzalez and Captain Figueroa had both been transferred to other posts, but there had been no punitive action against them.

27, 1982 certification that El Salvador was complying with the human rights conditions for U.S. military assistance. According to the certification message to Congress, 109 members of the Salvadoran armed forces and at least 20 civil defense members had been disciplined and/or remanded to the civilian courts for criminal prosecution in the previous six months.[11] A document obtained under the Freedom of Information Act subsequently revealed, however, that this information had been provided to the Department of State in a cable from the U.S. embassy in San Salvador, which pointed out, "The embassy cannot confirm it independently. Therefore, we recommend that it be used with proper caveats. Further, we have no information on final disposition of these cases."[12] Subsequent inquiries by Americas Watch and by members of Congress revealed that not one of the cases cited in the certification involved criminal sanctions for a human rights violation.[13] In fact, from 1979 through 1984, there was not a single case in which a member of the Salvadoran armed forces was criminally punished for a human rights violation against a Salvadoran, and just one case in which a civil defenseman was punished for such a violation.

In addition to the selective killings, there have been a great many deaths resulting from the armed forces' ground or air attacks on civilians in conflict areas or in guerrilla-controlled zones. Debate over the human rights situation in El Salvador in the early part of 1982 focused on a particularly grotesque episode in December 1981 in which a U.S.-trained battalion of the Salvadoran army had massacred between seven hundred and a thousand persons in the village of El Mozote and in several surrounding villages in Morazan Province, an FMLN stronghold. Despite firsthand investigation and revelation of the event by the *New York Times* and the *Washington Post*, Reagan administration officials, led by then Assistant Secretary of State Thomas Enders, denied that such a massacre took place, purporting to rely on an investigation of the episode by the U.S. embassy in San Salvador. In fact, however, the embassy's investigation did not support Enders's denial. As El Mozote was in a militarily contested zone, the closest the embassy's investigators came to it was a helicopter overflight; they interviewed no survivors; and such circumstantial evidence as they gathered tended to confirm that a massacre had taken place.[14] Nevertheless, Enders's denial of the massacre became the basis for a concerted Reagan administration campaign against press reporting of human rights abuses in El Salvador.*

Shooting the Messenger

In addition to attacking press coverage of human rights abuses, the Reagan administration also launched an attack on the other major source of information on this subject: the human rights organizations operating within El Salvador. The Reagan administration's own reports on human rights abuses in El Salvador were based exclusively on accounts published in the Salvadoran newspapers, which, as the U.S. embassy in San Salvador had pointed out in a cable to the Department of State, "only reports deaths in areas where they momentarily have correspondents or in areas into which correspondents do not fear to enter."[16] To this it could have been added that press reporting of abuses also reflected the fact that the two Salvadoran newspapers critical of the government from the left had been closed by violence from government forces: La Cronica in 1980 after its news editor and a photographer were hacked to death; El Independiente in 1981 after army tanks and trucks surrounded its building. The shutdown of these two papers considerably reduced the amount of information on human rights abuses reported in the Salvadoran press—and thus also the reporting of abuses by the Department of State.

In 1982, the Reagan administration's attack focused on Socorro Juridico, the legal aid organization affiliated with

---

* This campaign was strongly aided and abetted on the editorial page of the Wall Street Journal (see, for example, its editorial of February 10, 1982). It particularly focused on the reporting of Raymond Bonner of the New York Times and almost certainly played a part in his removal from El Salvador later that year and in a general decline of press coverage of human rights abuses there.[15]

the archdiocese of San Salvador. The U.S. embassy in San Salvador accused it of dealing with only one side of the conflict and insisted that the group reveal its methodology and sources in order to be credible as an unbiased observer.[17] The attack was unfounded and unfair. Socorro Juridico was "one-sided" in the sense that its definition of human rights abuses was the one standard in both international law and U.S. law—that they are abuses of citizens' rights by their governments. Though a handful of human rights groups (such as Americas Watch) had chosen to report abuses by antigovernment groups as well as by governments, the prevailing practice was the one followed by Socorro Juridico.* The charge of not revealing its methods was false, as Socorro Juridico made it widely known that it relied on testimony taken from witnesses to abuses and from family members; and the charge of not revealing its sources was partially false because Socorro Juridico's reports frequently listed the names of family members who provided testimony, and partially spurious because no organization can reveal the names of sources who fear reprisals for providing testimony.

An implicit—and sometimes explicit—element in the attack on Socorro Juridico was that it was left-wing. This was consistent with the Reagan administration's effort to interpret all actions in El Salvador, including the tabulation of human rights abuses, in terms of East-West conflict, and then suggesting that political left and pro-Eastern sympathies were in a one-to-one correspondence. It is a clever inference but a serious misrepresentation of an organization that perceived itself as performing a Christian mission, not as aiding one side or another in a geopolitical struggle.

The attack on Socorro Juridico had a significant deleterious effect. Though it did little to discredit the reports of U.S. organizations that relied on human rights data collected by Socorro Juridico, it undoubtedly played a part in persuading

---

* Indeed, the Reagan administration regularly cited the findings of such groups as authoritative when they were critical of governments it opposed— as in the case of the Permanent Commission on Human Rights, in Nicaragua, which has an adversary relationship to the Sandinista government but which until July 1984 did not report on abuses by the *contras* trying to overthrow that government.

Archbishop Arturo Rivera y Damas to end Socorro's affiliation with the archdiocese in May 1982. In its place, the archbishop established Tutela Legal as the Church's human rights monitoring office.

Since May 1982, Tutela Legal has been a major source of human rights information for groups in the United States and elsewhere attempting to determine the extent and nature of political violence in El Salvador. Departing from the practice of Socorro Juridico, Tutela Legal reports on human rights abuses committed by the Salvadoran guerrillas as well as on abuses committed by government forces and paramilitary groups allied to them. Like Socorro Juridico, Tutela Legal has relied on testimony from witnesses to abuses and from members of the victims' families to compile its reports. Also like Socorro Juridico, Tutela Legal has come under attack from the U.S. embassy in San Salvador and the Department of State, which have been eager to discredit reports indicating that the political violence attributable to the government of El Salvador is greater than reported by the embassy on the strength of accounts in the Salvadoran press. The fact that Tutela Legal reports on guerrilla abuses has not spared it from State Department efforts to define it as left-wing and, by implication, suspect.

Tutela Legal reported 5,143 political killings of civilian noncombatants by the Salvadoran armed forces and paramilitary forces allied to them during 1983 and another 535 disappearances after abductions by such forces. In addition, during 1983, Tutela Legal reported 67 political murders of civilian noncombatants that it attributed to the guerrillas. The organization had tabulated 40 such murders in 1982 in the period following its establishment in May of that year. Some of these were political assassinations in which the victims were right-wing politicians. Others were executions of suspected collaborators with the armed forces or death squads. Still others involved attacks in rural areas on buses that failed to stop at guerrilla roadblocks. In general, however, the guerrillas had little incentive to attack civilians, and the numbers were relatively low. Ironically, Tutela Legal's reporting of information on political violence against civilians by the guerrillas has been all the more damaging to the government because it showed the disproportion between the numbers.

Death Squads

The most widely publicized aspect of El Salvador's human rights problem concerns the activities of the death squads. Groups of heavily armed men, generally wearing civilian clothes, travel in vans, abducting targeted individuals and causing them to "disappear," or killing them on the spot. Since 1979 such death squads have killed several thousand civilian noncombatants.

Though press accounts of human rights abuses in El Salvador have tended to attribute most of the killings of civilian noncombatants to death squads, this has never been accurate. Even in 1981, at the peak of death squad activity, Socorro Juridico attributed more than 60 percent of civilian deaths to regular uniformed Salvadoran forces. During 1982 and 1983, Socorro Juridico and Tutela Legal attributed only about one-third of the killings of civilian noncombatants to death squads, or paramilitary groups not displaying military insignia, and the balance to uniformed forces. Of those attributed to the uniformed forces, the great majority were found to be committed by the army rather than by the National Police, the National Guard, and the Treasury Police —which are known collectively as the "security forces."

One reason that the U.S. press misperceived the army's paramount responsibility for killings—and the death squads' secondary, dependent role—is the way the situation has been presented by the Reagan administration. First, for a substantial period, the administration simply denied that most death squad killings were connected to the armed forces at all. The State Department's *Country Reports on Human Rights Practices* for 1982, for example, attributed political murders to "extremes of the right and the left" and conceded a relationship to government forces only insofar as "some groups associated with the military security forces identify and eliminate suspected collaborators" of the opposition.[18]

This refusal to acknowledge the direct responsibility of the government of El Salvador for such killings, and the effort to attribute them to the "extreme right" (along with the "extreme left"), persisted during most of the first three years of the Reagan administration. As late as August 1983, Assistant Secretary of State Elliott Abrams said publicly, "The assumption that the death squads are active security forces remains to be proved. It might be right, though I suspect it probably isn't right."[19] Four months later, President Reagan himself went a step farther and said that he suspected that death squad murders were actually committed by left-wing guerrillas trying to smear El Salvador's reputation because "the right wing will be blamed for it."[20] And as late as May 1984, President Reagan made the speech quoted at the beginning of this section attributing the political violence in El Salvador to the guerrillas and to "a small, violent right wing" that is "not part of the government."

No one familiar with El Salvador can take such explanations seriously. Though vehicle checks by the army and the security forces had been a regular feature of life in El Salvador for several years, there was no recorded instance in which a death squad was apprehended in such a check. Though a curfew was in effect for years and any unauthorized person on the streets during curfew hours could expect to be shot, death squads operated with impunity during nighttime hours. Uniformed forces have frequently blocked streets to permit death squads to perform their duties. No arrest or prosecution for death squad activities is known to have occurred.

The list goes on—increasingly discrediting the administration's argument. That the death squads have been responsible for relatively fewer deaths is a reflection not upon their zeal, or their freedom of action, but on their smaller operating units and their selectivity—as distinct from the army's often indiscriminate reprisals.

In the fall of 1983, as a new U.S. ambassador arrived in

San Salvador, the embassy abandoned the effort to insulate government forces from responsibility for death squad activity—although what embassy spokesmen began to say was not always consistent with the words of administration spokespeople in Washington. In a speech to a Chamber of Commerce group in San Salvador, the new ambassador, Thomas Pickering, asserted, "There has been little doubt of the commitment of the authorities to dealing with terror by the FMLN. There may be lack of means, but there is no lack of resolve. What has distressed my government is the lack of parallel activity against those who murder and kidnap university professors, doctors, labor leaders, *campesinos*, and government workers. We know by their selection of victims . . . [that they] are not guerrilla organizations."[21] To back up Pickering's public statements, Vice President George Bush traveled to El Salvador on December 11, 1983, and met with the country's thirty-one top military commanders. Though the exact details of that meeting were not disclosed, the U.S. embassy in San Salvador let it be known that the vice president made explicit threats that U.S. aid would end unless death squad killings and disappearances were curbed.

The Pickering-Bush efforts had a significant effect. During the six-month period from May 1983 through October 1983, Tutela Legal recorded 588 killings committed by death squads and 322 disappearances, for a combined total of 910. In the six-month period from November 1983 through April 1984, Tutela Legal recorded 241 death squad killings and 113 disappearances, for a combined total of 354. Of course, that is still a significant, indeed, a horrifying number. And the very fact that it was U.S. pressure on the Salvadoran armed forces that reduced the number of death squad killings and disappearances made all the more clear the direct links between the armed forces and such activity.

Unfortunately, disappearances and death squad killings were no more the sum and substance of human rights violations in 1984 than they had been three or four years earlier, when this variety of killing had been much more frequent. In 1984, as in previous years, the majority of deaths of civilian noncombatants involved operations by the army of El Salvador. And here the change of ambassador meant no change in the U.S. position; the embassy kept pretending that such death squad killings constituted the bulk of human rights violations in El Salvador. Indeed, the embassy in San Salvador used its attack on the death squads to reinforce the Reagan administration's claim that all, or virtually all, deaths resulting from army operations should be considered combat-related and, accordingly, should be omitted from tabulations of human rights violations.

Killings in Army Operations

According to a January 1984 cable from the US embassy in San Salvador to the Department of State, "Tutela Legal's figures on civilian deaths that occur during military engagements (mostly of guerrilla *masas*)* now account for almost 80 percent of Tutela Legal's overall reported total of civilian victims of political violence." The cable went on to say, "Although Tutela Legal regards *masas* as unarmed civilians, some of whom even may be helping the guerrillas involuntarily, *masas* do live in close proximity of and travel in the company of armed guerrillas. This intermingling with and support of the armed insurgents makes them something more than innocent civilian bystanders when they and their armed companions come under fire during military engagements." [22]

As it happens, Tutela Legal did not use the term *masas*; it was used by the guerrillas. In any event, it was not a useful term in determining whether killings by the Salvadoran armed forces may be properly described as human rights violations. Indeed, it had the pernicious effect of stigmatizing civilians who happened to live in conflict zones or guerrilla-controlled zones, appearing to legitimize attacks upon them. In any war, of course, some injuries to those taking

---

* *Masas* is a term used by the FMLN to describe civilians living in guerrilla-controlled zones or zones of conflict. The term also implies support for the guerrilla cause.

no active part in hostilities are the inevitable consequence of attacks on legitimate military targets. Tutela Legal did not include such killings in its tabulations and also excluded doubtful cases. By using the term "guerrilla *masas*," however, the embassy implied that it was the views of those who were killed that mattered: in its own words, that they were "something more than innocent civilian bystanders" because they supported the guerrillas.

Tutela Legal pointed out that many of those killed in connection with military engagements were killed at the conclusion of battle. Some were fleeing civilians who were attacked, often by air. Others were pulled from their homes and killed because it was thought that they had aided the guerrillas by furnishing food to them or by not disclosing their whereabouts. Others were prisoners who were killed. Still others were the wounded who were finished off. Such killings come under no proper category of combat deaths, yet were casually dismissed as just that.

In July 1984, the U.S. embassy in San Salvador shifted its position, finally acknowledging that international humanitarian law forbids attacks on civilian noncombatants even if they live in close proximity to guerrillas and support the guerrillas. An embassy spokesperson told Americas Watch, "*Masas* are not an appropriate military target of and by themselves, only insofar as they may be part of a legitimate target of armed guerrillas."[23] The shift, however, was accompanied by yet another attack on the investigation and reporting methods of Tutela Legal, specifically concerning this issue. Yet Tutela Legal's reports were also consistent with the testimony obtained by representatives of Americas Watch and of the Lawyers Committee for International Human Rights during several 1984 missions to El Salvador, and with information gathered by independent U.S. journalists who ventured into conflict zones and interviewed residents of those areas.[24]

At this writing, much of the Salvadoran government's military effort consists of aerial bombardments of areas controlled by the guerrillas. Available information on the effect of such bombardments indicates that the great majority of the victims are civilians. A seeming purpose is to deprive the guerrillas of a population from which they can obtain sustenance. It also has the effect of creating a large population of external refugees and internally displaced persons.

Refugees and the Displaced

By mid-1984, close to one-fourth of the Salvadoran population were either refugees outside the borders or internally displaced. Some 750,000 Salvadorans had fled the country entirely during the previous five years. Many had entered the United States (though some 10,000 or so each year were apprehended here and deported back to El Salvador); others had crowded refugee camps in Honduras, or immigrated to Mexico or Nicaragua. Though many of the external refugees endured severe hardships in escaping the country and attempting to establish themselves elsewhere, by and large they were relatively fortunate, given the lot endured by another 500,000 or so Salvadorans who fled their homes but not their borders. The refuge of displaced-persons camps operated by churches and various humanitarian relief organizations, the new slums on the edges of the cities and, in some cases, makeshift shelters by the sides of the roads offers little but misery. Considered automatically suspect for having fled the army, those residing in camps were virtual prisoners because of the extreme danger they would face from the armed forces if they attempted to leave. Few of the displaced, in or out of camps, have any prospect of rebuilding more or less normal lives until the conflict ends.

Army or government activity cannot be blamed entirely for the existence of these camps. That many had fled homes in guerrilla-controlled zones and conflict zones was evident from the underpopulation of these areas by mid-1984. Though the guerrillas effectively controlled about one-third of the country, it was generally estimated that some two hundred thousand civilians remained in the areas they controlled. This was about one-third or one-fourth of the number who had resided in those areas five years previously. Among those who remained in guerrilla-controlled areas, many had lost their homes in bombardments and were eking out an existence as best they could.

The guerrillas helped enlarge the displaced-persons population during 1984 by forcefully recruiting in zones of the country they did not control but in which they were able to operate sporadically. To avoid being press-ganged into joining the guerrilla forces, thousands joined the refugee population in Honduras or crowded into the slums around San Salvador and into displaced-persons camps.

The existence of the camps, however misery-ridden, still does not begin to address the refugee problem satisfactorily. Displaced-persons camps have not been safe havens. More than two hundred thousand of the internally displaced persons are not officially registered with the Salvadoran government—and thus are subject to deliberate attacks by the Salvadoran armed forces. Such attacks take place despite the fact that virtually all these people are women, young children, or elderly people and despite the fact that highly respected international voluntary organizations and religious groups attempt to provide them with care and protection. These attacks also extend to relief workers assisting the displaced. Forms of attack ranged from aerial bombardment to abduction, torture, disappearance, and murder. According to a report by Americas Watch and the Lawyers Committee for International Human Rights, based on two missions to the camps in 1984, the Salvadoran armed forces chose these targets because they thought them sympathizers with the guerrillas, or—preposterous as it may seem in connection with a population almost entirely composed of infants, young children, their mothers, and the elderly—themselves active guerrillas.[25]

The violence and harassment inspired by government mistrust created a vicious circle, because the reason so many displaced did not register with the government was fear. They did not give their names, relationships, and places of origin to the Salvadoran authorities out of fear that to do so would invite reprisals. They gave up the enhanced care and assistance available to the registered displaced in order to achieve relative protection. Yet the consequences of not registering prove devastating.

The attacks have not been limited to displaced persons alone. Refugee workers, medical personnel, and others who came in contact with the displaced were viewed with great suspicion and often faced harassment and direct attacks by the Salvadoran armed forces. Thus, for example, in 1983 and early 1984 twelve relief workers associated with camps run by the archdiocese of San Salvador and relief efforts of the Lutheran Church were abducted, and several of them were tortured.

The Lawyers Committee and Americas Watch also discovered a particularly horrendous abuse of human rights by the Salvadoran air force, which has bombed sites where displaced persons in conflict zones gathered to obtain medical assistance from the International Committee of the Red Cross. The ICRC, which gave the armed forces advance notice of the places where it would be providing such assistance, had been forced to discontinue much of its aid in conflict zones to avoid endangering the displaced. Americas Watch brought this practice to the attention of U.S. Ambassador Thomas Pickering and the Congress, and by mid-1984, embassy pressure on the Salvadoran armed forces had ended attacks on ICRC medical service sites. In July 1984 the ICRC reported that it was providing services to 105,000 displaced persons in conflict zones.

Duarte's "Democracy"

In May 1984, Jose Napoleon Duarte was elected president of El Salvador, ostensibly now with the mandate, or the legitimacy, he said was missing during his tenure as president of the junta from 1980 to 1982. In gaining this office, Duarte was apparently aided by substantial covert financial support from the United States, reportedly funneled through the CIA. This did not significantly deter the Reagan administration from hailing his election as a triumph for the democratic process.

In his second coming, Duarte became an even more effective public relations spokesman for the Salvadoran government than he had been previously. Following his inauguration, Duarte spent most of his first several weeks as president traveling in Europe and the United States. The allocation of time appeared to reflect a realistic assessment of his role, for though there was little he could do within the country, he could lobby persuasively for international assistance from abroad. His efforts helped the Reagan administration to obtain $70 million more for military aid to the Salvadoran armed forces, on the grounds that human rights conditions had improved.

The Reagan administration's effort to document such improvements was also aided significantly by the May 1984 conviction of five national guardsmen for murdering the four American churchwomen in 1980. The case had become by far the best-known symbol of human rights abuse in El Salvador. But despite Duarte, despite the conviction in the churchwomen's case, and despite the decline in death squad killings and disappearances that began in late 1983, the human rights situation in El Salvador continues to be bleak and heading for no significant improvement.

Duarte has little real power within El Salvador. Under the present constitution, the president appoints neither the attorney general nor the members of the Supreme Court. These are appointed by the Constituent Assembly, which is still controlled by a coalition of Roberto D'Aubisson's far-right ARENA party and the PCN (National Conciliation Party), the traditional party of the armed forces and wealthy landowners. At the same time that Duarte assumed office—June 1, 1984—an ARENA party stalwart became attorney general and a new Supreme Court was installed consisting entirely of members from ARENA, from the PCN, and from a splinter of the PCN. The chief justice of the Supreme Court is Jose Francisco ("Chachi") Guerrero, who was the PCN's 1984 presidential candidate against Duarte. The Supreme Court designates all lower-court judges. Accordingly, Duarte's domestic political opponents, not he, will determine whether there are any prosecutions for human rights abuses.

The conviction for the murder of the churchwomen resulted in no small way from three and a half years of intense pressure from the United States, including a determination by the U.S. Congress that $19 million in U.S. military aid to El Salvador would be withheld until there was a trial and a verdict in the case. There has been no comparable pressure with respect to the murders of Salvadorans—and accordingly, little prospect that members of the Salvadoran armed forces will be punished for murdering forty thousand of their fellow citizens since 1979.

Technically, Duarte is the commander-in-chief of the Salvadoran armed forces. His actual control over these forces is minimal, however. Some changes in command—though not at the highest levels—were made at about the time he took office, but these reflect pressure from the U.S. embassy rather than from Duarte. As to the decline in death squad killings and disappearances, it too required intense U.S. pressure. Even with it, the level of such killings and disappearances—thirty or so a month at this writing—remains appallingly high, especially in so tiny a country where there has been so great an orgy of killings that it must be a challenge for death squads to find politically suspect persons still alive to be killed. The numbers may be reduced, but they remain high enough to perpetuate terror in El Salvador.

The United States, meanwhile, continues to bankroll abuse. As Alexander Haig wished, the United States has drawn the line in El Salvador. It has made the conflict there, which was rooted in a struggle over land and over the methods used by El Salvador's landowners and their military allies to crush protests against their control over the country's wealth, loom as a significant East-West conflict. Having drawn such a line, the United States now finds it difficult to walk away from the conflict, for to do so would seem to involve geopolitical humiliation. Yet the methods by which the Salvadoran armed forces are attempting to prevail massively transgress international codes of permissible conduct.

In aiding the Salvadoran armed forces, the United States has felt compelled to serve as the apologist for these abuses and to undermine those who inform the world about them.

At this late date, it will be difficult—if not impossible—for the United States to retreat from its portrait of the civil war in El Salvador as a major East-West conflict. A negotiated settlement could save some face; abandoning the Salvadoran armed forces possibly to their defeat would certainly humiliate the United States internationally. Human rights advocates are painfully aware that if the choice is between enduring such humiliation on the one hand and continuing to sponsor gross abuses of human rights on the other hand, there is little doubt what decision will come.

HONDURAS

In mid-October 1984, when he called for a new, "more independent relationship on security issues,"[1] the foreign minister of Honduras reportedly took U.S. officials by surprise. For three years the United States had used Honduras as regional base for military training and maneuvers and had convinced it to provide a haven for *contras* fighting the Nicaraguan government. The Honduran military had acted as a willing ally in sealing the border with El Salvador against escaping refugees, and the civilian government had supported the entire framework of the regional strategy. For three years the Honduran armed forces had received massive U.S. military aid and welcomed thousands of U.S. soldiers, while the government had even allowed the U.S. ambassador to participate in delicate state meetings.[2] Honduras had been not only an important ally but also an especially tame one. Internal discontent with these developments had been firmly punished, and by the same administration whose foreign minister now sought independence.

But Honduras had paid for its allegiance, and the foreign minister suggested the price for maintaining it. "We want . . . more assistance in helping to build our economy and strengthening our democratic system," he said—a simple enough demand at first sight, but he complained of a lack of "concrete response" from the United States.[3] Dominated by its armed forces and strategically key to the U.S. policy for Central America, Honduras was drowning in the wrong kind of aid and had experienced the abuses that militarization can foster. The nation was, as three U.S. human rights groups pointed out in 1983, "on the brink" of becoming a disaster, in social terms and in terms of human rights;[4] the leadership, long defensive with its critics on this score, had apparently come to see that time was short.

Portrait of an Ally

With a per capita GNP of $561 in 1981, Honduras is one of the poorest countries in the Western Hemisphere. The illiteracy rate is 43 percent, and there are serious problems with inadequate health care and malnutrition. Of the 62 percent of the population that lives in rural areas, most are small farmers who produce at little more than subsistance level, and land reform legislated in the 1960s and 1970s has been bogged down by slow government action and endless litigation. The society, on the other hand, is less polarized between rich and poor than in other Latin American countries. Although some areas of the economy are highly concentrated—notably the banana industry, where U.S. private investment is strong—Honduran society is not dominated by a powerful, small, landed oligarchy.

Perhaps for this reason, political and social conflict, while active, is not as violent as elsewhere in Central America. There are strong and highly organized trade union and peasant union movements. Political parties are also relatively diverse and active in the National Assembly. The dominant parties are the conservative Partido Nacional and the Partido Liberal, now in power. The latter is completely controlled by its more conservative wing. A faction called ALIPO, representing the reformist tendencies of the Villeda Morales presidency in the early 1960s, was displaced from the party in the 1980 primaries and later organized as an opposition party. Smaller and recently created parties, such as PINU (Party of Innovation and Unity) and the Christian Democratic Party, also have some congressional representation. By contrast, the Socialist Party of Honduras (PASOH) and several other leftist groups are very divided and have no parliamentary representation.

The single most important source of political power is the army, which controls not only the air force and navy under a single command, but also the police (FUSEP) and its investigations unit (DNI). Honduras has a long history of political instability and military coups, even in the recent past. In 1963, the army ousted the reformist government of Ramon Villeda Morales, using the excuse of the dangers of Communist infiltration, and for the next decade a succession of harsh military regimes and weak civilian governments were legitimized by fraudulent or meaningless elections. The armed forces were not highly trained or professional—in 1969 they lost a war to the Salvadoran army in a matter of days—but they were increasingly eager to take state power. In 1972, the military once again did so, this time against both major parties, and controlled the government until 1981. Despite a shy attempt to institute halfhearted reforms early in that period, the ten-year military government was generally corrupt and inefficient. The return to parliamentary democracy in 1981 resulted in the election of President Roberto Suazo Cordova, a last-minute substitute for the Liberal *caudillo* Modesto Rodas Alvarado, who died right before the election.

Because of Honduras's relative internal peace, the military regime had not been notably repressive, though a combination of political motives and inefficient administration of justice resulted in long-term detentions of trade union and peasant leaders. Then, as now, the courts and police were highly susceptible to pressure from landowners and large corporations. At the same time, Honduras—like Costa Rica —maintained neutrality in the growing internal conflicts of neighboring countries, providing safe haven to refugees and refusing to deport Sandinistas fighting against Somoza, or armed opponents of the regimes in El Salvador and Guatemala.

The presidential elections of 1981 were held because the discredited military regime had exhausted its possibilities. They did not result, however, in a reduction of the military's privileged role in shaping public policy—quite the reverse. The transition to civilian rule coincided with a series of internal changes in the army command structure from which General Gustavo Alvarez Martinez emerged as its most powerful figure. Attempting to establish an image of "professionalism" and enjoying the active support of the United States, the armed forces under Alvarez did not need to occupy institutional positions in the government in order to increase their power and influence. Under the military's *de facto* authority came such key aspects of public policy as internal security, foreign affairs, refugee policy, and civil liberties.

Thus after 1981 Honduras became the model of government for which the Reagan administration has shown particular fondness in the hemisphere: a constitutional democracy where the armed forces have undisturbed and uncontrolled power over those large areas of the decision-making process that are considered of strategic importance in terms of both internal and regional security. Such a model allows the United States to have a double relationship with the country: a diplomatic contact with its civilian leadership and a direct, fluid relationship between the Pentagon and the military.

The Costs of Militarization

Like the new U.S. administration, General Alvarez saw Central America as an East-West testing ground and soon brought about a complete reversal of Honduran neutrality in the conflicts in the region. As early as 1980, and increasingly in 1981, Honduran police and immigration authorities began arresting and illegally deporting Salvadoran nationals suspected of involvement in activities against their government. Hondurans who were considered supporters of the Salvadoran left were also targeted for arrest and disappearances. Also in 1981, the CIA began recruiting and training Nicaraguan exiles to conduct violent actions against the Sandinista regime.

The Honduran government did not simply tolerate the presence of rebels fighting a neighbor government, as it had done before 1979 when the Sandinistas were fighting Somoza, but lent considerable logistical support through army personnel, materiel, and facilities. Honduran officers were engaged as trainers, side by side with officers sent covertly by the military dictatorship of Argentina, though these were later replaced by CIA personnel. Honduran officers also participated in limiting public access to training camps, provided transportation, and assisted in forcible recruitment among Nicaraguan refugees.

Finally, in 1983 the United States began a series of military exercises called Big Pine, ostensibly designed to provide training to the Honduran army. In a matter of months, the exercises grew in scope, providing training also for Salvadoran troops and establishing permanent bases for U.S. troops throughout Honduran territory. By 1984 the bases were also being used to send reconnaissance and espionage flights into El Salvador and Nicaragua.

In the meantime, U.S. military assistance programs for Honduras grew dramatically, with hardly a complaint in the U.S. Congress. From $3.9 million in 1980, such aid more than doubled, to $8.9 million in 1981. It then skyrocketed to $31.3 million in 1982 and $37.3 million in 1983,[5] and the figure for fiscal year 1984 was $78.5 million—a twentyfold increase over the amount just five years earlier. For fiscal year 1985 the original request was $62.5 million, but the final amount was certain to be greater because the pattern set by the administration is to request supplemental appropriations during the year. As high as these figures are, it is important to note that they do not include any of the costs involved in military construction, nor any of the expenses for military maneuvers and training, nor the cost of covert operations against Nicaragua launched primarily from Honduras.

Honduras has become a country permanently occupied by U.S. troops. In September 1984, the State Department asserted that seven hundred U.S. troops were permanently stationed in Honduras. At certain peaks, during maneuvers, the number goes still higher. The figure was two thousand in March and April of the same year, and U.S. troops participating in maneuvers were approximately fifty-five hundred from August to December 1983, twenty-six hundred in January and February 1984, and eighteen hundred in May 1984. The U.S. influence is pervasive not only in military terms but also in the actions of the Suazo government in other matters. For example, Honduras has steadfastly refused to enter into bilateral discussions with Nicaragua, preferring instead to follow the State Department line of favoring regional talks including other governments. When Secretary of State Shultz surprisingly opened talks with Managua on May 30, 1984, and it was revealed that secret bilateral talks had been conducted for months at Costa Rica's behest, the Honduran foreign policy suffered an embarrassing blow.

The Honduran government's complete acquiescence in

subordinating the country to the regional military and diplomatic policies of the United States has fueled widespread
nationalist feeling and criticism of Suazo from all opposition
quarters. But such criticism was not easily tolerated after
1981. A significant change brought about by the new militarization of Honduras is that human rights violations became
paradoxically more serious under the civilian government
than they had ever been in the twenty years since the military coup of 1963. The government's defensiveness on the
human rights issue and its failure to respond to complaints
appeared not to concern the Reagan administration, which
itself denied, as far as possible, that any such problem existed
—either by misrepresenting the nature and scope of actions
actually taken, or by explaining away the government's refusal to take positive action.

There is no significant, nationally organized leftist movement in Honduras, and political dissent is legal. Nonetheless, under the civilian government there have been
systematic disappearances of individuals involved in political
activities. The first few cases occurred in 1981, with the practice generally directed against members of the Salvadoran
guerrillas, or Hondurans who supported them.

Disappearances and Torture

Disappearances did not cease with Suazo's inauguration but
rather increased in 1982 and 1983. At the same time, the
targets became more diversified, as has been the pattern also
in other countries. Victims of disappearances soon included
labor and student activists and Hondurans suspected of belonging to leftist organizations. They were abducted in the
street, or in their homes or workplaces, or arrested by uniformed security agents at the borders. Their arrests were not
acknowledged by the authorities, and administrative or judicial inquiries on their whereabouts and fate were met with
denials or simply ignored. According to some who survived
the experience, the *desaparecido* was typically taken to a
clandestine detention center run by intelligence officers of
the army, where he or she was subjected to beatings and

torture in the course of interrogation. In some cases, there is evidence that the interrogators ultimately murdered the victim. A clandestine burial ground was found near Tegucigalpa in early 1982, and at least one of the remains identified there belonged to a person who had disappeared after his arrest by security forces the previous year.

The number of disappeared persons in Honduras has not reached the proportions that have made the practice so notorious in Guatemala, El Salvador, Chile, and Argentina. The figures are nonetheless significant, because the proportion of disappearances is high in relation to all cases of political arrests in the same period. The practice was, moreover, centrally directed and apparently was carried out with at least the general knowledge of the civilian authorities as well as the military command. A new practice since 1981, disappearance was firmly identified with the civilian accommodation to military priorities under Alvarez.

By mid-1984 the Tegucigalpa-based Committee for the Defense of Human Rights in Honduras (CODEH) had tabulated 112 cases of unresolved disappearances since 1981. CODEH also lists "temporary disappearances," 20 of them in 1983 alone. The term "temporary disappearance" refers to abductions followed by unacknowledged detention periods of several weeks, after which the victims are eventually released or brought before the courts.

Political murders and acknowledged detentions without charges also have occurred. Between 1981 and 1984 there were 219 extrajudicial executions by security forces, many of which appeared to have political motives. Included in that figure are 24 cases in 1983 that CODEH documented as political murders. By the end of 1983 there were between 35 and 40 persons in prison awaiting charges for political offenses. Six months later, the courts had yet to convict one of them.

In a very high proportion of cases there were verifiable reports of torture inflicted on prisoners. Of 41 political arrests in 1983, CODEH reported 34 cases of torture. On at least two occasions prisoners have died as a result of torture while still in custody. Methods included beatings, and suffocation with hoods; also in many instances more sophisticated means were employed, including electric shocks in the course of interrogation.

Several prisoners' complaints of torture have been published in the press and formally denounced to the courts, but no investigation has ensued. This is typical of the complete breakdown of judicial due process in Honduras during the past few years, which is reflected not only in the lack of serious prosecutions of political cases but also in the absence of any investigation into reports of abuses by security forces. Indeed, legal experts suggest that the complete ineffectiveness of *habeas corpus* is a prime factor making systematic disappearances possible.

Denial and Distortion

The Reagan administration's response was initially to deny this bleak picture altogether, or to attempt apologetic explanations about the subversive threat perceived by the Honduran government. State Department and U.S. embassy officials stated privately in 1982 that disappearances simply were not happening, thus accepting the official Honduran explanation that persons reported as missing were actually in hiding or abroad. The *Country Reports on Human Rights Practices* for 1982 and 1983 mention those cases as "allegations" by local groups and report their incidence with considerably lower figures than those cited by CODEH and others in Honduras. The *Reports*, in addition, imply that Honduras faces an emergency in which extreme internal-security measures would be justified. The 1982 *Reports* in particular goes to great lengths in explaining the concern supposedly expressed by most Hondurans about the military buildup in neighboring Nicaragua. "Hondurans," it states, "believe that the Sandinista regime in Nicaragua has an active interest in weakening democratic Honduras and hurting its image through a combination of subversion, military intimidation, and malicious propaganda."[6] The same report also states, "The year 1982 was one of transition for the extreme left, moving from an earlier strategy of an 'Oasis of Peace' for

Honduras to one of preparing the ground for local revolutionary violence in collaboration with Salvadoran and Nicaraguan Marxist revolutionaries."[7]

There has been some terrorist activity in Honduras, particularly in 1982, as well as an aborted attempt to start a rural guerrilla group in the south-central province of Olancho in 1983. No connection to an international conspiracy, however, has been established, and authorities have not convicted any defendant in court for terrorism or such conspiracy. The influence of these groups in Honduran political life is negligible.

In 1983, possibly because of the pressure of public opinion, FUSEP and DNI began producing, and filing charges against, prisoners who had been "temporarily disappeared." Though cases of unresolved disappearance still occurred in late 1983 and early 1984, the trend was clearly toward the use of "temporary disappearances" instead. Almost immediately State Department and embassy officials began hailing "progress," citing the fact that disappearances were no longer occurring (after having denied previously that they were taking place at all). The *Country Reports* for 1983 mentions ten cases for that year as reported by CODEH and the Commission of Relatives of the Disappeared, a group established in 1983 to press the government for information on their loved ones. (The figure published by these groups for unresolved disappearances was actually twenty-six.) As with other country reports—Nicaragua's being a notable exception—statements by independent human rights monitors were, at best, "allegations," inasmuch as their findings were inconvenient for the administration.

The *Country Reports* on Honduras for 1982 and 1983 also seriously misstate the attitude of the Honduran government vis-à-vis human rights violations, giving the impression it was carrying out serious investigations and prosecuting abuses by the security forces. In fact, only in some well-publicized cases were there arrests of the agents involved, and the charges were subsequently dropped even when eyewitnesses were willing and able to testify. The *Country Reports* for 1983 includes a case from January 1984 in which a student died under torture, and it claims that as a result of this death the chief of DNI was fired. This is incorrect. Lt. Colonel Juan Blas Salazar was not fired but transferred to the intelligence unit of the army (G-2), reportedly as second-in-command. In October, he was again transferred to logistics. Not mentioned in the *Country Reports* is the fact that the victim in that case belonged to an influential right-wing group with connections in the army and that the cause for the arrest did not involve the exercise of his rights but seemed related to illegal currency traffic.

The *Country Reports* also give glowing accounts of the legislative protection of freedoms of expression and of assembly and association. Indeed, Hondurans are permitted a relatively healthy exercise of these freedoms; there is at least one independent newspaper, and strong trade unions, student associations, and political parties are able to function. But it would be a mistake to ignore the steadily growing number of incidents in which the government has reacted against debate, criticism, and independent organization. In 1983 a UPI correspondent was expelled from the country after covering a human rights case; a reporter for *Diario Tiempo* was threatened by unknown assailants who fired a shot at him; photographers for the same newspaper were beaten while covering police repression of demonstrations. In 1984 a German journalist was imprisoned while DNI translated an article he had written; eleven peasant leaders of the Union Nacional de Campesinos Autenticos de Honduras (UNCAH) were arrested for demanding land rights; a columnist for *Diario Tiempo* who had frequently criticized the government was arrested for several hours, presumably under investigation for his possession of a calendar issued by Radio Vencerenos, the Salvadoran rebels' radio station; and two trade union leaders were arrested at the airport upon their return from a conference in Nicaragua. Demonstrators by the hundreds were arrested when protesting the disappearance of labor leaders or when peacefully demanding land. A Spanish journalist was denied permission to work in Honduras. In such a situation it is not surprising that self-censorship is widely practiced and public gatherings tend to be small.

The State Department's willingness to ignore such problems only reinforces the tendency in the Suazo administration to dismiss all human rights complaints or to attribute any criticism to obscure forces attempting to discredit the democratic process. An important opportunity thus is lost to make corrections and redress grievances at a time when human rights violations still can be controlled. If any private pressure is exerted by U.S. officials, it is lost in the shuffle of numerous public statements that defend the Honduran military and government.

Even when privately admitting the occurrence of disappearances and arbitrary arrests, U.S. officials seek to portray abuses as outside the scope of official misconduct. They take pains to portray police frustration when allegedly known terrorists go free for lack of evidence. Conversely, judicial inaction is attributed narrowly to the existence of old-fashioned codes and regulations, not at all to the Suazo administration's lack of political will to allow an independent judiciary. Where the courts are concerned, the State Department seems to favor just minimum independence. When the new Honduran Supreme Court—appointed by the National Assembly at the proposal of the executive branch—took over in January 1982, U.S. Ambassador John D. Negroponte took the unusual step of paying a visit to the members soon after their inauguration and, according to a reliable source, told them that the first priority of the judiciary was to combat subversion.

Refugee Policies

In one other important aspect of the Honduran human rights record, the United States has a more visible participation: the treatment of refugees from neighboring countries. Honduras considers refugee policy a military problem rather than a humanitarian concern. Accordingly, the government's Commission on Refugees is coordinated by an army officer. And in line with U.S. policies, the Honduran military treats the refugees as extensions of the internal conflicts in their home countries. State Department officials in charge of refugee matters, for their part, have repeatedly defended Honduran government actions and plans while vaguely accusing international observers, including U.N. personnel, of violating their neutrality.

Honduras refuses to sign the U.N. Convention Relating to the Status of Refugees but allows the U.N. High Commissioner for Refugees (UNHCR) to run relief and protection programs in Honduras. In this fashion, international efforts carry all of the financial burden involved in hosting refugees, while the government is not bound by any commitments to implement the principles of international refugee law. There is a striking variation in treatment of refugees, reflecting the government's political partnership with the United States. Salvadorans and Guatemalans totaling some twenty-six thousand are not afforded any freedom of movement; they must remain within camps under close and often hostile surveillance of the Honduran army and are not allowed to work. In contrast, the approximately eighteen thousand Nicaraguan refugees are allowed to resettle anywhere in Honduras, particularly close to the Nicaraguan border, and they enjoy freedom of movement.

All of these refugees suffer serious and frequent security problems from forces with which the United States—and thus Honduras—are allied. Salvadorans and Guatemalans have been imprisoned or abducted from the camps by security agents from their countries with the help of Honduran army personnel. Some of the Salvadorans and Guatemalans have been killed near the camps. Many Miskito Nicaraguans have been forcibly recruited by *contra* organizations, also with the help of the Honduran army.[8] In late 1983 this problem became so serious that a conservative relief organization threatened to terminate its programs assisting Miskito refugees unless the forced recruitment was stopped.

The UNHCR insists on removing refugees from borders, but the Honduran government takes no such action in regard to Nicaraguans, who receive international assistance

country to the United States. Early in the twentieth century, four invasions by U.S. Marines, sent by different administrations, supported pro-American factions in internecine struggles, and between 1909 and 1934 U.S. Marines occupied Nicaragua twice for extended periods. Augusto Cesar Sandino led the struggle against the latter occupation until he was murdered in 1934 in a plot organized by Anastasio Somoza Garcia, who became the U.S.-supported president. The U.S.-created National Guard replaced the marines and became the Somoza family's security corps for the next four decades. As the staunchest U.S. allies in the hemisphere, the Somozas not only endorsed every diplomatic stance taken by different administrations but also loaned Nicaraguan territory and support to U.S.-inspired actions against other sovereign states, as in 1954 against Arbenz in Guatemala, and in 1962 against Cuba. The Somoza years also provided a sympathetic environment for U.S. business ventures, including mining, forestry, agriculture, and in the 1960s, industry.

The domestic face of this strongly pro-U.S. regime was one of the most repressive and corrupt in the Americas, although it maintained the outward trappings of a democratic process. Critics were jailed for their opinions and tortured, and the National Guard had a reputation for enjoying its job. Under those circumstances, it is not surprising that Nicaraguans who resisted the Somozas were almost invariably anti-American also. Sandino in the 1920s and 1930s and the Frente Sandinista de Liberacion Nacional (FSLN) in the 1960s and 1970s were able to command appreciable popular support by taking clear anti-Somoza and anti-U.S. stances.

After the earthquake in 1973, President Anastasio Somoza Debayle took control of foreign emergency and development assistance to benefit his family and his close followers. This new evidence of corruption antagonized large elements of Nicaragua's business and middle class, and the opposition against Somoza grew in numbers and in political and social diversity. By 1979 the Nicaraguan people as a whole had joined the active struggle to overthrow Somoza by political, military, and insurrectional means. The dictatorship responded by bombing Nicaragua's principal cities and indiscriminately murdering thousands of civilians.[1]

The Carter administration's human rights policy weakened Somoza by placing attention on his abominable record of human rights violations. Military assistance was cut off in spite of Somoza's powerful lobby in the United States. But when his fall seemed inevitable after the 1978 and 1979 insurrections, the Carter administration attempted to avoid an absolute Sandinista takeover by promoting a transitional government and trying to convince the opposition to preserve the National Guard after Somoza's ouster. This plan for "Somocismo without Somoza" failed because of the stubbornness of Somoza first and of his short-lived successor government later; both refused to negotiate a cease-fire. But it also failed because the survival of the National Guard was unacceptable to the overwhelming majority of Nicaraguans.

The ambivalence of the Carter policy did not win the United States any friends in Nicaragua because it was seen as unnecessarily prolonging a bloody civil war in which forty thousand people had already died. It had drawn harsh criticism within the United States from the beginning, with conservatives presenting the policy as an example of all that was wrong with criticizing allies on human rights grounds. Members of what would become the Reagan administration openly advocated rescuing Somoza at any cost. Even before the 1980 presidential campaign, the Democrats were accused of "losing" Nicaragua to Communist influence—although the Sandinistas had indicated their plans for a mixed economy and elections. As future U.N. ambassador Jeane Kirkpatrick wrote in 1979, "In neither Iran nor Nicaragua did the U.S. adequately appreciate the government's problem in maintaining order in a society confronted with an ideologically extreme opposition." The Carter administration, she charged, had remained "passive in the face of Communist expansion."[2] The new administration would not. During the campaign the Republican Party platform pledged to terminate the Carter administration's economic assistance package for Nicaraguan reconstruction and to "support efforts of the Nicaraguan people to establish a free and independent government."

Thus, from the start, the Reagan administration's policy toward Nicaragua was based on the premise that there can be no coexistence with Sandinismo. The example of a guerrilla-based movement defeating a pro-U.S. government could not be allowed to spread into neighboring countries— to "export" itself. The administration embarked on a consistent policy of economic, political, and diplomatic isolation of Nicaragua, and of active military action to destabilize and eventually overthrow the FSLN. The only limitations to the plan have been those imposed by domestic concerns within the United States, particularly the extent to which the American people after Vietnam still oppose any direct involvement of U.S. troops abroad.

Open Hostility and Covert War

In January 1981, as the new administration took office, reconstruction aid to Nicaragua was frozen, and in March it was completely cut off. In February, the State Department released a "white paper"[3] purporting to show that the Salvadoran guerrillas were receiving massive external support, specifically that arms shipments and communications help were being channeled through Nicaraguan territory. Although press reports later discredited the white paper—even its authors admitted the document was in parts "misleading" or frankly in error[4]—the charge that Nicaragua was part of a Soviet-Cuban plan to spread communism in the region served to isolate the Sandinistas and became the pretext for later U.S. aid to anti-Sandinista forces.

U.S. assistance and loans dropped from $60 million in 1981 to $6.3 million in 1982 (mostly in grants to the private sector) and then to zero in 1983. Simultaneously, U.S. representatives to international financial institutions began voting systematically against loans to Nicaragua. Assistance from multilateral lending agencies, where the U.S. influence is proportionate to its contributions, went from $118 million in 1981 to $51 million in 1982 and to $30 million in 1983. The administration has also applied diplomatic pressure on countries that maintain development assistance programs in Nicaragua. In early 1984, when the newly elected government of Argentina announced a modest agreement to exchange industrial goods and technology with Nicaragua, the State Department discreetly "asked questions" about it.

The administration had simultaneously launched a far-reaching program of covert operations. Even under Carter, the CIA seems to have begun a program to channel funds to opponents of the Sandinistas within the country. The Reagan administration converted this assistance into training and equipment for war.

By February 1981, high officials of the administration were planning a protracted destabilization program. In a November 1981 meeting of the National Security Council, President Reagan approved a $20 million covert military program presented to him by the CIA.[5] By mid-1984 more than $100 million had been spent in recruiting and training more than ten thousand Nicaraguan rebels, arming them and setting up camps in Honduras and Costa Rica. Initially the plan included the participation of agents of the Honduran and Argentine armed forces as trainers. Gradually the CIA took over training roles, although at least until the end of March 1984, while General Gustavo Alvarez was in command, the Honduran army continued to provide important logistical support.

After two years of operations it became clear that in spite of this impressive apparatus, the *contras*—short for *contrarevolucionarios* (counterrevolutionaries)—were capable of controlling neither population nor territory for any significant period of time; they did not enjoy popular support, nor did they represent any serious threat to the stability of the Nicaraguan government. The CIA then began directing its operations against economic targets, escalating the tactics and weapons of war. Air and sea raids attacked refineries, industrial plants, roads, bridges, and airports. In early 1984 —and without reporting to the congressional intelligence committees, as required by law—the CIA started mining the ports of Nicaragua. When several cargo ships were damaged, many nations friendly to the United States are said to have protested, including Great Britain, and France offered to help sweep the mines. Nicaragua took the case to the International Court of Justice in The Hague in April. But just a few days before the complaint was lodged, the State Department filed a brief suspending U.S. acceptance of the court's jurisdiction for two years on matters dealing with Central America. Thus, when the court handed down a preliminary injunction at Nicaragua's request, the United States could shrug this off. (The court subsequently ruled that the United States' suspension of its acceptance of the court's jurisdiction was not valid, and projected a decision on the merits of the case for 1985.)

As a result, by mid-1984 both Congress and the public were so opposed to the policy that the House of Representatives refused to vote funds for the covert action program. In its insistence on funding the covert war, the White House attempted several legislative tactics, including tying the aid to domestic job bills and to African famine-relief measures. In spite of this, the Senate effectively suspended the *contra* aid by first allocating $29 million, then making the appropriation subject to a new Congressional approval to be discussed in March 1985.* The White House decided not to press the matter in Congress during an election year, but the actions of the *contras* continued unabated, giving rise to speculation that the CIA had secured alternative financing.

This concerted and illegal military campaign† has been accompanied by a steady stream of accusations against the Nicaraguan government (GRN) that seek to justify U.S. pol-

---

* The request to Congress for funds described covert operations to be conducted by the CIA, using anti-Sandinista Nicaraguans, with the primary purpose of interdicting arms supplies allegedly going from Nicaragua to the Salvadoran rebels. In spite of this limited purpose, the recipients of the funds have made it abundantly clear that their aim is to overthrow the Nicaraguan government.
† Committing military resources abroad without an act of Congress arguably violates the War Powers Resolution and possibly the separation of powers clause of the Constitution. The aggression against Nicaragua also violates international law, specifically the prohibitions in the U.N. and OAS charters against use of force to settle disputes.

icy. These criticisms and characterizations of the Sandinistas
are based on two central arguments: first, that Nicaragua is
"exporting revolution" and "subverting her neighbors," and
second, the alleged repressive nature of the Sandinista regime itself. According to these arguments the U.S. policy
. tries to save neighboring countries from Nicaragua and Nicaraguans from Marxists' violations of human rights. The
first claim has yet to be proven—indeed, has been contradicted by a former CIA official.* The second has prompted
several human rights organizations, including Americas
Watch, to examine conditions in Nicaragua. We have found
the administration's claims quite out of proportion to abuses
—though we have noted and condemned abuses to the extent we have found them—and can only conclude that the
administration has used human rights arguments with a profound cynicism and disregard for the truth.

President Reagan has reserved for himself the most inflammatory words against Nicaragua. In a major televised speech
on May 9, 1984, he called the Sandinista rule "a Communist
reign of terror." On July 18, 1984, he said that the Nicaraguan people "are trapped in a totalitarian dungeon" worse
than the Somoza dictatorship. Many other administration
officials have used similar language to attack Sandinista practices on human rights. The White House public liaison office
has organized the Central America Outreach Program, one
principal aim of which is evidently to offer a carefully staged
series of presentations to the media and the public purporting to portray Sandinista atrocities. About half of the "outreach" seminars in 1984 were devoted to discrediting the
Nicaraguan government for an audience ranging from private corporations to the Moral Majority to Jewish organiza-

* Nicaragua does provide political support to the Salvadoran rebels of the
FMLN as well as safe haven in its territory for their leaders. But the State
Department has failed to provide the American public with any serious
evidence that the Nicaraguans provide weapons or other military assistance
to the Salvadoran guerrillas. The administration claims that this evidence
exists but that it must remain secret to protect its sources. Skepticism about
the nature of the evidence is growing in Washington, however, particularly
since David McMichael, a CIA contract agent who spent two years looking
for such evidence, revealed in April 1984 that he could find none.

tions. For that program and for press attention generally, the Human Rights Bureau of the State Department has taken particular care in promoting visits of alleged Nicaraguan victims of abuses, something it seldom does in regard to violations by other governments and has not done with regard to a single other country in Latin America. In addition, several private organizations with ties to the administration, such as the National Forum, the Institute on Religion and Democracy, and the Heritage Foundation, which in the past have expressed contempt for human rights policy, have taken great interest in promoting the testimony of victims or alleged victims of Sandinista abuse and in defending the *contras* from accusations of crimes against the civilian population. And the administration and its allies characterize representatives of the *contra* groups ARDE, FDN, or Misura as authoritative experts on human rights violations by the Nicaraguan government, although numerous claims by these groups have proven false and their political motivation is evident. To the extent that violations have taken place, the Reagan administration has seized every opportunity to publicize them, to exaggerate them out of proportion, and to add unsubstantiated allegations to them. When the Sandinista authorities have done anything to correct them, the U.S. government has been either completely silent about these improvements or has downplayed their effect.

A major case in point is the matter of extrajudicial executions, which in other Central American countries are by far the most common and disturbing feature of human rights violations. The State Department's *Country Reports* on Nicaragua for 1982 mentions fifteen to twenty "credible reports of deaths at the hands of security forces, most of which have been confirmed."[6] The *Country Reports* for 1983, in turn, claims that the private Permanent Commission on Human Rights (CPDH) "documented the cases of twelve persons who died while in custody of government authorities."[7] In fact, the circumstances of these deaths are less than "documented." And in all cases, the deaths are reported to have happened in remote areas and in the context of sweeps against *contra* forces. Therefore, though extrajudicial killings may well have taken place, there is no evidence that they are encouraged or tolerated by the Nicaraguan government, nor do they represent a consistent pattern.

The Miskitos

President Reagan has made special cause of the Miskito population, some 100,000 Indians living on the Atlantic coast of Nicaragua and near the border with Honduras, along the Rio Coco. The Miskitos have never been fully integrated into Nicaraguan national life, and they maintain a cultural independence as well as a skepticism about the central government. *Contras* have recruited heavily from the Miskito population both for geographical and cultural reasons; between December 1981 and late 1983 this made the entire Miskito population suspect in the eyes of the GRN. Correspondingly the Miskitos have been held up by administration officials as the definitive example of Nicaraguan intolerance.

In his speech of May 9, 1984, President Reagan stated,

> [T]here has been an attempt to wipe out an entire culture, the Miskito Indians, thousands of whom have been slaughtered or herded into detention camps where they have been starved and abused. Their villages, churches, and crops have been burned.

It is completely untrue that "thousands . . . have been slaughtered"; even the *Country Reports* fails to make such a serious allegation. Indeed, a week after the president's speech, the Inter-American Commission on Human Rights (IACHR) of the OAS released a long-awaited report on the situation of the Miskitos that included only one incident, on December 23, 1981, when Miskito prisoners were killed by Sandinista guards in Leimus, near the Honduran border. The Leimus incident had been the subject of wild allegations by dissident Miskito leaders, and the matter was made worse by the GRN's refusal to publicize its own investigation of the matter. It is now quite clear that between fourteen and seventeen Miskitos who had been detained in Leimus a day earlier were taken out of the prison and shot, apparently in reprisal for the attacks on border towns that had taken place in preceding days. The government conducted an investigation but has not shown convincing evidence that it punished anyone for this.

The IACHR found this one incident of noncombat killing. Americas Watch has learned of one other case, in Walpa Siksa in 1982. There, seven young Miskitos were killed by Sandinista soldiers, who were later severely punished by their officers. These episodes are indeed serious and merit condemnation. But they fall far short of the "thousands" that have been "slaughtered" according to the president.

When he accused the GRN of having "herded" the Miskitos into "detention camps," the president was referring to—but vastly misrepresenting—the government's decision to move the Miskito population away from the border area where hostilities were most active. Relocation of Miskito Indians from border hamlets along the Rio Coco had been conducted in December 1981 and January 1982 in response to a series of attacks by Miskito *contra* forces operating from Honduras. The *contra* attacks had resulted in sixty deaths in less than five weeks and several acts of rape, kidnapping, torture of civilians, and other atrocities. Most importantly, the nature and location of the attacks made the Sandinistas fear that a portion of Nicaraguan territory could be seized by their enemies.

Under those circumstances, the Americas Watch report on Nicaragua in May 1982 found that it was not unreasonable for the GRN to remove civilians from a border area to facilitate the defense of the country's territorial integrity. The Catholic bishops of Nicaragua, whose anti-Sandinista statements are so often quoted by U.S. officials, expressed exactly the same position in a pastoral letter about the problem in February 1982. Similarly, the IACHR report of May 1984 reaches the same conclusion after a careful analysis of the facts and of the international law applicable to noninternational conflicts.

To find the relocation decision justified is not to say that the manner in which it was conducted should not be criticized. The conflict between the Nicaraguan government and the Miskito minority is the area where Nicaragua's human rights record is most open to criticism, and the events that began in late 1981 have brought much suffering to the Miskito community. In this regard, Americas Watch has objected to the lack of notice given to the Miskitos; their lack of participation in the relocation decision; the inadequate and harsh means of transportation used for all of them except the elderly, pregnant women, and infants; and the destruction of the property they left behind, for which they have not been adequately compensated.

Contrary to what Ambassador Jeane Kirkpatrick and General Haig said at the time, however, there was no slaughter during the relocation. These high officials were simply repeating allegations made by Stedman Fagoth, the leader of Misura, one of the CIA-sponsored *contra* organizations of the Miskitos. When he visited the United States in February 1982, sponsored by the American Security Council and Freedom House, officials of the State Department's Human Rights Bureau helped arrange Mr. Fagoth's appointments with nongovernmental organizations. Based on other accusations by Mr. Fagoth, Freedom House published a report that accused the GRN of "summary execution, during the process of evacuation of women and children" and of "burying Indian people alive."[8] All of these allegations have been thoroughly discredited by more serious research.[9]

It is also misleading to characterize the new settlements as "detention camps," as the president did in his May 9 speech. Our firsthand observation, in 1982 and 1984, confirmed that though there is no question that the Miskitos did not go to the camps of their own free will, from the beginning it has been possible for them to relocate elsewhere. Many of them are able to travel on errands to nearby towns, or for prolonged periods to Managua and other cities, and each day they go into the countryside to farm, hunt, or fish. The camps have minimal security, and visitors are allowed. A blatant falsehood in Reagan's statement is that in the settlements the Miskitos "have been starved and abused." Indeed, the GRN has made a significant effort to provide the Miskitos with housing, health care, education, and food supplements, and has provided jobs for them and assisted them in developing crops.

Due Process and Detention

The administration has found relatively little to say about more structural aspects of the Nicaraguan situation, perhaps because these are not sufficiently emotionally laden. It is true, for example, that violations of due process have occurred frequently in Nicaragua as the country rebuilt its judiciary from scratch after the 1979 revolution. The record, however, is mixed, as most observers agree that the Supreme Court and lower courts have exercised control through judicial review and have even dismissed judges who were blatantly arbitrary.

The state of emergency imposed in March 1982—another result of the *contra* war—has tightened procedures and limited rights to appeal. In 1983, the GRN used its state of emergency powers to create special "popular tribunals" outside the judiciary to prosecute security-related offenses. Two of the three tribunal members are selected by grass-roots organizations. Although these courts provide a measure of free access to counsel, judicial review of their decisions is very limited, and their sentences have tended to be harsh. Human rights organizations have appealed to the GRN to disband these courts and strengthen the regular court system. On the other hand, even during the suspension of rights due to the state of emergency, several courts—ultimately the Supreme Court itself—upheld the availability of *habeas corpus* relief against arbitrary imprisonment. In August 1984, *habeas corpus* relief was fully restored except for cases under the jurisdiction of the "popular courts."

Since the declaration of the state of emergency, the increase in violent antigovernment activity has been met with a sharp increase in the number of security-related arrests. The state of emergency allowed the authorities to detain people without charges for indefinite periods. In practice, however, every detainee was either charged or released after several weeks of detention. When charges were actually brought, they related to offenses involving violent activity or collaboration with it. In a few cases, although there were charges filed, the prosecution was suspect because of the defendant's otherwise legitimate activities in opposition to the government.

As the number of security-related arrests increased, especially after 1982, there have also been more allegations of mistreatment of prisoners. The Permanent Commission for Human Rights (CPDH), a private group, has documented some cases in which detainees were subjected to prolonged incommunicado pretrial detention, even though the laws in effect did not provide the security forces with the authority to place detainees in incommunicado detention. In the course of these periods of detention, prisoners reportedly were threatened and psychologically coerced into making confessions. In some cases reported as taking place in remote areas, detainees were also beaten. There is no evidence that this is a widespread practice; CPDH, though generally critical of the government, has not shown that these abuses are committed pursuant to deliberate governmental policy or are tolerated by the authorities. While incommunicado detention is a source of concern to human rights groups in Nicaragua and abroad, it does not appear to have been accompanied by mistreatment except in some apparently isolated cases.

The Reagan administration nonetheless has attempted to describe torture as a common occurrence in Sandinista Nicaragua. The *Country Reports* for 1981 stated:

> there were credible reports of physical abuse of prisoners during interrogation and assertions that torture is practiced at the El Chipote state security detention center. There were also credible reports of secret prisons throughout Nicaragua, where prisoners are tortured.[10]

When Americas Watch was preparing its first mission to Nicaragua, in February 1982, we asked for the sources of this information and were referred to a U.S. official in the Managua embassy and to CPDH. Both sources stated that torture was not practiced in Nicaragua; the embassy official said there might be some isolated cases but not such as to constitute a pattern. We then requested, under the Freedom of Information Act, a copy of the original embassy report on which the *Country Reports* had been based, but the State Department refused to disclose it. By the end of 1984, the case was still under litigation.

In the *Country Reports* for 1982, the administration modified its position. The report began by stating: "Torture is not widely practiced by the government." Though it continued with the statement "There have been . . . at least half a dozen documented cases of torture committed by security forces in 1982," [11] the paragraph went on to explain that the government had in fact taken action to investigate and punish those abuses.

In the *Country Reports* for 1983, the charge was revived. CPDH was cited as having "compiled data on 102 instances of physical abuse and torture." [12] The examples given in the following sentences are of bad conditions of detention, of prisoners being fed at irregular intervals in order to disorient them, and the like. There is no mention of specific testimony of systematic use of physical abuse to punish or to extract confessions or information. The State Department does not ordinarily use the word "torture" to describe abuses such as those reported by CPDH.

Similarly misleading have been the State Department reports on disappearances. CPDH has long contended that there are a number of persons who are arrested and who are not acknowledged to be in prison afterward. However, CPDH uses the word "disappearance" more loosely and with a different meaning than the expression is used in other countries where disappearances are indeed a major feature of repression, conducted as part and parcel of a deliberate governmental policy. What happens in Nicaragua is that in remote areas, arrests sometimes are not readily acknowledged to relatives, especially when detainees are transferred to different locations. For the most part, however, prisoners are eventually located in detention or released. In countries where disappearances are a common practice the opposite is true: The majority is never heard of again, and a few are eventually located. CPDH includes cases of disappearances in its monthly reports. Unfortunately, until July 1984, it did not take note of when these persons actually "reappeared" or were located. This led the State Department to include a highly misleading statement in the *Country Reports* for 1983:

> The security forces often hold suspected guerrillas and subversives incommunicado indefinitely without notifying family members. The Permanent Commission on Human Rights documented 167 unresolved cases of disappearances in which it said security forces were implicated but in which the government has not acknowledged involvement.[13]

Evidently the figure of 167 was arrived at by adding CPDH's monthly figures. Perhaps unbeknownst to the State Department, in January 1984 CPDH published an Annual Report for 1983 that placed the figure of "unresolved disappearances" for that year at 31. By February, that list was down to 28. All of these cases had taken place in remote areas, in the course of sweeps against *contra* forces. Though in many of the cases there was some evidence of an arrest by security forces, failure to acknowledge arrests did not amount to a government policy. This does not contradict the fact that the Nicaraguan authorities must be held responsible for failing to devise a system that would ensure prompt acknowledgment of all arrests. The outstanding Miskito cases are especially important in this respect.

Between July and September of 1982, 69 Miskitos disappeared after their arrest by security forces. Though the practice ended abruptly after October 1982, the GRN is nonetheless responsible for investigating these cases and providing information to the relatives.

Freedom to Dissent

The Nicaraguan government's intolerance of freedom of expression has been a serious concern of Americas Watch and other human rights organizations. The state of emergency permits prior censorship of all media, but until August 1984 that authority was exercised beyond the needs imposed by the emergency. Before 1982, there was no prior censorship, but news organizations were subject to sanctions if they printed material detrimental to military security or susceptible of causing economic shortages. When prior censorship was imposed, however, in March 1982, it was not restricted to these narrow grounds, and since then it has been applied to prohibit the free circulation of opinion. In 1982, independent radio news programs were suspended, though gradually some of them have been allowed to resume broadcasting. Toward the end of 1983, prior censorship of the opposition daily La Prensa was considerably eased, though the system remained very much in place. In August 1984, in connection with the electoral campaign, the GRN announced that prior censorship would be applied only to security-sensitive items.

Freedom of expression should be demanded of any government without regard to the content of the opinion to be expressed. Thus, support for La Prensa's right to publish is not indicative of support for what La Prensa has to say. This does not appear to be the standard used by the Reagan administration, however. Every action taken against La Prensa elicits strong comment from the administration, while the murder of journalists in El Salvador, and routine violations of the right to free expression elsewhere in the hemisphere, are not condemned.

Related to freedom of expression is freedom of religion. The GRN has been repeatedly accused by the Reagan administration of persecuting the Catholic Church, and without a doubt one of the most serious domestic conflicts faced by the Sandinista regime is its confrontation with the bishops. This conflict is strident and involves exchanges of charges, but the right of the Church to express its views and of the faithful to worship is not compromised. On occasion, measures taken by the GRN do in fact violate these rights, as when ten foreign priests were summarily expelled after demonstrating publicly against the house arrest of a Nicaraguan priest that the government accused of complicity with

the *contras*.* The criticism from the U.S. government, however, goes far beyond these legitimate matters for concern
and portrays any verbal confrontation between the GRN and
the bishops as another sign of the totalitarian and antireli-
gious inclination of an atheistic ideology. The truth is more
complex. The conflict cuts across Church lines: An estimated 30 percent of the clergy sides with the Sandinistas
against the hierarchy. And it also touches upon a wide range
of issues, from private education to negotiations with the
contras (both of which the bishops support) and the military
draft.

Response to Criticism on Human Rights

Unlike several other Latin American governments that have
come under harsh criticism (though not from this administration), the GRN has responded to human rights organizations with efforts to improve the situation. Equally as
significant as the administration's strident complaints against
Nicaragua is its silence regarding these improvements. In
early 1984, for example, the GRN conducted several investigations of abuses in remote areas, which resulted in the
prosecution and appropriate punishment of members of the
security forces. In the most important of these cases, forty-
four security agents and civilians were prosecuted for several
cases of murder, rape, theft, and other abuses that had taken
place in a border region of Matagalpa and Jinotega. Thirteen
of them received heavy sentences. Later, three members of
the army were sentenced to long prison terms for running a
truck against a Catholic Easter procession, which had resulted in twelve deaths. In April 1984, an army sublieutenant
was sentenced to eighteen years in prison for raping a Miskito woman in the village of Lapan.

In regard to the Miskito minority, there has been a clear
effort to improve relations and resolve past conflicts. Urged
by the Inter-American Commission on Human Rights, the

---

* The priest was pardoned in October 1984, but the ten foreign priests were
not allowed to return to Nicaragua in spite of many requests from abroad.

GRN decreed a general amnesty on December 1, 1983, for all Miskitos arrested and tried for security offenses since November 1982. Some three hundred Miskito prisoners were released that day and another sixty later, leaving in prison only those whose cases were under review by courts to determine whether the amnesty decree was applicable. Also in response to the IACHR, the government has pledged to allow all the Miskitos who were evacuated from the Rio Coco area to return there when the hostilities subside.

After the December 1981–January 1982 evacuation from the Rio Coco to the settlements known as Tasba Pri, there have been several other evacuations of people from the border areas where there is heavy fighting. For the most part, those evacuations have been voluntary and without controversy. In the course of one evacuation, a helicopter crash caused the deaths of more than seventy Miskito children, but this was clearly an accident and no other deaths have been documented or alleged.* The last evacuation of Miskitos took place in July 1983, involving some nine hundred persons from ten villages in northern Zelaya province who have been resettled in a camp called Sangni Laya. The military justification for this move was less clear, because although there had been fighting in the area, there was no risk to territorial integrity because the villages were not near the border. Since then, the regional government in Zelaya has pledged that there will be no further relocations; in fact, in the two subsequent instances of heavy fighting where people were temporarily dislocated,† they were allowed to return to and receive emergency assistance in their villages.

Finally, Moravian Church sources report that there has been a visible change in attitude by the security forces toward the Miskito population. In 1982, the government forces would round up suspects in villages where there had been *contra* activity, detain large numbers of men, take them into detention centers, and hold them for several weeks pending

* In October 1984, American observers visited the four camps near Wiwili, Jinotega, where these Miskitos have been resettled, and found that living conditions there were more crowded and primitive than in Tasba Pri.
† Wounta-Haulover in October 1983 and Sandy Bay in March 1984.

investigations. According to the Moravians, in 1984 the security forces still conducted raids in those areas but arrested individuals only when there was probable cause to believe they were involved in criminal offenses. On October 20, 1984, the GRN allowed Brooklyn Rivera, leader of the Indian rebel group Misurasata, to return to Nicaragua and begin talks designed to further a peaceful settlement with the Miskitos. This was an important step because Rivera is the most representative leader of the Miskito community.

The U.S. Double Standard

These developments should be encouraged and the GRN should be expected to follow through with more and deeper corrections and remedies. More importantly, these measures should be recognized out of sheer respect for the truth. Instead, just as these events were unfolding, the Reagan administration was stepping up its accusations of mistreatment of the Miskitos with unsubstantiated or wildly exaggerated charges. Simultaneously the IACHR released its long-awaited report on the Miskito conflict that, though rightfully critical of Sandinista violations, at the same time demonstrated that the charges of widespread "slaughter" (Reagan), "genocide" (Haig), and "an attempt to wipe out an entire culture" (Reagan) were completely untrue.

In another attempt to portray the Sandinistas as antiminority and antireligion, President Reagan has repeatedly accused the GRN of anti-Semitic acts. He has based his accusations mainly on the confiscation of an abandoned synagogue belonging to one leader of Nicaragua's tiny Jewish community who had been a staunch Somoza supporter and as such left the country in 1979. Four days before the president first leveled these accusations on July 20, 1983, the U.S. ambassador in Managua sent a confidential cable to Washington stating he could find "no verifiable ground" to accuse the GRN of anti-Semitism.[14] This cable and its subsequent publication by the Associated Press were no obstacle to the president's and other officials' stream of arguments that the Sandinistas harbor prejudice against Jews.

Perhaps the highest expression of the Reagan administration's double standard vis-à-vis Nicaragua is the administration's attitude toward human rights violations by the rebels it generously supports. The State Department's Human Rights Bureau employs entirely different measures for evaluating *contra* abuses than it uses for guerrillas elsewhere in the region.

When discussing El Salvador, the bureau consistently contends that local and international human rights organizations that report on the government's violations cannot be credible unless they report on violations by the guerrillas as well; otherwise their data are inherently flawed and unreliable. Yet the administration makes no mention of the violations by the Nicaraguan rebels in its public remarks on Nicaragua. References to these episodes in the *Country Reports* are always referred to as "allegations" and doubt is cast on them, whereas violations by the GRN are always said to be "documented." The president also consistently refers to the *contras* as "freedom fighters," while Mrs. Kirkpatrick calls them "democratic" and other high officials insist that they are fighting for the true ideals of the 1979 revolution. Thus the illegality of the campaign to overthrow the Sandinistas is given a gloss of traditional American values.

The fact is that the Fuerzas Democraticas Nicaraguenses (FDN) has routinely attacked civilian populations. Their forces kidnap, torture, and murder health workers, teachers, and other government employees. The Indian organization Misura has engaged in forcible recruitment of refugees in Honduras, and the rival Indian organization Misurasata has been known to execute civilians they accuse of collaborating with the Nicaraguan government. Several of these episodes have been reported in the U.S. press. In August 1984 an article in the *Washington Post* reported evidence of a massacre of seven captured peasants and Sandinista militia members whose throats were slit by the FDN in Tapasle, Matagalpa.[15]

On April 20, 1984, Misura forces attacked the Miskito settlement of Sumubila, one of the Tasba Pri camps where evacuated Miskitos live, directing rockets and machine-gun fire against the houses and causing six deaths among the civilian population, including women and children. They burned down the hospital and other buildings, destroyed the ambulance, and kidnapped the only doctor and other government employees. As noted above, the views of the Nicaraguan insurgents are frequently paraded in Washington as irrefutable evidence of Sandinista abuse without regard for the fact that they are a party to a violent conflict and therefore manifestly unreliable. On the other hand, when three Miskito residents of Sumubila testified in the U.S. Senate about the episode of April 20, organizations such as the National Forum and others in the Reagan camp[16] attempted to discredit their testimony and offered, as evidence, the contradictory views of those responsible for what was presented as an attack on a legitimate military target.

In October 1984 the press revealed that the CIA had written and distributed a handbook for "psychological operations" to be used by *contra* forces. The handbook called for executions of civilians and of prisoners, and for the hiring of paid criminals to carry out certain crimes, including the murder of *contra* sympathizers to create martyrs. National Security Adviser Robert McFarlane promised that an investigation would be conducted and that any agent associated with the manual would be removed. After the November 6 U.S. elections, however, President Reagan himself downplayed the handbook scandal, calling it "much ado about nothing."[17] The CIA's internal investigation, in turn, concluded that there had only been "lapses of judgment,"[18] not breaches of the law.

Elections

When the Sandinistas came to power in 1979, they promised to hold elections, but opposition groups objected to elections being held immediately after the Sandinista victory. At their request, a decision was made in 1980 to wait until 1985. Although this process was public and well known, the administration accused the GRN of reneging on its election promise and used the delay in elections to portray the

Sandinistas as totalitarian. In February 1984 the GRN announced that elections for the presidency and for a constituent and legislative assembly would be held that November just two days before the U.S. elections. The administration then chose to dismiss the planned elections beforehand as inherently fraudulent. President Reagan called them "Soviet-style sham elections,"[19] although at the time conditions for opposition participation were still being negotiated. This again is in sharp contrast with the Reagan administration's insistence that an election in El Salvador, no matter under what conditions it is held, is the ultimate test of that regime's commitment to human rights.

A portion of the political opposition inside Nicaragua withdrew from participation in the elections because the GRN refused to postpone them again; or to negotiate with the *contras* and allow them to participate; or to terminate the state of emergency altogether. The first two issues were of questionable relevance, for the period of electoral preparation and time permitted for registration had been substantial and the *contras* did not demonstrably represent any Nicaraguan constituency, nor had they shown a serious desire to negotiate. The third condition, involving the state of emergency, did relate legitimately to human rights. In fact, although the government refused to terminate the state of emergency altogether, because violent attacks were continuing, it had relaxed restrictions considerably in July and August 1984 in preparation for the electoral campaign.

A number of other positive measures accompanied the campaign period. Prior censorship, although maintained, was cut back to apply only to news that might endanger security. The GRN decreed the full effectiveness of *habeas corpus* and reinstated the right to strike, freedom of association, and freedom of assembly. The Popular Anti-Somocista Tribunals were maintained for security-related offenses. It would, of course, have been highly desirable to disband these exceptional courts and return full jurisdiction over all criminal matters to the judiciary. Given the continued violence and the seriousness of the threat posed by attacks against the stability of the government, it is hardly unreasonable for the GRN to maintain some exceptional measures; these are clearly permissible under both Nicaraguan law and the international law principle of derogation or temporary suspension of certain rights during an emergency.

Registration for the election was mandatory, and it took place in late July; 93 percent of those eligible were registered. The deadline for presentation of candidates was extended several times to allow negotiations between the government and the opposition to proceed. Finally, the parties grouped under the Coordinadora Democratica Nicaragüense refused to participate, and two weeks before the election the Partido Liberal Independiente announced its withdrawal.* The government refused to allow it to withdraw, however, and some PLI candidates continued to campaign.

The electoral atmosphere was less than ideal. Some of *La Prensa*'s articles dealing with the elections were censored, although they had no relation with military matters.† Some rallies were interrupted by harassment, by crowds for the most part sympathetic to the FSLN. There were no injuries, however, in any of the four or five more serious incidents. And, at the same time, *La Prensa* and the other dailies exhaustively covered campaign speeches and activities, most of which were harshly critical of the FSLN and of the GRN. Radio and television time was guaranteed to all parties running in the elections.

When the elections were held on November 4, the FSLN obtained around 67 percent of the vote. Most of the remainder went to three moderate-conservative parties and about 7 percent were void. Turnout was very high, although voting was not mandatory. Even before the election, however, the Reagan administration actively lobbied the opposition to abstain or withdraw, seeking to diminish the significance of the election by their nonparticipation.

It may well be that this tiny country of fewer than three

* In January 1985, Arturo Cruz, the CDN's candidate, announced his support for continued U.S. aid to the *contras*.
† Immediately after the election, censorship tightened. *La Prensa*'s assistant editor, Pedro Joaquin Chamorro, Jr., protested the restrictions by going into self-exile in Costa Rica.

million people has been the target of more criticism on human rights grounds from the Reagan administration— and especially from the president himself—than any other country in the world. Significant abuses of human rights have taken place in Nicaragua. It is plain, however, especially when set alongside apologies for human rights abuses in nearby countries where far greater violations have taken place, that promotion of human rights in Nicaragua is not the Reagan administration's principal aim. Rather, the aim is to overthrow the Sandinista government, an aim that the administration also pursues through overt-covert support for armed forces attacking Nicaragua. In effect the Reagan administration's human rights policy with respect to Nicaragua is a degradation of the human rights cause, for it makes human rights criticism an instrument of military policy.

GUATEMALA

"Everyone has said that there is a lot of violence in the country," said Guatemalan chief of state General Oscar Humberto Mejia Victores at a June 1984 press conference. "But that is not true. In the newspapers they announce violence in huge headlines, but when you read the inside pages you find it isn't major."[1]

During the two weeks preceding Mejia's statement, the Guatemalan press reported nineteen abductions or disappearances; twenty-six others had been murdered or found mutilated in clandestine graves. In a sense, though, the general had a point. Often events are seen as noteworthy only if they deviate from the norm. In contemporary Guatemala, political violence has become more than merely commonplace. Under a series of army-dominated regimes that have ruled Guatemala since 1954, political terror has firmly established itself as the principal means of governance.

The everyday reality of today's Guatemala is a thing to stun the senses—but only if those senses are exposed to it. Even in a time when Central America has emerged as a major issue, Guatemala remains, at best, on the margin of the North American political consciousness. In his May 1984 television address on Central America, President Reagan gave it one sentence. The last congressional hearings focused on Guatemala were in March 1983. A country whose recent political death toll matches or exceeds that of El Salvador and dwarfs that of Nicaragua, Guatemala regularly disappears from U.S. newspapers for months at a time, and from network television for periods of up to a year. For this reason, any discussion of human rights there must take into account the misconception and relative ignorance that surround it.

The Reagan administration and its critics agree that in terms of Central American geopolitics, Guatemala is the greatest prize. It has a larger population, a stronger economy, more natural resources, and heavier U.S. investment than its neighbors. It borders Mexico and the Yucatan oilfields. Secretary of State Haig characterized it as "strategically the most important Central American republic" and "clearly the next target" for revolutionary forces.[2] Yet while the rest of Central America occupies center stage of the U.S. political debate, Guatemala remains in the shadows.

The reason for this inattention is twofold. First, unlike Nicaragua, Guatemala has maintained the political status quo; its government remains in the hands of a friendly army. Second, unlike Honduras and El Salvador, Guatemala receives no extensive direct U.S. military aid. There are no congressional debates over continuation of assistance. There are no teams of U.S. advisers to count and photograph. Like El Salvador, Guatemala has death squads and guerrilla battles and army massacres. Yet without the context of big American money and nearby American troops, all those dead Guatemalans in and of themselves do not add up to a major story.

But Guatemala *is* a major story—albeit one that the administration has tried to play down. The three military regimes in power since 1981 have all enjoyed U.S. patronage (though the first was criticized afterward as if no support for it had ever existed); all have been distinguished by their brutality, which unpublicized U.S. aid has indirectly abetted; and all have derived their power from an army (one of the hemisphere's most systematically violent) organized, trained, and armed by the United States for more than twenty years.

No Respect or Mercy

On May 17, 1982, the conservative daily *El Grafico* abandoned the Guatemalan newspapers' traditional reticence on the subject of official violence. "Massacres have become the order of the day," it stated in an editorial that then President Efrain Rios Montt later conceded as directed at the army. "In the hamlet of Semeja II in Chichicastenango . . . eight members of a family were murdered by armed men. There was no respect or mercy shown for grandparents, children, or grandchildren, all were exterminated equally. . . . How is it possible to behead an eight- or nine-year-old child? How is it possible for a human adult to murder in cold blood a baby of less than a year and a half? . . . Nor is it acceptable to murder pregnant women, for these acts of bestiality only serve to sink the nation deeper into the most degenerate immorality."

The national bishops' conference declared in 1984 that "violence has taken possession of Guatemala." They decried "the irrational use of torture; massacres of entire families and groups, above all Indians and *campesinos*, including children, pregnant women, and old people; massive displacement of families and segments of the population seeking security and losing their homes and possessions, giving rise to refugees abroad who have to endure the most inhuman levels of misery and uncertainty."[3] The resulting ripples of fear spread beyond the immediate victims, they wrote, citing "violations of homes, correspondence, private communications, and all norms which make up the fabric of human rights in all civilized societies."[4]

Violence actually took possession of Guatemala some time ago. Since the CIA-sponsored coup of 1954, each of Guatemala's heads of state has been a military man, with the sole exception of Julio Cesar Mendez Montenegro (1966–70), who was permitted to assume office only after promising the military unfettered control of internal security matters. A small guerrilla opposition that surfaced in the 1960s was quickly and efficiently crushed—at the cost of thousands of civilian lives. Even after the armed opposition had subsided, the government began targeting unions, peasant cooperatives, and religious and professional groups for death squad disappearances and assassinations. When guerrillas reappeared in the late 1970s, reprisals against the nonviolent opposition intensified. Centrist leaders and reformers were murdered, polarizing the country further. The regime of General Romeo Lucas Garcia (1978–82) became identified with an almost haphazard brutality, as in the landmark incident of May 1978 at Panzos, a northeastern town: When peasants gathered at the town hall to petition for their rights in a dispute over land tenure, the rural military police (PMA) opened fire, killing a hundred men, women, and children.

In the northwestern highlands of Quiche and Huehuete-nango departments, where the guerrillas were strongest and the population is predominantly Indian (like 60 percent of Guatemala), massacres became commonplace during these years, as Lucas and his brother, Army Chief of Staff Benedicto Lucas Garcia, sought to eliminate support for the rebels. By late 1981, the regime had added to its straightforward violence a plan for counterinsurgency that included displacing the highland peasants and gathering them under army "protection" so that they could not aid the opposition.

When a coup supplanted President Lucas in March 1982, his successor, General Efrain Rios Montt, curtailed the army-sponsored death squads in Guatemala City, offering the world a façade of calm and peacefulness. At the same time he announced his intention to "begin a merciless struggle"[5] against subversion. Explaining his approach on television, Rios Montt forthrightly said that he had "declared a state of siege so we could kill legally"[6]—a reference to the death penalties to be handed down by the secret tribunals he had established to try those accused of political crimes.

The Counterinsurgency Model

Rios Montt turned the counterinsurgency model that had been applied on a limited scale by Benedicto Lucas Garcia into a systematic national campaign. The army swept methodically through rural villages. "Never in our history have such extremes been reached," the Catholic bishops declared in May 1982, "with assassinations now falling into the category of genocide."[7] The toll of killings reported by local newspapers—a fraction of the actual number—totaled more than 530 in June alone. In August, the *Miami Herald* reported that over 50 villages had been destroyed.[8] Between 20,000 and 30,000 Guatemalans, mostly Indians, fled across the border into southern Mexico as, according to Amnesty International, some 2,600 civilians were killed in over 100 separate incidents between March and July.[9]

The task of gathering detailed human rights information in Guatemala is more difficult than elsewhere in Central

America. The country's terrain is one obstacle; in the highlands many villages are made remote by poor roads and infrequent transport. The armed forces' hostility to observers, whether Guatemalan or foreign, also complicates research, for in areas controlled by the army, a combination of surveillance and general fear make Guatemalans hesitant to state their grievances. No local human rights group has functioned safely in Guatemala since early in the Lucas period, and information is gathered by a network of individuals who run extreme risk and enjoy no protection like that provided by the Church in El Salvador. An investigator therefore relies in part on testimony from the likes of soldiers who are willing to discuss their tactics. Such evidence shows that during the Rios Montt period the violation of the right to life was systematic and cold-blooded, a simple part of policy, while such abuses as torture and forced displacement were also common.

In October 1982, for example, a corporal who was participating in Rios Montt's rural sweeps described the reaction of villagers when the army approached: "They flee from their homes," he said. "They run for the mountains." When asked what the soldiers do in such cases, he answered: "When they run and go into the mountains, that obligates one to kill them" because "they might be guerrillas. If they don't run, the army is not going to kill them. It will protect them." He admitted to killing women as well as men in "lots of" villages. But like General Mejia, the corporal had learned to adjust his standards of normality and excess. Asked how many people he had killed in each village, he said "about twenty . . . not many."[10]

A sergeant who commanded such sweeps in El Quiche has explained the procedure step by step. "We go into a village and take the people out of their houses and search the houses. . . . You ask informers who are the ones that are doing things outside the law. And that's when you round up the [guerrilla] collaborators. You question them, interrogate them, get them to speak the truth. Who have they been talking to? Who are the ones who have been coming to the village to speak with them?"

The interrogations, he said, were conducted in the village square with the population looking on. To induce the suspects to talk, the sergeant explained, one would "beat them to make them tell the truth, hurt them." Wrapping his hands around his neck and making a choking sound, he demonstrated, "more or less hanging them. . . . You just have to subdue them a little to make them tell the truth."

The army then offers villagers an alternative. After the interrogations, as the sergeant put it, "We tell the people to change the road they are on, because the road they are on is bad. If they don't change, there is nothing else to do but kill them. . . . If they don't want the good, there's nothing more to do but bomb their houses." [11]

The practice of offering the villagers the option of "the good"—collaborating with the government—was an innovation usually credited to Rios Montt. The message was clear and forceful. An army officer in Cunen, El Quiche, explained it to the *New York Times*: "If you are with us, we'll feed you, if not, we'll kill you." [12]

On July 16, 1982, the army evidently decided that the residents of Finca San Francisco in Nenton, Huehuetenango, were no longer with them. The army had recently enlisted twenty of them into two local civil patrols. According to the report of the Inter-American Commission on Human Rights (IACHR) of the Organization of American States:

On Thursday, July 15, the soldiers arrived unannounced and called the recent recruits and told them to go to the mountain, something that did not arouse any fears because they considered it a routine call. Once they were outside of town, the army shot the twenty men that were accompanying them. The next day . . . the army gathered part of the population in the Catholic chapel and in the town's biggest houses. According to the account of the only survivor, they then proceeded to burn the houses. There was no mercy shown for anyone; in one house they burned forty people, in three others twenty-five people and ten in another. Others were tortured and when they could not get any more information from them, they were finished off with machetes. Angered with others that did not respond in Spanish [many Guatemalans in rural areas speak only their Indian languages], they decapitated them on the streets. Afterward, according to this account, the soldiers rushed the people they had gathered at the town's chapel. For that they used hand grenades, bazookas, and machine guns; those who could flee from the chapel were gunned down or killed with machetes. The houses and the people that were still alive in them were burned.[13]

The final death toll exceeded three hundred.

Two days later, according to several eyewitnesses, another army unit entered the village of Plan de Sanchez, Rabinal, Baja Verapaz. They rounded up the inhabitants, raped the young women, and ended by setting 250 villagers on fire.

Since the killings at Panzos in May 1978, the steady repetition of such incidents has created a massive community of internal refugees. In 1982, even before the Rios Montt sweeps began, the Catholic Church placed the number of displaced people at one million, fully one-seventh of the Guatemalan population.

As Americas Watch discovered during visits in 1982 and 1983, Guatemala's displaced are virtual prisoners of the army, suspected of guerrilla sympathies, and treated accordingly. Driven from their homes, the displaced must starve or surrender and be resettled in "protected villages," where life is policed by the authorities and food is provided in exchange for work and collaboration. The price of safety for those living under army control is participation in civil patrols, officially described as self-defense units organized voluntarily by villagers to fend off guerrilla attacks. These are in fact forced-participation auxiliary units—claimed to number seven hundred thousand by late 1983—some of which the army sends out on forays, uses as a shield in combat with guerrillas, and, according to testimonies from patrol members, orders to carry out the murders of civilians. The policy of displacing the highland population, holding them, and pressing them into quasimilitary service has continued under Mejia Victores. It effectively divides Guatemalans into "good" and "subversive," permitting no one to be seen as neutral.

In the fall of 1983, a soldier standing outside the barracks in Santiago Atitlan, Solola, in western Guatemala, explained the implications for refugees of living on the run. Asked how the army treated refugees, he replied: "Those that don't turn themselves in, they die. Even if they're not in the guerrilla. If they don't want to collaborate with us, they get killed."

Children are included in the army's roster of legitimate targets. As this soldier explained, "By the time they're seven years old, they're capable of killing you. . . . They're not in [the guerrillas] yet, but if their father is, then they are too."[14]

Refugee testimony gathered by numerous human rights organizations corroborates this. Children may be taken by the feet and bashed against trees, or clubbed to death. Sometimes they are cut into pieces by soldiers' machetes, according to these statements. A ten-year-old girl from Centro La Esperanza, Ixcam Grande, Huehuetenango, described her memories by drawing a picture of "what the army has done to us" and explained what it portrayed:

They have killed; the helicopter has shot at us and bombed our homes and dropped fire on our farms. They shoot the ones they capture, they cut off our hands, our heads, our feet, sometimes all that's left is a little piece of the body, and when they capture families they massacre them. They shoot bullets in their stomachs and hang them from trees.[15]

About one month after the August 8, 1983 coup that replaced Rios Montt with Mejia Victores, twenty-two villagers were killed by soldiers in the town of Xebaj, Rabinal, in the northcentral province of Baja Verapaz, according to eyewitnesses. It is estimated that some 10 percent of Rabinal's population of thirty thousand to thirty-five thousand have died by political violence—the overwhelming majority of it government perpetrated—in the past five years. After the Xebaj incident, one woman recalls: "They left the poor mothers hanging, one with a little baby on her back . . . they cut the throats of the little ones."[16]

The Guatemalan press operates under self-censorship, but often it has carried revealing material. An October 1983 edition of *Prensa Libre*, Guatemala's largest and most conservative daily, carried an item headlined "Pilgrimages to the Morgue," which describes an eerie scene of death and grief. Numerous people whose relatives have disappeared or been abducted gather daily in the morgue of the La Verbena cemetery in Guatemala City, with the hope of locating a disappeared loved one. People of diverse social and economic backgrounds stand watch near the autopsy room, said the article, and "when they see the ambulance squad arriving with a body they run toward the unit to ascertain if it contains the relative whom they long to find, if even in this somber place. The watch continues every day, including all hours of the night."[17]

· The previous month the Guatemalan press had begun to report "a wave of abductions" in the southwestern coastal region. On September 29 the newspapers reported thirty-one that had occurred in San Marcos, four in Escuintla, four in Santa Rosa, and three in Guatemala City. On that same day, General Mejia told a press conference that death squads do not exist and that "there are no violations of human rights in Guatemala."[18]

U.S. public inattention to the Guatemalan conflict has fostered an apparent inability in some quarters to grasp political and military phenomena that are more complex than a crude black/white polarity. This was dramatically demonstrated during Rios Montt's counterinsurgency when his "beans and bullets" program of using economic aid to elicit collaboration and to control and relocate the survivors of army massacres was misinterpreted by a number of foreign observers as a social reform program and a sea change in government attitudes.

Perhaps the most embarrassing piece of work inspired by this phenomenon was the November 1983 report prepared for the United Nations Human Rights Commission by U.N. Special Rapporteur Viscount Colville of Culross, a Conservative member of the British Parliament. In what the *Times* of London called "a breach of diplomatic protocol that is almost unthinkable for the United Nations,"[19] the study was later repudiated by the Human Rights Commission. Colville lavished praise on the Rios Montt counterinsurgency program, buttressing his argument with false statements such as the claim that service in the civil patrols is voluntary—this despite the fact that such service was made compulsory by decree-law No. 44-82 and that numerous officials had threatened reprisals against those who failed to participate.[20] Colville was much impressed by the village relocation programs, reporting, "I visited on Saturday a new village under construction near Nebaj—San Juan Acul. The people working with such enthusiasm to build the new community included the same group of Ixil people whom I had met, wretched and hopeless, last June."[21] He failed to note that the people in question had left their villages after surviving three major army massacres in the previous year and a half.*

Egregious though his factual errors may have been, Colville was not alone. More recently, a change in tactics under the Mejia administration wherein urban street assassinations have been in part superseded by quieter and less obvious abductions, has led some visitors to believe mistakenly that all is calm. In September 1984 the *New Republic* editorialized, in praise of changes ostensibly brought by the July 1 constituent assembly elections, "The massacres of Indian villages have ended, and the ambiance of generalized violence is gone."[22] Though one could be led to this conclusion by failing to overhear gunshots on the street, it could not withstand a simple reading of the local newspapers. "The level of violence striking the country in the last two months dropped notably in the days immediately before and after the July 1 elections," reported the respected local journal *Central American Report* on July 13, 1984. "Nevertheless, since the last week of June a steady flow of kidnappings, disappearances, and assassinations has been reported."

* The Ixil people are a group of Indians who traditionally have lived in an area of El Quiche known as "the Ixil triangle."

The U.S. Military Legacy

The Reagan administration's commitment to keep the Guatemalan regime from falling under guerrilla pressure has never been in doubt. "There is a major insurgency under way in Guatemala," acting Assistant Secretary of State John Bushnell told Congress in May 1981. "I think given the extent of the insurgency and the strong Communist worldwide support for it, the administration is disposed to support Guatemala."[23] In practice, however, large-scale support has never been required. Unlike El Salvador's, the Guatemalan army has been able to hold its own without emergency U.S. aid.

The reason lies partly in the differences between the two societies. The Guatemalan oligarchy is wealthier and more politically cohesive than its Salvadoran counterpart. The Guatemalan oligarchy has larger investments at home and historically has been more inclined to stay and defend them rather than settling for a condominium in Miami and a Swiss bank account. The Guatemalan economy is larger, more diversified, and more complex than that of El Salvador and is less subject to disruption by the destruction of a few key bridges or sabotage of a particular crop.

But one crucial, perhaps overriding factor is the Guatemalan army. It has been called by military experts the best organized and best trained in Central America—as well as the most experienced in counterinsurgency. What is rarely remarked upon, however, is how it got that way. The strength of the Guatemalan army is the linchpin of the country's current strategic situation. Because it is strong, it has held off the guerrillas. Because it has held off the guerrillas, Guatemala has not required open U.S. aid. Because it has not required open U.S. aid, Guatemala has not become an issue in the United States. And because Guatemala has not become an issue in the United States, the government's political murder of tens of thousands of its citizens of the past decade has largely escaped the attention of the American public. All of this is due, in large part, to the fact that most of what the United States is doing for the army of El

Salvador today, it did for the army of Guatemala twenty years ago.

Until the late 1970s, the United States was economically, politically, and militarily much closer to Guatemala than to El Salvador. From 1931 to 1945, the commandant of the Escuela Politecnica, Guatemala's military academy, was a U. S. Army officer. In 1954 the CIA organized a coup that toppled Guatemala's last elected, reformist government and installed the first in the series of military regimes still in power. The CIA chose Guatemala in 1960 as the training site for the Bay of Pigs invasion force. When dissident young Guatemalan officers staged a barracks revolt on November 13 of that year, CIA pilots flew bombing missions to help put down the uprising.

Under U.S. auspices, Guatemala's police force was made an instrument of counterinsurgency policy. The AID Public Safety Program (1957–74) helped train and reorganize the Guatemalan national police and their political subdivision, the *judiciales*, a unit that a 1962 State Department report described as "employed in the investigation and harassment of political opponents and in the carrying out of this or that unsavory assignment."[24] After nine more years of U.S. training, a 1971 U.S. Senate report said, "The police are widely admitted to be corrupt and are commonly held to be brutal. . . . After fourteen years, on all the evidence," the report charitably concluded, "the teaching has not been absorbed. Furthermore, the United States is politically identified with police terrorism."[25]

From 1954 to 1972, some two thousand Guatemalan army officers were trained in U.S. schools. By 1965, U.S. military advisers in Guatemala numbered thirty-four, the largest U.S. contingent in Latin America. For the next three years they carried out a thorough reorganization of the Guatemalan army—among other things, helping to organize and equip the Mobile Military Police (PMA), the unit implicated in Panzos and many of the early Lucas-era massacres.

Through the 1960s and early 1970s, U.S. aid averaged 12 percent of the Guatemalan defense budget. The tasks performed by the U.S. advisers paralleled those of their successors now in El Salvador. They organized special combat units, intelligence networks, and command and control centers. In the words of a study by two RAND Corporation analysts, "Among the new missions was the creation of a 'rapid reaction force' made up of airborne companies, which first implemented the tactics of airmobile counterinsurgency warfare in Guatemala. . . . [N]ew communications and transportation equipment . . . added greatly to the mobility of the Guatemalan military. It has given them the capacity for sustained field operations which were of extreme importance to the counterinsurgency campaigns of the late sixties. . . ."[26]

These campaigns, in the eastern provinces of Zacapa and Izabal, represented the first application in Central America of the "civic action" style of counterinsurgency that would be used so widely in Vietnam and later on a systematic scale by Rios Montt. An examination of the tactics used then provides a reflection of the entrapment of civilians and the abuses of human rights that recurred in 1982 and 1983. Directed by U.S. Green Berets, the original operation had two key components: economic projects to aid peasants who collaborated with the army or had been relocated from their villages, and the organization of local residents into paramilitary patrols. Colonel John Webber, the U.S. military attaché, was quoted discussing the campaign in a *Time* magazine article in 1968. According to the article, "armed local bands of 'civilian collaborators' licensed to kill peasants whom they considered guerrillas or 'potential guerrillas' had been used. 'That's the way the country is,' [Webber] said."[27] According to the RAND analysts, "[An] element in the destruction of the guerrillas was the employment of terror. Military authorities in the early stages of their counterinsurgency operations permitted clandestine anticommunist groups to wage a campaign of violence as the 'counter-terror' to frighten possible guerrilla collaborators. Further, blacklists were compiled which included not only those suspected of working with the guerrillas, but those suspected of Communist leanings."[28]

Estimates of the final civilian death toll between 1966 and

1968 range from three thousand to ten thousand.[29] Before the campaign began, the entire guerrilla force was estimated at only a few hundred combatants.

The problems of concentrated land tenure, the extreme poverty of the Indian population, and the lack of political participation were not seriously dealt with in subsequent years. In the mid- to late 1970s, when export prices rose and the Guatemalan economy as a whole grew rapidly, peasant living standards actually declined as speculators and military officers seized increasing amounts of their land. Channels of political redress remained closed to the poor majority as the army retained power through fraudulent elections and as unions, the Church, and grass-roots organizations were repressed. It was predictable that guerrilla opposition would resurface, attracting more Indian participation than before and boasting several thousand combatants by 1980.

In 1977, indignant over a critical human rights report from the Carter State Department, Guatemala refused further U.S. military aid. General Kjell Laugerrud, the president, announced that if such aid were contingent on having to endure human rights criticism, his army was not interested. Congress and the State Department responded by imposing a *de facto* ban. Other countries, including Taiwan and Argentina but most substantially Israel, stepped in to fill the gap. Israel plugged new hardware and manpower into the structure built by the United States. Israel equipped the army, national police, *judiciales*, and air force, and Israeli advisers assisted in the Lucas, Rios Montt, and Mejia counterinsurgency campaigns. With such day-to-day assistance to maintain the foundation built by years of U.S. aid, the Guatemalan army has held its own.

The Costs to a Community [30]

As in the past, land distribution continues to be the central economic problem underlying both opposition to and repression by the government. Most of the nation's land, including the most easily cultivated holdings, are concentrated in the hands of the less than 2 percent of the population who run the agricultural export sector. Many large plantation owners cultivate only a small portion of their landholdings, while hundreds of thousands of rural Guatemalans work as landless farm laborers, or possess such tiny *parcelas* that they can barely produce enough food to feed one individual, let alone an entire family. Efforts to alter this structural inequity, or even to mitigate its day-to-day impact, have been fiercely resisted by Guatemala's military regimes.

The story of Santa Cruz del Quiche is in some ways typical. As in most of the highlands, the people are Maya Indians. They speak Quiche and the women wear non-Western dress. Infant mortality is high; curable diseases are among the most frequent causes of death; nutrition is poor; illiteracy is widespread.

During the late 1950s and 1960s the average peasant holding was 3.4 acres of mostly steep, eroded land; 22 percent of the farms had less than 1.7 acres; and 75 percent lacked sufficient land for subsistence.* During the harvest season, thousands of peasants were trucked to the lowland plantations of the southern coast to reap the export crops, sleeping there in crowded, open sheds and earning about $1.00 a day. By the early 1970s, however, local self-help organizations had emerged that functioned effectively with wide participation by the rural population. Initially many of these were established with the help of the Catholic Church. By the mid-1970s they had achieved impressive results. Agricultural, savings and credit, consumer, and industrial (weaving) cooperatives incorporated and benefited thousands of Quichelenses. Agricultural productivity increased as new methods of cultivation, as well as fertilizers and insecticides, were introduced along with more efficient distribution. People began to see alternatives, though limited, to their plight. By 1980, few from this *municipio* went to the southern coast for seasonal work, in contrast to the enormous proportion of the population that went from other *municipios*. They were gradually improving their economic situation.

* These figures are from the 1964 census. The 1979 census shows that 93 percent of the farms in the *municipio* of Santa Cruz had insufficient land to support a family.

There were also educational programs devoted to literacy and substantive instruction. Radio Quiche—a community-service station unique in Guatemala—could be heard on every mountain around Santa Cruz for most of the day. The most effective programs of Radio Quiche were literacy classes, which were supplemented by "promoters" who visited the communities at least once a month. Though they themselves did not have much formal education, the "promoters" served as teachers, and at any one point, about three thousand students were involved. Radio Quiche also broadcast religious education programs reflecting a liberation theology. Civic education programs dealt with political issues and encouraged participation in the evolving cooperatives.

The Committee of Peasant Unity (CUC) was established throughout the highlands starting in 1978. Although it was necessarily a clandestine organization, it would hold mass meetings of up to two thousand people. Building on the years of educational work already done in the area, CUC drew much of its membership from Santa Cruz. Previously, because of a long history of repression that discouraged public organization, the Indians had been allowed few institutions of their own beyond their families and immediate communities. The system of *alcaldes indigenas* and *alguaciles* (locally elected indigenous officials) was a mediating institution but one that was limited and localized. There had been no institutions that tried to break out of the established order to deal effectively and independently with the social and economic problems of the community. The impact of organizational experience on the people of Santa Cruz was to instill confidence and hope. To the national elite, however, these developments were worrisome. They appeared as a revolutionary movement that had to be stopped.

The cooperatives in the northern Quiche were among the first to suffer repression. The clergy were persecuted, forcing them to abandon the province and requiring the bishop to close the diocese in July 1980 after a number of priests were murdered. In 1980, community leaders in Santa Cruz began to be killed, and still others were forced to flee. The army moved into rural villages massacring people and destroying crops and material possessions. By the end of 1981, repression in Santa Cruz had become generalized. There was not a single hamlet nor hardly a single household in the municipality that had not felt the effects. It is difficult to know the number of victims, but one can say that almost no family has been spared a death, or a disappearance, or the terror of fleeing for their lives.

Aid and Apologetics

The inattention to Guatemala in the United States has had perhaps its greatest impact on shaping the terms of debate between Congress and the administration on the question of U.S. military aid to Guatemala. Since mid-1981, in lieu of any big-ticket budget proposals, the controversy has centered on one question: whether the United States would sell from $2 million to $6 million in helicopter spare parts and maintenance services requested by Guatemala under the Foreign Military Sales (FMS) program. Lacking formal legal authority to prevent the sale, Congress struck an agreement with the administration, recorded in committee report language, providing that it be consulted prior to any such sale.

For nearly three years, the debate wore on. The administration would say it was going through with the sale, and Congress would balk. The administration would pull back and try again later. The administration finally went ahead and announced its approval of the deal in January 1983. But Guatemala did not take delivery until a year and a half later.

At no time during this drama did either side give an inkling that they realized they were in fact arguing over a red herring; for from 1981 through 1982, while all eyes focused on spare parts and repair allowances for three helicopters, twenty-three brand-new helicopters (worth $25 million) were sold by the United States to Guatemala, promptly fitted with .30-caliber machine guns, and taken into the field. Between January and March 1982, more than twenty Guatemalan air force pilots came to Texas for flight training and received advice on how to mount the guns.[31] The Bell helicopters played their first major role in the October 1981 civic-action offensive in the western province of Chimaltenango, in which Benedicto Lucas Garcia initiated his counterinsurgency plan. Throughout the following year, according to Congressman Michael Barnes, "the Guatemalan army was systematically massacring the Indian population. Helicopters . . . [were] used in those massacres."[32]

This assistance was in addition to other forms of backdoor military aid, including the provision of rifles for civil patrols, the presence of a Green Beret counterinsurgency trainer at the military academy, clandestine shipment of A-37 spare parts, and the activities of a U.S. embassy military officer who trained Guatemalan officers[33]—all of which were virtually ignored while Congress, most of the press, and the interested political community went on saying that military aid to Guatemala had somehow been forestalled because the helicopter spare parts were yet to be delivered. The rifles were of particular importance, for they were used to arm civil patrollers that accompanied the army.* The frequency of civil patrol participation in massacres—as admitted by patrollers themselves—makes it more than likely that the U.S. rifles were responsible for civilian deaths in Guatemala.

These instances of backdoor aid plainly contravened the spirit—if not the letter—of pertinent human rights legislation. In no case did the administration call them to the attention of Congress (they leaked out by other means), though they dwarfed the matter of the helicopter spare parts by any objective standards.

Such an active desire to assist Guatemala's military required justification. In the realm of description and analysis, the administration has compiled a consistent record of apologetics. It has devoted more energy to attacking human rights groups that try to report on crimes against the person than it has to criticizing those who commit them. After President Lucas fell in March 1982, the administration, seeking to praise his successors by comparison, gave a harsh and

---

* Captain Romeo Sierra, commander of the 250-man La Perla patrol base in Quiche Province, told the author in September 1982 that the rifles had come from the United States via the CIA. Three other officers confirmed his claim.

accurate appraisal of his human rights record. Assistant Secretary of State Langhorne Motley decried "indiscriminate
use of violence to force [the peasants'] allegiance."[34] Deputy
Assistant Secretary of State Stephen Bosworth called Lucas's
actions "as abhorrent as they were counterproductive"[35] and
said that "civilian violence was an implicit part of government policy"[36] during his regime. Assistant Secretary of
State for Human Rights Elliott Abrams called the Lucas
counterinsurgency a "war against the populace."[37] A senior
U.S. diplomat in Guatemala was more graphic still: "We
knew perfectly well that they were raiding villages and taking
out all males from fourteen up, tying their hands behind
their backs, torturing, and killing them."[38]

While Lucas was in power, however, the administration
conceded none of these facts and at times actively denied
them. During a 1981 visit to Guatemala, its special envoy,
retired CIA Deputy Director Vernon Walters, embraced
Lucas and said the United States would help defend "peace
and liberty" and "constitutional institutions."[39] The 1981
Country Reports on human rights attributed most of the violence to "self-appointed vigilantes" and elements beyond
the government's control.[40] Bosworth blamed the left and
discerned "positive developments" in security forces "taking
care to protect innocent bystanders."[41]

It was under Lucas that the administration first publicly
broke the military aid embargo, announcing a sale of jeeps,
trucks, and field radios on June 5, 1981. It was Lucas who
received the Bell helicopters and pilot training. Indeed, the
aid proposals that would later dominate debate during
the Rios Montt and Mejia years—helicopter spare parts and
the restoration of IMET (International Military Education
and Training) funds—were first requested on behalf of General Lucas.

When Rios Montt's supporters overthrew Lucas on March
23, 1982, the administration rushed to embrace the new
leader—comparing him favorably to one whom, it was now
claimed, the United States had "carefully refrained from
backing" due to his "record of serious human rights violations."[42] In April, the National Security Council authorized

$2.5 million for a covert CIA "arms interdiction program"—in light of "the recent junior officer coup [which] has given us new possibilities for working out an improved relationship with that country." [43]

As Rios Montt's staggering toll of lives began to become known, the administration defended him as if against slander and malice. This performance was epitomized by President Reagan when, after meeting Rios Montt in Honduras on December 4, 1982, he declared that the Guatemalan government had received "a bum rap" [44] on human rights and suggested that it had earned the right to renewed military aid. There is nothing to suggest that the administration gave pause when Rios Montt responded by telling reporters, "We have no scorched-earth policy; we have a policy of scorched Communists." [45] The following month, the administration announced it would lift the spare-parts embargo.

The administration was willing to deny even self-evident facts in its defense of Rios Montt. "The killings have stopped. . . . The Guatemalan government has come out of the darkness and into the light," said Ambassador Frederic Chapin on April 17. [46] "The number of killings are really down," said a State Department human rights officer, Dale Shaffer, in May. "There haven't been the massacres in the countryside like we had before." [47] "Since Rios Montt came to power in March 1982," the State Department's 1982 *Country Reports* stated flatly, "there has been a decrease in the level of killing." [48]

As a steady stream of reports made it harder to deny the existence of the rural massacres, the administration shifted ground and tried to blame the guerrillas. Bosworth told Congress that "in the majority of cases the insurgents . . . have been guilty." [49] In fact, however, in an October 1982 interview the embassy official whose research and analysis provide the basis for State Department human rights reports gave Americas Watch the entirely contradictory estimate that roughly "two out of ten" noncombatant killings could be attributed to the guerrillas. [50]

After Rios Montt was ousted by Mejia on August 8, 1983, the administration praised the new general for reversing practices it had previously lauded Rios Montt for initiating. Mejia closed down the special tribunals, which an embassy official background paper had described as "streamlined"[51] judicial institutions designed to fight corruption; the State Department called the abolition a "positive step."[52] Mejia reversed Rios Montt's counterinsurgency pattern as urban killings and abductions soared while rural massacres became relatively less common. The 1983 *Country Reports* hailed this as "a dramatic decline in reports of violence and political deaths in the countryside, in sharp contrast to 1982, when there were many allegations of abuses against Guatemala's Indian population, some of which were confirmed."[53] In September 1983 as the rate of assassinations doubled and abductions quadrupled (to a hundred per month),[54] a State Department official told the *New York Times* that "we see a trend toward improvement in human rights."[55]

More than just ignoring and distorting evidence, the administration has gone so far as to create new analytical tools to explain away and even implicitly to justify the government's political killings. Two arguments have been notable: first, the claim that many killings are the fault of renegade elements beyond the central government's control, and second, the argument that regardless of who is doing it, such actions are understandable and excusable when committed by a government fighting an insurgency.

The administration's willingness to invoke the renegade argument insincerely—in knowing disregard of the truth— was demonstrated most dramatically under Lucas Garcia. But even the State Department's own retrospective condemnations of that regime have not shamed them into abandoning this argument, and it is still used occasionally in defense of Mejia.

The second argument is more interesting and more politically ominous, for it does not turn on questions of fact. It does not need to deny government culpability. It merely needs to establish a historical context of insurgency, which thereby mitigates anything the government might do—or believe itself to be doing—in its own self-defense.

This argument was stated in its clearest form by Rios Montt and his chief aide, Francisco Bianchi, during a June 1982 interview while the village sweeps were at their most intense. Asked about army killings of unarmed civilians, Rios Montt replied: "Look, the problem of the war is not just a question of who is shooting. For each one who is shooting, there are ten working behind him, and you know that very well."[56]

"The guerrillas won over many Indian collaborators," Bianchi explained. "Therefore, the Indians were subversives, right? And how do you fight subversion? Clearly you had to kill Indians because they were collaborating with subversion. And then they would say, 'You're massacring innocent people.' But they weren't innocent. They had sold out to subversion."[57]

The Reagan administration began to experiment publicly with a modest prelude to this argument in 1981 during the Lucas administration. In congressional testimony, Deputy Assistant Secretary of State Bosworth defended the sale of military trucks and jeeps by attributing the violence to a "cycle of provocation from the left and overreaction from the right." For such an argument the starting point—who initiated hostilities—is all-important. According to Bosworth, "The most recent cycle of violence began in October of 1978, when the leftist opposition exploited an economic issue to lead street riots in which thirty people were killed."[58]

The sentence was a masterpiece of careful phrasing. In the incident to which Bosworth referred, tens of thousands of Guatemala City residents staged a peaceful protest march against an increase in bus fares. According to local newspapers, eyewitnesses, and newsfilm of the incident, the army and police attacked the crowd: fifteen hundred were arrested, four hundred were wounded, and thirty-three were killed.

But the facts were beside the point. Any other incident at any other time could have been cited to trigger the logical chain reaction that constitutes such an argument, and the argument would still be flawed. For the Guatemalan army's abuses, the Guatemalan army is obviously responsible. Bosworth did not see it that way, however. His conclusion was, "In Guatemala, improved human rights will not be possible unless the overall level of violence and provocations by the insurgents are reduced."[59] This, of course, could be accomplished only by aiding the army.

After the passing of Lucas and the advent of Rios Montt's more presentable civic-action approach, the administration took the argument one and sometimes two steps farther— first, dropping the opprobrium of calling the antileftist violence "overreaction"; and second, at times not bothering to foist the responsibility off on the "renegade right," letting it instead reside with the government said to be engaged in a legitimate labor of self-defense.

In January 1983, shortly after the president's "bum rap" statement, Assistant Secretary of State for Human Rights Elliott Abrams appeared on television to defend the announced resumption of military aid. "The price of stability in the middle of a guerrilla war is high," he said, "but I don't think you blame that on the government. You blame that on the guerrillas who are fighting the government. . . . When the guerrillas are in the middle of a war against the government and increasing the amount of violence that they are using, you don't blame the government for the creation of refugees."[60]

Using such an argument, there is no conceivable fact about government atrocities against civilians during an internal war that could permit one to "blame the government." Once the self-evident reality that guerrillas are fighting the government has been established, all further evidence is ruled immaterial.

In the Guatemalan case, further evidence included the political murders of three American clergymen in 1981 and 1982, as well as the manifold testimony of terror gathered by human rights groups from refugees in Mexico and sources inside the country. Assistant Secretary of State for Human Rights Elliott Abrams dismissed the refugee accounts of massacres as fabrications of "guerrilla sympathizers"; the U.S. embassy in Guatemala tried to slur Amnesty International's reporting on civilian deaths as the product of a "Communist-backed disinformation plan."*

Hard as it was on those who tried to report human rights violations, the administration showed no end of indulgence for the conduct of the violators themselves. In November 1983, the head of Guatemala's Franciscan order was assassinated, the bishops were threatened by the government when they protested,[61] and the mutilated bodies of two abducted Guatemalan AID employees appeared in a ravine.[62] Shortly thereafter the State Department announced it was ready to go forward with the delayed helicopter parts sale. In December the U.S. embassy official investigating the AID killings fled Guatemala in "fear of his life,"[63] and in turn, U.S. Customs released twelve thousand hitherto impounded rifles bound from Israel to Guatemala, while President Reagan announced Guatemala's inclusion in the Caribbean Basin Initiative.[64] In January the Kissinger Commission reported that the Guatemalan security forces "have murdered those even suspected of dissent."[65] Two weeks later the administration finalized the helicopter parts sale.

This administration's construct of legitimate defensive action implies that a government becomes logically incapable of performing a culpable act. Whatever it might do, the argument goes, it was provoked into doing.

In addition to permitting one to justify literally anything, this argument has obvious practical implications for the way the Reagan administration collects human rights information and weighs it in policy. In October 1982, the author discussed human rights data gathering and reporting with a senior U.S. diplomat in Guatemala. The official said that the Rios Montt government "has a policy against torture." Told of recent conversations with officers who described how they

* The charge was made in a document based on reports by the embassy but not circulated after its faulty research was pointed out by nongovernmental experts on Guatemalan issues. The document also attacked the Washington Office on Latin America and Guatemalan and solidarity offices concerned with human rights. This was the embassy's second major attempt to undermine Amnesty International's credibility—the first being a September letter signed by Assistant Secretary of State Thomas Enders and widely circulated in Washington and Guatemala (see Chapter 1).

tortured and had been trained to do so, he replied: "That's not what we conclude on the basis of our information." Asked what that information was based on and whether it included talking with troops in the field, the official admitted that this research was haphazard. When asked whether the embassy's human rights reporting drew on forensic information, the diplomat replied sharply, "We are not a coroner's office. No, we don't talk to the forensic doctors. I only have two people in the whole political section. And they spend a hell of a lot of time analyzing and correcting the false charges made by a lot of organizations. It takes a lot of research to answer these allegations. But we do correct the factual errors in a lot of Amnesty International reports."

When asked how these reports could be evaluated if the embassy generally did not collect field and forensic information and instead relied on newspaper and government accounts, the senior official got to the crux of the matter. "These human rights statistics are unnecessary and irrelevant. We do the grim grams [monthly human rights reports cabled to the State Department] because there's a requirement for it. It's a very sterile and useless exercise. It's not relevant to the central issue: Should we help Guatemala or shouldn't we? I want to help Guatemala. I don't think the numbers matter."[66]

By "numbers," of course, he was referring to the dead, people who had had names and homes and families. That they have enjoyed no rights or respect is the fault of thirty years of violent rule, a pattern in which the United States has been compromised and to which the Reagan administration has contributed more than its share.

5

DEMOCRACIES
UNDER FIRE
Peru
Colombia

The civilian presidents of Peru and Colombia were both elected on waves of hope and expectation. Not the least of that hope was for increased political participation and respect for human rights. In 1980 Fernando Belaunde Terry of Peru followed an unpopular and economically harsh military regime; in Colombia, Belisario Betancur took office in 1981 after a civilian who had permitted the armed forces free rein to arrest and intimidate. Both face internal armed challenges—Peru from Maoist guerrillas whose own brutality has terrorized peasants, Colombia from more typically leftist and populist guerrilla forces with roots in a history of aborted reform and limited democracy. These groups' existence, in both cases, highlights the discontent felt by poor majorities who do not take up arms but also do not feel that the traditional power structure represents them.

These are democracies under fire from two directions: from the guerrillas who challenge their legitimacy, and from the armed forces who challenge their authority to control abuses of human rights. Whether Peru and Colombia can develop as stable and genuine democracies will depend on how their governments respond to social problems that have led to both peaceful and violent protest, and whether they and their armed forces respect the right of protest itself. Both countries have a potential for polarization and bloodshed that equals that of El Salvador, a potential for institutionalized military rule to rival that of Argentina or Chile. These dangers are apparently of little moment to the Reagan administration, which has failed to concern itself in any visible way with human rights in either of these countries.

This is a different failure than is found elsewhere in Latin America; the administration has not made a campaign of apology for these democratic governments caught in a violent cycle, as it has for military-dominated or simply military governments nearby; it has not rushed to make an issue of their fragility and of the U.S. commitment to democratic rule, peace, and stability. It has neither offered public support for positive steps taken—as in Colombia—nor has it publicly remarked, or conditioned its aid decisions, on the serious abuses that persist and are traceable to the military. The administration, in short, has developed no human rights policy with respect to these two nations with immense human rights problems, nations whose decline into further violence could only undermine progress toward democracy elsewhere.

In both countries, the administration's important ties are not with civilian leaders but with military institutions; in Colombia's case these ties have been close for many years. Yet these are countries that, above all, require economic help, diplomatic support for their positive efforts, and an attitude of U.S. cooperation with long-term social development. Such cooperation, emphasizing basic human needs and recognizing the social cost of the heavy foreign debt burden, would demonstrate support for civilian institutions and understanding of structural social problems.

The Reagan administration's misuse of military aid and its apologies for military rulers are often noted. In these two cases, on the other hand, we see the reverse side of Reagan policy. This administration, so committed to military solutions, has been, when given the opportunity, unwilling to give meaningful support to solutions short of force. Struggling democracies, flawed and fragile but perhaps the last chance for peaceful resolution in their countries—in Colombia's case a popular, vital program for internal peace—are a challenge this administration appears not to understand.

PERU

The situation of Peru is unenviable. In Sendero Luminoso, the country faces the most violent and enigmatic guerrilla organization that has yet appeared in the Western Hemisphere. Yet despite its dogmatic ideology and repugnant character, Sendero seems able to exploit the misery and alienation in an impoverished section of the country that the central government has neglected for centuries.

In coping with Sendero Luminoso, Peru is greatly handicapped by institutions designed to promote law and order but inadequate for the task. The Peruvian judicial system has suffered for years from corruption, political manipulation, and acute underfinancing. The courts are ineffective in administering justice in ordinary times, and they cannot begin to cope with the present crisis.

One of the consequences of the weakness of these institutions is that, of some 18,000 inmates in Peruvian prisons, 76 percent (some 13,700) are awaiting trial and only 24 percent (some 4,300) are serving sentences.[1] This helps to make many Peruvians cynical about the legal process in dealing with crime, a cynicism enhanced by the fact that the contraband drug industry, reaping enormous profits from the export of cocaine, could not thrive unless many police, prosecutors, and judges were being paid off handsomely by the *narcotraficantes*.

Competition and resentment between the military and police forces, and between different police branches, has led to violent conflict in the streets between uniformed men. Particularly under military governments, the police forces were badly treated and inadequately funded. Their poor facilities, poor training, and low salaries left them vulnerable to bribes, and frequently they are charged with abuse, especially beatings and torture in connection with common crimes.

To the extent that Peru has used the legal process to deal with Sendero Luminoso, it has been principally through an antiterrorist law. Adopted by the administration of President Fernando Belaunde Terry in 1981, this law facilitates police abuse of those detained on suspicion of terrorism by author-

izing fifteen days of detention before the courts may inter-
fere. It also defines terrorism broadly to include such
offenses as "adversely affecting international relations or the
security of the state," or "using the news media to incite
people to terrorism," or "speaking out publicly in favor of an
act of terrorism or a terrorist." Thousands of Peruvians have
been detained under this law and, as of July 1984, more than
1,500 persons were in prison on charges of terrorism. According to the president of the Supreme Court, only 12 to 15
were serving sentences, though he said that some 475 others
were in the process of being tried.[2]

As might be expected of a law worded so broadly, Peru's
antiterrorist statute has been used against many persons who
have nothing to do with the kinds of acts committed by Sendero Luminoso. Among those who have been detained
under the law are leaders of trade unions and peasant groups
who have taken part in nonviolent protests, and priests who
have aided them.

Though the abuses that have taken place through the legal
process are very serious, they are not the crux of the human
rights problem in Peru. It is rather what appears to be the
abandonment of legal process, which seems to be leading
the armed forces to believe that anything goes in the battle
against Sendero Luminoso, and likewise, anything goes also
against any other Peruvian—even those not remotely suspected of involvement in armed conflict.

On July 27, 1984, Jesus Oropeza Chonta, a well-known
peasant leader with centrist political affiliations, was detained by members of the Civil Guard (police) in the Andean
town of Puquio. He had been attending a meeting of the
local agrarian league. Thereafter, Oropeza disappeared. The
Peruvian press has reported that he was transferred from the
local jail to an armed forces truck and driven away. Two
weeks later, the police brought his charred and mutilated
corpse back to Puquio.[3]

On August 2, 1984, Jaime Ayala Sulca, a correspondent
for the opposition daily newspaper *La Republica*, went to the
military barracks in Huanta, a highland town near the de-
partmental center of Ayacucho, to file a complaint against

police abuse. He was last seen publicly as he entered the barracks. Ayala has disappeared.[4]

The Oropeza and Ayala cases, which attracted unusual attention, have made clear to Peruvians that those who are well connected are not immune to the political violence sweeping the country. The greatest number of victims, however, are Indian peasants from isolated communities in the south-central, Andean department of Ayacucho, few of whom speak Spanish. Several incidents of mass murder of Quechua Indians have occurred in 1983 and 1984, and reports of the discovery of mass graves now appear with some regularity in the Peruvian press.

One of the best-known cases of mass murder in Ayacucho took place in the village of Soccos on November 13, 1983. It grew out of an argument between some "Sinchis"—members of a police antiterrorist unit, now notorious for brutality —and the guests at a wedding party. After some of the wedding guests were shot by the Sinchis, the rest were herded off to a gully and machine-gunned, apparently in an effort to eliminate witnesses. Thirty-four bodies have been found. At this writing, it remains unclear whether any of the police involved will be criminally punished.[*]

Reform and Retreat

Belaunde is serving his second term as president of Peru after an interruption of twelve years of military rule, and he faced similar crises in his first term. There had been widespread peasant uprisings from 1958 to 1963 in the valley of La Convencion near Cuzco. Later, in 1965, following the example of Cuba, a group of urban intellectuals launched a guerrilla war in the Andes. Both phenomena signaled the need for agrarian reform and the integration of the peasants into the national society and economy.

---

[*] The police attempted to blame the massacre at Soccos on Sendero Luminoso. Eventually the public prosecutor indicted the police, but the minister of the interior, Luis Percovich, who told Americas Watch a month after the episode at Soccos that there was a "real possibility" that the Sinchis had committed the massacre, subsequently insisted in a newspaper interview that it was actually a massacre by Sendero.

The guerrillas, who had not blended into the peasant communities, were easily isolated and crushed by the newly formed police special forces or Sinchis (the same forces used in Ayacucho today). Belaunde legislated a reform, but there were few real changes, and his administration was troubled by cases of corruption, including questionable contracts with foreign petroleum companies. In 1968 his term ended in a military coup led by General Juan Velasco Alvarado.

In the mid-1960s, a new school had developed within the Peruvian armed forces that, partially in response to the peasant uprisings, began to express the growing need for profound social changes in Peru. The Velasco regime (1968–75) imposed a liberal-statist development model that sought to modernize the economy while increasing state participation,* and to mobilize Peru's poor by creating grass-roots organizations controlled from above.

To finance its projects, the government borrowed large sums. Then, in 1975, Peru's economic fortunes changed dramatically. World copper prices plummeted, and oil production proved barely sufficient to meet national needs. At the time Peru had contracted close to $8 billion in foreign loans. Velasco's experiment ended, and a conservative military regime led by General Francisco Morales Bermudez came in to impose austerity. Confronted with stringent IMF guidelines as a condition for refinancing and new loans, public spending contracted rapidly. For a nation accustomed to a large state apparatus, the results were dramatic. The currency was devalued; basic food subsidies were cut; and wages rapidly lost ground to rising inflation. Mounting protest and resistance aimed at the military (including four national strikes) were met with increased repression. This unrest and

---

* In this process, some foreign petroleum and mining companies were nationalized; the press was nationalized; worker-management enterprises were established; and a sweeping agrarian reform was initiated in 1969. Considered the most advanced in Latin America at the time, the land reform law transferred some 25.9 million acres belonging to large haciendas to landless peasants working on those haciendas. Four hundred thousand rural families were affected. Sixty percent of the land expropriated was consolidated in agrarian cooperatives formed by farm workers. The redistribution broke the economic and political dominion of Peru's agricultural oligarchy.

the economic crisis itself led the military to call for elections to establish a constituent assembly in 1978. A new Constitution was drafted in 1979, and Belaunde was reelected in 1980 with 43 percent of the popular vote.

The second Belaunde administration began with broad support from a military-weary country. Yet, to address the problem of the foreign debt, it began to reverse many of the economic reforms. At the urging of the IMF, Belaunde implemented a conservative free-trade economic model, facilitating the flow of foreign imports and lifting protectionist laws that favored national products. Agrarian reform, paralyzed under Morales Bermudez, was effectively reversed under a 1980 law that halted redistribution, reduced legal protection to cooperatives, and made reappropriated land salable. In some areas, it is reported, as much as 80 percent of the land has already returned to the ownership of the *hacendados*.

The international recession—coupled with the cheap-import policies that undercut domestic industry—have meant the loss of some 900,000 jobs in a country where less than half the work force of 6 million is fully employed and where 150,000 new jobs are needed every year to keep pace with the growth in the population.[5] At the same time, salaries and wages, in real terms, decreased 50 percent from June 1980 to May 1984. With a foreign debt of over $13 billion, the debt per capita is about $720 per person, as much as 20 months' minimum wage for a Lima worker.

As the economic crisis deepens and social spending is cut back farther, protest has increased. Municipal elections in November 1983, serving as a referendum on the current government, reflected a major shift to the left. The elections gave Belaunde's party only 18 percent of the vote; the social-democratic APRA Party, 33 percent of the vote; and the Left Unity coalition, 29 percent of the vote.

Sendero Luminoso

On the same day in May 1980 that Peruvians cast ballots, returning to constitutional democracy after twelve years of military rule, Sendero Luminoso (Shining Path) began its guerrilla war by dynamiting ballot boxes in a small Ayacuchan town.

Sendero Luminoso was not new to Ayacucho. The group dates back to the early 1970s, when Maoist factions split from the Moscow-line Communist Party. The "Peruvian Communist Party in the Shining Path of Jose Carlos Mariategui" * moved to the Andean countryside to live with the peasants. Its leadership was predominantly middle-class intellectuals who gathered in the University of Huamanga (Ayacucho), and Sendero grew among students and first-generation urban dwellers. Very different from the Cuban-style *foquista* groups of the 1960s, which were isolated from the people and easily suppressed, Sendero for almost a decade has absorbed the language, customs, and culture of the Quechua Indians of the region.

Sendero's only international link—and that link seems only ideological, not material—appears to be with a remnant of Maoist "Gang of Four" followers, including the U.S. Revolutionary Communist Party. It has equally denounced the U.S.S.R., the People's Republic of China, Cuba, and Albania, as well as Peru's traditional left, which has taken the parliamentary route and controls some municipal governments and parliamentary seats. From all appearances, Sendero Luminoso is rigidly dogmatic, and it has proven to be vicious and bloody in its quest for power. It has combined a classic Maoist strategy for guerrilla war—that of a "prolonged popular war" encircling the cities from the countryside—with the traditional Incan messianism of the indigenous population.

After four years of terrorist activity and two years of open conflict in Ayacucho, the Peruvian government and the military have yet to locate the leadership, effectively infiltrate the organization, ascertain its size, or seriously inhibit its expansion. But from a survey of prisoners in El Fronton

* Mariategui, founder of the Peruvian Communist Party who died in 1930 at the age of thirty-five, wrote a series of essays on Incan communal life, among other works.

prison who admit to being "Senderistas,"[6] among those wounded in battles and involved in the few public demonstrations of support, it seems that high school students as young as twelve and thirteen and university students are Sendero's most numerous followers. Sendero has offered a violent alternative to young people without a future.[7] Perhaps, also, part of its attraction is its demand for intense commitment and sacrifice from young people from whom few other demands are made—an attraction similar to that of some religious cults elsewhere. It is hard to determine the size of the group. In 1981, the army estimated the core to include about five hundred militants. In July 1984, however, Army General Julian Julia estimated that this core numbered some two thousand militants.[8] This suggests that the group has multiplied four times in only three years. The New York Times reported government estimates ranging from two thousand to seven thousand militants in September 1984.[9]

Sendero began its war by dynamiting public buildings and electrical towers. Armed confrontations began in March 1982. In a major show of strength and intelligence work, the group dynamited key power stations, leaving Lima in darkness, in August 1982. Since then this has become one of its trademarks. That same month, Sendero began to target certain local groups—policemen, landowners, government officials, loan sharks, merchants, and informants—in Ayacucho. Senderistas staged "popular trials" and executions. This initially strengthened their popularity among the Indians, many of whom held officials in contempt. Yet as Sendero began to control "liberated zones" of Ayacucho in late 1982, it imposed an antitechnology, subsistence peasant model that, along with its brutality, has led the group's actions to be compared to Pol Pot's reign of terror in Cambodia. Sendero closed regional markets; forced peasants to plant only enough for their own subsistence; and brutally killed those who opposed them. As Sendero has implemented its own kind of terror, some of its support has waned, yet its strength apparently has not.

Since the counterinsurgency began in January 1983, many peasants in Ayacucho now claim that they are terrified by both Sendero and the security forces. Yet the polarization seems to have benefited Sendero more than the government. Even as Sendero is put on the defensive in Ayacucho, it has effectively been able to exploit economic and social discontent in other areas. It is reported to be growing in the Lima shantytowns, on the southern coast (Nazca, Ica, Pisco), in both the northern and southern Andes (Cajamarca, Huancayo, Puno, Cuzco), and now in the high jungle of Tingo Maria.

Uchuraccay

World attention to Sendero began when eight Peruvian journalists were killed by members of the Indian peasant community of Uchuraccay in Ayacucho on January 26, 1983. The journalists had traveled to the Andean village to investigate reports that seven persons had been killed earlier in the month by members of the Indian community of Huaychao. At this writing, nearly two years later, it remains unclear why the journalists were killed. The initial assertions by the Peruvian military commander in the region, General Noel, who claimed that the journalists had entered Uchuraccay carrying a red flag and chanting antigovernment slogans, and that their cameras were mistaken for guns,[10] has been shown to be false by a government investigating commission headed by novelist Mario Vargas Llosa. The commission accepted the view, however, that the journalists were mistaken for Sendero Luminoso guerrillas coming to avenge earlier killings of guerrillas. Its report blames the entire peasant community for the killings and, in addition, suggests the guilt of all Peruvians for the failure to incorporate the Indians into modern society. Amnesty International, on the other hand, blames the local *teniente gobernador* (lieutenant governor), a local official appointed by the central government and acting under the authority of the armed forces in the region, for carrying out summary executions.[11] The implication is that in doing so, he carried out what he understood to be government policy in the area. Nearly two years later, the case has not been resolved by the Peruvian courts; the lieutenant governor has disappeared; his wife is dead; other key witnesses have disappeared; and Uchuraccay is virtually a ghost town, as most of its residents have fled.

Terror vs. Terror

Since the beginning of 1983, Ayacucho and several other provinces where Sendero Luminoso is active have been militarized, with all civilian functions subordinated to the authority of a political military commander. From all appearances, the armed forces operating in the region have made a deliberate decision to use terror as their principal weapon against Sendero Luminoso's terror. A counterinsurgency expert in Ayacucho told the New York Times that the security forces purposely leave bodies on public display. "This raises doubt about who did it and dissuades people," he said. "The idea is to reduce the terrorists to their hard core by using greater terror."[12] In this regard he alluded to the Argentine antiguerrilla campaign of the 1970s, when thousands of guerrillas, sympathizers, and peaceful opponents of the government were killed.*

The army has implemented a two-track strategy to dissuade peasants from supporting Sendero Luminoso. On the one hand, it offers food, seeds, and protection from the guerrillas to those villages that side with the army. On the other hand, Sinchi patrols terrorize communities where Sendero Luminoso has passed through. Reports by villagers cite how Sinchis and marines rape women of all ages, steal valuables and animals, and burn homes. In some cases they take prisoners, while in other cases prisoners are summarily shot.

A consequence of the methods used by the armed forces is that, in scenes reminiscent of Argentina's mothers of the desaparecidos, every day there are long lines of women, in this case Quechua Indian women, outside the offices of the police and the public prosecutor's office in Ayacucho seeking

---

* The New York Times also cites Peruvian intelligence sources who said that Peruvian officers had been trained in intelligence and interrogation by the Argentine military, both in Peru and Argentina.[13]

news of relatives who have not been heard from since they were arrested. Along the roads outside Ayacucho, rotting bodies can be found as well as mass graves.

Reports of disappearances and extrajudicial executions— many following detention by official forces—are not limited to Ayacucho but come also from the departments of Andahuaylas, Huancavelica, Pampas, and Tayacaja.[14] In urban areas the victims are mainly teachers and university and high school students—thought to be the base of Sendero Luminoso's support. In the rural areas, mass executions have occurred. But the disappeared include people of all ages and political stripes, and in some instances, entire families.

The Belaunde Government

President Fernando Belaunde Terry enjoys an international reputation as one of the Western Hemisphere's leading democratic figures. But he is faced with a staggering international debt, high unemployment, uncontrolled inflation, and a system of social services that does not begin to serve the needs of either the rural poor in the Andes or the millions who have crowded into Lima's shantytowns in recent years. Under such circumstances, it would require extraordinary leadership to ensure that human rights were respected during the battle against Sendero Luminoso. Unfortunately, far from supplying such leadership, he has made matters worse by the public stands he has taken when abuses are called to his attention. Characteristic was his comment in August 1983, when Amnesty International sent him a comprehensive report documenting extrajudicial executions, disappearances, and torture.[15] He announced that Amnesty's report went "right into the trash can." He has similarly denounced foreign priests for bringing "ideological garbage" into the country;[16] and has criticized the country's research centers and foreign foundations that support them for "dedicat[ing] themselves to divisive activities and to planting the evil seed in the souls of the people."[17] The president's brother, a member of the Parliament, has acted as his surrogate in publicly attacking Peru's cardinal for speaking out on human rights matters. Members of the Belaunde administration echo the president, as when then Prime Minister Fernando Schwalb told Americas Watch, "Those criticizing Peru on human rights grounds are not acting in good faith. They are trying to harm the democratic government of Peru to serve their own political purposes." [18]

Many Peruvians who are committed to human rights have been reluctant to criticize abuses for fear that this will undermine the Belaunde government and that the armed forces will again seize power. Some expressing this fear say that, if that were to happen in the context of the war against Sendero Luminoso, it would lead to a bloodbath comparable to what took place in Argentina in 1976 or in Chile in 1973. Whether or not this is a rationalization, the effect is that many whose voices should be heard denouncing abuses have remained silent. In addition, the country lacks a prestigious human rights organization that crosses political party lines, such as exist in Argentina, Chile, and Colombia.* In the absence of such a group, the most visible critics of human rights abuses have been a few members of the Peruvian Parliament, who by themselves do not represent a sufficient cohesion of purpose to create a strong human rights pressure.

The Role of the United States

As of the end of 1984, the Reagan administration has refrained from any public criticism of human rights abuses in Peru. Such public statements as the United States has made are in keeping with the comment attributed to Vice President Bush in the Peruvian press that President Reagan "has confidence that the leaders of the democratic government of Peru are making an effort to protect civil liberties in the military campaign against Sendero Luminoso." [19]

Aside from expressing confidence in the Belaunde administration, the Reagan administration has attempted to in-

---

* There is an excellent Catholic Church-sponsored human rights organization, CEAS, but it is small and the Church has kept it low-key.

crease U.S. military support for Peru. In 1983, such aid amounted to $4.6 million; for 1984, the Reagan administration proposed $25.7 million, though this was cut by Congress to $10.7 million. The purpose seems not so much to aid the armed forces in fighting Sendero Luminoso as to prevent the Peruvian armed forces from becoming dependent on the Soviet Union. (During the period of military government, Peru purchased a large quantity of arms from the Soviet Union.) Whatever the purpose, U.S. military support appears to ally the United States with the Peruvian armed forces, which are committing gross abuses of human rights.

1985 and Beyond

In early 1985, Amnesty International published a list of more than one thousand Peruvians who had disappeared after detention by the security forces. True to form, President Belaunde used the occasion of Pope John Paul II's visit to Peru, when the eyes of the world were on his troubled country, to hold a press conference in which he railed at Amnesty for this report. For its part, the Reagan administration did not comment on the disappearances, but proposed to Congress a $128 million aid package for Peru for fiscal year 1986. Though most of this would be for desperately needed economic assistance, the proposal includes more than $20 million in military aid.

National elections, scheduled for April 1985, will give Peru a new government and a new president starting in July 1985. The new government will face a mountain of problems, including the need to stop the disappearances and to provide an accounting for cases documented by Amnesty and others. Unless the new government acts quickly and resolutely on these matters, the human rights situation in Peru could become as nightmarish as it has been anywhere in the hemisphere.

COLOMBIA

Though larger than Peru and more strategically placed, at the neck of South America, Colombia shares with Peru many superficial and a few profound similarities. As in Peru, though to a lesser degree, Colombia's varied topography interferes with communication and understanding among regions, contributes to the isolation of Indians and other cultural groups,* and inhibits nationwide grass-roots organization. In both countries the leadership of the Catholic Church remains generally conservative and identified with ruling elites. Like Peru, Colombia faces a guerrilla challenge coupled with the lawlessness—and economic importance—of an over $1 billion-a-year cocaine and marijuana industry. Both countries face difficult debt problems; Colombia's foreign debt of $11 billion, relatively small by hemispheric standards, is nonetheless draining funds from desperately needed social programs. In both countries, law enforcement and judicial procedures are inefficient, and the police are corrupt; in Colombia as in Peru, corruption—a product both of the political system's favors and of easy drug money—extends to members of Congress as well. Thus, while both Colombia and Peru currently possess democratic forms of government, democracy is a relative concept—made more so by strong military institutions that are capable of resisting civilian control and have a record of human rights violations.

But Colombia may be able to avoid the trap into which Peru more typically has fallen. In May and August 1984, the nonaligned, innovative leadership of Belisario Betancur produced limited-duration cease-fire agreements with Colombia's major guerrilla organizations, offering the first credible hope for internal peace in forty years. On this possibility for peace rests an entire economic and social agenda—and on the cease-fire agreements, therefore, Betancur staked much of his considerable prestige and popularity. This gamble was

---

* Colombia's Indians, a half dozen different groups, number about five hundred thousand and live in reservations throughout the country. Their standard of living is extremely poor, including widespread malnutrition, tuberculosis, and other diseases.

especially courageous and especially necessary in a period of economic trouble and in a country so pervasively violent as Colombia.

Violence and Social Conditions

According to a 1983 study by the World Bank, Colombia's wealthiest 10 percent received 40 percent of the national income and owned fully 80 percent of the land. By contrast, the poorest 20 percent received only 5 percent of national income, and the bottom 10 percent owned a pitiful 0.2 percent of the land.[1] The scarcity of land coupled with rural violence have provoked mass migrations from the countryside throughout the past thirty-five years, such that now nearly three-fourths of Colombia's twenty-nine million people live in or around the four main cities[2] in conditions that for the poor are worse than unhealthy. An estimated seventy thousand children die each year before the age of five; more than a third of the population lack access to safe water.[3] With unemployment at 14 percent in 1984 and the gradual devaluation of currency eroding the salaries of those with jobs, the prevalence of criminal behavior, including but not limited to employment in the drug industry, is hardly surprising.

Colombia's criminality, however, goes well beyond the expected level of response to deprivation and is therefore often traced to historical factors as well. In 1983 alone, close to 200 persons were kidnapped, a few by political groups but most for ransom pure and simple; since 1950, the total number exceeds two thousand.* In 1981 there were over ten thousand murders, the vast majority nonpolitical; compared to population, this is about three and half times the rate in the United States, another very violent country.[4] In Colombia the cocaine and marijuana trades generate violence as well —like the activity of gangs reputedly organized by drug traffickers to protect themselves and their families from kidnapping, but at least one of which, MAS (acronym for Death to Kidnappers), recently became a nationally active death

* Figures released by the Colombian armed forces in December 1983.

squad attacking political oppositionists, peasant and Indian leaders, and trade unionists and terrorizing the residents of rural areas. (MAS has been linked to large landowners as well, and according to Colombia's attorney general has been directed by active-duty military personnel up to the rank of colonel.[5])

These social contradictions are hardly new; their existence has stamped Colombia with its tradition of violent political conflict and limited democracy. From the 1930s until a military coup in 1953, the two major parties, the Liberals and Conservatives, amassed private armies and fought for the spoils of government power, while peasants of conflicting allegiances slaughtered one another in the countryside. From 1947 to the mid-1950s, up to 450,000 Colombians died in this orgy of retaliations, known as "La Violencia."[6] The only beneficiaries of this time of horror were the political strongmen of both parties and the large landowners who, as thousands of peasants fled to the cities, consolidated their holdings at little or no expense.

After a brief period of military rule,* in 1958 the Liberals and Conservatives devised a resolution to their conflict that effectively closed off the democratic process while preserving regular elections. Under this agreement—the National Front, 1958 to 1974—the two major parties alternated control of the presidency and shared equally in running the bureaucracy. The Supreme Court and Congress were deprived of effective power, while maintaining the bloated bureaucracy became the government's principal function.

A state of siege has been in force for almost all the past thirty years. Military courts handled political offenses, and violations of the rights of the person and rights to due process for oppositionists became widespread. But in the 1960s,

---

* A military coup in 1953 brought to power a junta headed by General Gustavo Rojas Pinilla, a brutal populist who permitted only the partial exercise of political and civil rights. After convincing guerrillas to accept an amnesty and lay down their arms, he was responsible for the murder of scores of their leaders and rank-and-file fighters. Removed by plebiscite in 1957, he remained a force in national politics for many years.

U.S. administrations were calling Colombia a "showcase" of reform. A client of the Alliance for Progress, a major recipient of U.S. counterinsurgency "civic action" training, Colombia received $1.4 billion from the United States during the National Front period, making it at various times the largest beneficiary of U.S. economic and military aid in Latin America.[7]

Protest and Repression

Modern guerrilla warfare in Colombia can be traced to these years after 1958, when armed movements broke away from the traditional parties. The Revolutionary Armed Forces of Colombia (FARC), the largest and oldest of five currently active guerrilla groups, was formed by a fusion of Liberal Party dissidents and Communist Party guerrillas. (The Communist Party has long been legal in Colombia and participates in electoral politics. It denies links to guerrillas, though that denial is often contested.) The Army of National Liberation (ELN) was formed soon after. The tradition of guerrilla warfare, however, is substantially older than these expressions of it. Since independence from Spain in 1819, the country has experienced more than twenty civil wars, many of them fought as guerrilla conflicts. During La Violencia, the political parties' troops were several thousand strong, and in response, peasants protected their families and fields by forming local self-defense units.

The initial battle of modern counterinsurgency in Colombia was an army attack on such self-defense units in four southwestern areas, to dislodge the farmers from what Conservative spokesmen were calling their "independent republics." For this maneuver—Operation Laso, in 1964—some seven thousand troops were put into the field, with artillery and aerial bombing support. Since this first example of U.S. training in action, the counterinsurgency has continued with varying intensity for twenty years.

Urban protest took on a new energy at the same time, with corresponding repression. During the 1960s and 1970s, the

combination of land scarcity * and virtually nonexistent social services provoked mass mobilizations of peasants, students, and workers as movements such as the leftist United
Front † and the populist ANAPO, working outside the traditional parties, tried to offer an alternative for the dispos-
sessed. In 1970 the country was on the verge of an
insurrection after allegations that the National Front had
stolen electoral victory from ANAPO; ‡ in September 1977
the historically splintered labor movement united to launch
a nationwide, highly successful general strike—for which the
army killed an undetermined number, arrested three thousand, and began a crackdown that lasted several years.

The legacies of these experiences are voter apathy, and
low levels of participation in either major party; "civil
strikes," in which tenants and workers close down poor city
neighborhoods with demands for water, light, and other
basic services, in an atmosphere of extreme tension as police
and the army respond like an occupying force; and not least,
the emergence of the guerrilla group, the April 19 Movement (M-19). Though not the largest—FARC has operated
over twenty-five fighting "fronts" to this organization's fourteen—M-19 drew much attention for its flamboyant early
actions in the mid-1970s and represented a new surge of
social protest, a response to tighter military control; for in
1972, in addition to the state of siege, portions of Colombia
had been militarized, and in these zones, the zones of guer-

* Under the Alliance for Progress, Colombian officials agreed to implement
an agrarian reform. Then as now, this implied dismantling the power base
of the landed oligarchy. In 1966, President Carlos Lleras Restrepo founded
the National Agrarian Reform Institute (Incora) to manage the reform. But
by 1971 the effort had come to a halt. The land that had been distributed
addressed the needs of only some 10 percent of Colombia's landless families.
Incora still exists but only as a marginal entity. With representatives from
the Church, army, and cattlemen's and agribusiness associations, it includes
only a token representation for peasant organizations.
† The United Front was organized and led by Father Camilo Torres, a priest
who later took up arms with the guerrilla group ELN and died in battle.
‡ ANAPO's candidate in that election had been former dictator Gustavo
Rojas Pinilla, and the organization charged he had won a clear victory. Rojas
Pinilla worked out an agreement with the government to withdraw his
charges of fraud; this conciliation laid the basis for subsequent splits in
ANAPO, one of which led to the formation of M-19.

rilla strength, the army essentially ruled autonomous of the civilian government. As an Americas Watch report concluded in 1982, the existence of militarized zones, combined with military court jurisdiction over political offenses, had created a Colombia that was two countries: a "functioning democracy concerned about human rights and [a] militarized society in which human rights are grossly abused."[8]

The guerrillas in Colombia control neither population nor territory. Capable of taking even relatively large towns for brief periods, they are quite sophisticated in military terms, and certainly longevity has contributed to their skill; but they are not, and never have been, a military threat to the government.* Nor have they engaged in violent actions against civilians, with the exception of kidnapping, which they have carried out with sufficient regularity to give a group such as MAS an antiguerrilla, as well as an antidelinquent rationale. The guerrillas' continued fighting serves mainly to keep in the public mind their demands for social changes—agrarian reform and wider political participation being primary demands—and also maintains a climate of social anxiety, for it serves to rationalize the armed forces' abuse of power.

Colombia's sixty-five-thousand-man armed forces are among Latin America's most professional and, after thirty years of U.S. military education and relatively steady counterinsurgency experience, among its most seasoned. Their professionalism, however, has not prevented them from engaging in a reign of abuse where their power has been most absolute—in the militarized zones that cover one-fourth of Colombia, including parts of the regions of Caqueta and Putumayo in the Southwest; the Middle Magdalena, along the banks of the Magdalena River; Puerto Boyaca in the East; and Uraba in the North. Colombian novelist and journalist

* Estimates of the number of guerrillas vary widely. The FARC has published the figure of 5,000 to 6,000 for its own fighters. By contrast, former Defense Minister Fernando Landazabal put the number at 12,260 for FARC alone—his estimate being perhaps less reliable due to the armed forces' interest in portraying a major threat. It is generally believed that the ELN is about half the size of FARC, M-19 perhaps a fourth as large, EPL somewhat smaller still, and ADO insignificant (even Landazabal credited this group with only 30 fighters).

Gabriel Garcia Marquez wrote recently of the Middle Magdalena: "It is not a small El Salvador, but another, much
larger one than that of Central America, and it is even worse,
because it is more chaotic and neglected."[9]

The militarized zones, which as of this writing have not
been altered by the cease-fire agreements, have amounted to
territories of occupation, where freedom of movement is restricted by checkpoints and where safe-conduct passes are
required; where death squads, generally perceived as working at the behest of large landowners, drug traffickers, and/
or the army, act with impunity against trade unionists, peasant organizers, and Communist elected officials, some of
whom disappear, some of whom are shot outright; where the
army's counterinsurgency troops, the elite, have tortured
peasants suspected of guerrilla sympathies[10]; and where the
police intelligence unit, F-2, has been connected to many
disappearances.

The Permanent Committee for the Defense of Human
Rights, Colombia's principal human rights monitoring
group, tabulated 267 murders during 1981 that it ascribed to
official repression, most in militarized rural areas.[11] In the
year August 1982 to August 1983, in spite of the advent of
Betancur, this figure jumped sharply to 1,289, accompanied
by some 4,400 arbitrary arrests and more than 1,200 cases of
torture.[12] In Puerto Berrio, in Antioquia Department, part
of the militarized zone of Middle Magdalena, all but one
opposition elected official were murdered in 1983.[13]

The army often identifies the victims in such cases as guerrillas. But the reliability of the army's figures on guerrilla
deaths has been challenged by human rights organizations,
which report that many of the dead are in fact civilians—
taken, for example, from their homes in the wake of a guerrilla occupation of a town; tortured and killed for supposed
information on the guerrillas; dispatched by death squads
linked to the armed forces; or simply terrorized, as in an
incident in January 1984 in the Vuelta Acuna district of San-
tander Department. According to the Permanent Committee, "An army patrol of some forty men, which included
well-known members of the [death squad] MAS . . . reached

the home of [the peasant] Oscar Yepes. . . . The house was raided. . . . Oscar Yepes and Jesus Munoz attempted to find out what the troops wanted, but were shot several times. . . . The corpses showed signs of torture; Isaura Lascaro's stomach had been cut open, her eyes pulled out, [and] it seems acid was poured on her."[14] These methods of terror are indeed reminiscent of El Salvador. And also reminiscent was the armed forces' version of the event, which appeared in the Bogota daily *El Tiempo*: "Eight guerrillas of the FARC's XI Front were killed in two clashes with troops . . ." and included the peasants' names.[15]

Despite the extent of military control in these areas, they remain the major operational base of the phenomenally profitable drug industry.* This is not so surprising as it may seem. Some members of the military are reportedly bought off, as are many of the police (the latter being the force in charge of narcotics control); in addition, the difficult terrain and vastness of these rural areas, which serve as refuges for the guerrillas and have helped them to elude the army for over twenty years, provide the same service to Colombia's richest outlaws.

From Turbay to Betancur

When Belisario Betancur was elected in May 1982—with the highest voter turnout in Colombian history[16]—he replaced an administration that even for Colombia was unusually harsh. Under Julio Turbay Ayala (1978–82), the state of siege was coupled with a security statute that created new criminal categories and broadened military jurisdiction over political offenses. With this kind of license the Defense Ministry arrested 68,000 people in the single year August 1978 to August 1979[17] and militarized the cities. In the first months of 1981, over 16,000 peasants were detained and over 400 of them were killed.[18] The crackdown—according to documents released after the change of regime in 1982—was requested by

* The income of the drug industry is estimated at between $1 billion and $4 billion a year.

the army in response to the successful general strike of September 1977; it was not, in other words, a response to a military threat.

The repression had caused a broad-based reaction, however. One sign was the appearance of a major human rights organization, the Permanent Committee for the Defense of Human Rights (CPDDH), which represented a spectrum of political opinion. Another was the ability of Betancur—renegade within the Conservative Party, honest, a man of peasant origins—to capture the presidency on a platform of national reconciliation and respect for human rights. After Turbay's last-minute lifting of the state of siege, Betancur promoted active debate. In November 1982 he implemented his campaign promise to offer guerrillas a genuine and generous amnesty, which released over 300 political prisoners. He also established a peace commission to meet with rebel leaders and discuss the basis for achieving peace. And in 1983, his attorney general published results of an official investigation of the death squad MAS—a list of 163 alleged members, of which 59 were active-duty military men up to the rank of colonel.

In each of these courageous efforts the president faced, in one way or another, the institutional resistance of the armed forces. The chiefs of staff opposed any talks with the guerrillas. MAS murdered amnestied political prisoners, sometimes within hours of their release or before the release was widely known; the human rights organization CINEP learned that *amnistiados* in Caqueta were living in hiding and had been warned by the governor that they were unsafe in this militarized zone. The Defense Ministry and the rest of the high command refused to allow civilian courts to try the 59 accused military members of MAS and fought Betancur publicly on that issue till they won.* Meanwhile, disappearances

---

* Technically, the issue was resolved by a special panel, the Tribunal Disciplinario, which decides jurisdictional questions. In this case there were precedents suggesting that since the nation was not under state of siege, the ordinary courts should try all the accused, including the military. At the same time, past experience suggested that in military courts these suspects would not be seriously prosecuted. The decision, which granted the military

were increasing. A comparison of the first seven months of 1983 with the same period of 1984 shows disappearances more than doubled, from 43 to 94.[20] For all his efforts, Betancur was not capable of controlling the abuse of human rights.

In April 1984, Betancur's justice minister, who had been investigating and attempting to prosecute the drug "Mafia," was assassinated. With public support—but public trepidation as well—the president reimposed the state of siege in order, he said, to pursue the drug traffickers and rid the country of their violence and corruption. Despite fears that the military would use the state of siege to step up armed hostilities, the first of the cease-fire agreements—signed on March 28—went into effect at the end of May as planned. In succeeding months, this and the second cease-fire agreement—the former to last one year, the latter to last six months—seemed evidence that the guerrillas were willing to take Betancur at his word, to believe the government would limit the state of siege to tracking drugs. The armed forces' position was more complex: Though publicly supporting the cease-fires, and focusing their rhetoric on the "Mafia," the military violated the first cease-fire several times in its early months. The guerrillas appear to have instigated very few skirmishes, according to the CPDDH.* But on May 31— three days after FARC and the government reached agreement—the army high command sent a communiqué to all counterinsurgency troops instructing them "to liquidate and repress any guerrillas" they encountered.[21] The following day a patrol killed two FARC guerrillas who did not fight back, and in June and July several similar incidents reportedly took place. On August 10, just two weeks before M-19 was due to sign its cease-fire pact, the leader of its political

---

courts jurisdiction, was called political by the attorney general. And this view was shared by other knowledgeable Colombians. The president of the Permanent Committee for the Defense of Human Rights had anticipated a promilitary verdict, noting that if it decided differently, the tribunal's members "would have to leave the country the next day" for security reasons.[19]

* While there remained a few minor groups and factions that were not covered by the agreements, and these continued to fight, the guerrillas covered by the agreements were reportedly respecting them.

wing was assassinated, and on the day of the signing, guerrillas on their way to the ceremonies in Cauca Department accompanied by foreign journalists, were ambushed by a police unit.[22] Betancur removed the police forces from the area immediately. He also announced his determination to convene a "national dialogue" (as demanded by M-19) to bring together representatives of the poorest social sectors and government officials. But peasant leaders continued to be fearful of the military, and death squads kept functioning, though not at the nationally publicized level of MAS in the previous year. Human rights organizations in Colombia have called for the lifting of the state of seige.

Betancur had managed a peace of sorts, and that achievement was extraordinary. Yet it was a peace so fragile, so dependent on his personal appeal and reputation, that its future was far from assured. If it lasted, the government could attempt to deal with structural economic and social problems. But Betancur would have to work fast, for his own term of office ends in 1986. Neither the guerrillas nor the problems can wait for long, and the military has not been trained for peace.

Relations with the United States

To a much greater extent than in Peru, in Colombia the United States possesses influence with the armed forces. The history of close relations has its genesis in military training and U.S. military aid since 1950. In return, Colombia's armed forces—by themselves and in concert with the traditional parties—have supported U.S. political initiatives in the hemisphere and elsewhere even more loyally than their counterparts in neighboring countries.

During the Cold War's early years, Colombia severed relations with Moscow and was the only Latin American nation to send troops to South Korea. In 1962 Colombia introduced the U.S.-orchestrated resolution to expel Cuba from the OAS; in 1981, Colombia blocked Cuba's election to the U.N. Security Council and, also with U.S. support, began a minor but harassing territorial dispute with Sandinista Nicaragua. Colombia sent troops to the Sinai—along with Uruguay, the only Latin American nations to do so. And except for Chile, Colombia was the only Latin American country to support the United States' pro-British position in the 1983 Falklands/Malvinas war between Britain and Argentina.

It is therefore not surprising that the Reagan administration, like others before it, has refrained from criticizing the Colombian armed forces on human rights grounds. The armed forces have remained committed to the national-security tenets of counterinsurgency, at home and in Central America, fully in tune with the Reagan approach. The existence of a drug problem fortifies this link still further; the police, which are part of the military, receive U.S. aid to fight the cocaine traffic and recently have enjoyed some success.

Diplomatic relations, on the other hand, have been notably cool. Betancur brought Colombia into the nonaligned movement and refused to involve Colombia with the U. S. military strategy in Central America.* When he visited Washington in 1983, Betancur was bluntly critical of the U.S. Central America policy. Conversely, Ambassador Lewis Tambs, an architect of the administration's approach to Latin America as a member of the Committee of Santa Fe, outraged the Colombian government and public in March 1984 by publicly stating that FARC guerrillas were in league with the drug traffickers. At a time of delicate cease-fire negotiations with FARC, these unsupported comments were inflammatory and were criticized as such by officials and even a former president.[23] Tambs was essentially taking the military's side against civilian policy, for his remarks echoed the military's argument for rejection of all talks. As a

---

* Betancur was an instigator of the Contadora group—composed of Colombia, Mexico, Venezuela, and Panama—which has sought a nonmilitary solution to the Central American crises since January 1983. In addition, when approached by the Reagan administration with a plan to expand Colombian airfields for use by U.S. military aircraft—expansion that would have converted them into potential staging points for a Central American invasion, for surveillance, or for other U.S. airborne missions in that region —Betancur refused.

result the CPDDH, at a major national meeting on human rights, urged Tambs's removal from the country.[24] When the cease-fire agreements with both FARC and M-19 had been completed, in September 1984, the State Department's only comment on this landmark event was, in its entirety: " We hope these agreements promote the rule of law in Colombia."[25]

U.S. policy toward Colombia reflects the Reagan preference for military ties over long-term support for reform. The administration gives no developmental aid to Colombia but in its first year increased military assistance thirtyfold—to $10.5 million. Proposed amounts for later years were larger. For fiscal 1983 and fiscal 1984, again with no development aid proposed, the administration requested, respectively, $12 million and $24.5 million in military aid, though the administration did not get all it requested. The rise in military aid took place at a time when the Colombian armed forces were engaging in well-known and systematic violations of human rights. It was not coupled with an aid policy that benefited civilian institutions and the poor, nor with a public display of interest in Betancur's initiatives that would have shown the Colombian armed forces some U.S. support for his efforts. Overall the policy denotes an analysis of Colombia's problems—and the U.S. capacity to help—that ignores the social, the nonviolent, the structural. Betancur's quite exceptional determination to achieve internal peace has received no visible or audible support from the United States; the military, despite its abuses, has been treated vastly better.

6

RECOMMENDATIONS

An ancient maxim of medical practice cautions: *Primum non nocere* (First do no harm). It is a maxim that is also relevant when recommending a policy to guide the United States in dealing with human rights practices in other countries.

The Reagan administration has done harm by its public praise for governments that systematically abuse human rights, as when its first secretary of state, Alexander Haig, proclaimed "dramatic, dramatic reductions" in human rights abuses in Chile, Paraguay, Argentina, and Uruguay while they were still under brutal military rule;[1] when Ambassador Jeane Kirkpatrick purported to see "elements of constitutionalism" in the military dictatorships in Chile, Argentina, and Uruguay;[2] when Kirkpatrick praised the "moral quality" of the government of El Salvador at a time when its army and death squads were killing thousands;[3] and when President Reagan asserted that then President Rios Montt of Guatemala was "totally dedicated to democracy" and that complaints of human rights abuses by the Rios Montt government were "a bum rap."[4]

The Reagan administration has done harm by its public embrace of those responsible for gross abuses, as when Ambassador Kirkpatrick traveled to Chile to greet President Pinochet and announce a desire "to fully normalize our relations"[5] and as when then President (General) Viola of Argentina, a principal author of the "dirty war," traveled to Washington to become one of the first foreign heads of state to be received officially in Washington by the Reagan administration;[6] and when another Argentine general with blood on his hands, Leopoldo Galtieri (subsequently president; later imprisoned like Viola) was sponsored by the Defense Department on an official visit to the United States.[7]

The Reagan administration has done harm by attempting to discredit victims of human rights abuses and those who report on abuses, as when Ambassador Kirkpatrick circulated a false story accusing Argentine torture victim Jacobo Timerman of interfering with the work of Nazi-hunter Simon Wiesenthal;[8] when Assistant Secretary of State for Human Rights Elliott Abrams branded Guatemalan refugees who fled into Mexico as "guerrilla sympathizers";[9] when the State Department engaged in a sustained campaign to discredit human rights groups in El Salvador;[10] and when the State Department's Human Rights Bureau labeled the Chilean Commission for Human Rights as "political," asserting that it "openly devotes its efforts not only to human rights issues but to bringing about major changes in the nature of the government."[11] The latter assertion is especially nefarious in that, among other things, it implies a contradiction between promoting democracy and practicing human rights even though, at other times, the Department of State has insisted that promoting democracy is the best way to protect human rights.

The Reagan administration has done harm in attempting to shift the blame for human rights abuses, as when Elliott Abrams told a congressional committee, "I do not believe it to be accidental that the increase in violence in El Salvador has occurred since 1979, precisely the period of Sandinista rule in Nicaragua";[12] when Under Secretary of Defense Fred Ikle said the death squads in El Salvador "are in fact enjoying the protection of the Communist guerrillas";[13] and when Elliott Abrams said that death squad members "are fairly well known" but "there's no action taken by the far left because they like to see Salvadoran society divided."[14]

The Reagan administration has done harm by systematically disregarding U.S. law and international law on human rights and, in the process, undermining efforts to protect human rights by establishing the rule of law.

In part, a policy that promotes human rights involves doing the opposite of those things that do harm. Abusive governments should be publicly condemned. Public praise should go to those leaders who improve the protection of human rights, and the United States should distance itself from those responsible for abuses. Those who report on human rights abuses, often at great risk to themselves, should be honored. Blame ought to be placed squarely where it belongs, on those committing abuses. Demonstrating respect for both domestic and international law should be a constant concern.

The record of the Reagan administration in dealing with the death squad issue in El Salvador illustrates both the harm that can be done by U.S. policy and what can be accomplished when that policy shifts.

From its first days in office, the Reagan administration stoutly denied that the death squads were controlled by the security forces, attributing the murders they committed to "extremes of the right and the left."[15] As late as August 1983, Elliott Abrams asserted, "The assumption that the death squads are active security forces remains to be proved. It might be right, though I suspect it probably isn't right."[16] If anything, such assertions helped to embolden the death squads and, in the fall of 1983, their victims included well-known labor leaders and political figures, including an official of the Salvadoran Foreign Ministry judged to be insufficiently anti-Communist. The U.S. Congress became increasingly alarmed about the links between the armed forces and the death squads, which were widely publicized in the press,[17] and pressure on the Reagan administration increased. Finally, on December 11, 1983, Vice President Bush visited El Salvador, and in a meeting with thirty-one top military commanders, he issued an ultimatum: The death squad activity must be curbed, or continued U.S. aid was in jeopardy. Death squad killings in the first half of 1984 dropped to less than a quarter of the number in the first half of 1983. By mid-1984, the number of such killings each month was less than 10 percent of what it had been a year earlier.

The decline in death squad killings shows that money talks. This was also demonstrated in the May 1984 trial and sentencing of five Salvadoran national guardsmen convicted of murdering four U.S. churchwomen. For three years, the churchwomen's case had hung in limbo. Finally, wearying of the State Department's promises of "progress" on the case, the U.S. Congress enacted legislation that withheld $19 million in military aid pending a trial and verdict in the case. Faced with the loss of a significant portion of their military assistance, the Salvadoran military authorities allowed the trial to go forward.

Given the demonstrated effect that withholding—or seriously threatening to withhold—military aid has had on the Salvadoran armed forces, it is tragic that the Reagan administration has not employed the same strategy to end more pervasive atrocities: army and air force killings of civilian noncombatants in guerrilla-controlled zones. One would think that the United States would have an even better chance to end human rights violations committed by uniformed military personnel than by shadowy auxiliary gunmen. In fact, the United States has trained an entire generation of young officers and outfitted them with everything from uniforms to 750-pound bombs. Yet targeted bombings of homes, schools, crops, and civilians themselves; ground attacks against defenseless women, children, and old people; and rape, torture, and execution of captured guerrilla soldiers and civilians happen so frequently that these acts may be considered the Salvadoran armed forces' policy. It may be that the United States has not used its influence, financial and otherwise, to end such indiscriminate killings because it considers that these are necessary to win the war. Yet among those committed to that end, there are some who consider indiscriminate attacks to be counterproductive. Re-

tired Major General John Singlaub, who has become something of a hero to the extreme right in the United States,
chaired an advisory panel to the Department of Defense that
prepared a classified report highly critical of the bombing
practices of the Salvadoran air force. "Dropping 500-pound
bombs on insurgents is not the way to go," according to
Singlaub. He says, "There is a need for very discriminate
firepower." Another member of the Singlaub panel, Colonel
John Waghelstein, chief of the United States military advisory group in El Salvador in 1982–83, says that civilian casualties must be minimized for the Salvadoran government
to win the guerrilla war, because it must "gain and maintain
the support of the civilian population." [18]

The views expressed by Singlaub and Waghelstein suggest
that, in the case of El Salvador, promoting human rights is
consistent with promoting the maintenace of a government
considered friendly by the United States. But what if there is
a conflict? What should the United States do if a policy designed to promote human rights would undermine a government allied to the United States? Indeed, what if promoting
human rights would undermine the security interests of the
United States itself?

For a human rights policy to be meaningful, it should be
pursued even when other interests, or perceived interests,
suffer as a consequence. Yet there are limits, of course. International law permits the restriction of certain rights in
times of national emergency to the extent strictly required
by the emergency; domestic law in the United States permits
the restriction of even the rights to speak and assemble in
circumstances of clear and present danger. By the same
token, efforts to promote human rights internationally may
be suspended to the extent necessary to preserve the national
security of the United States in circumstances of great danger. The damage to a general effort to promote human rights
need not be severe—so long as it is explicitly acknowledged
that efforts to promote human rights are being suspended
and for what reasons.

Acknowledgment permits debate over whether the circumstances are so threatening to national security as to war-

rant the suspension of efforts to promote human rights. On the other hand, failure to acknowledge that this is what is being done puts an administration in a position where it falsely claims to be maintaining an effort to promote human rights and to be accomplishing that end through the self-same policy being implemented to pursue national security interests. This is the position into which the Reagan administration has put itself in the case of El Salvador. The contradiction is unfortunate from several standpoints.

It is unfortunate because it limits the opportunity of Americans to debate forthrightly whether their national security interests are so vitally affected by the war in El Salvador as to warrant suspension of efforts to promote human rights. It is unfortunate because it requires the administration to misrepresent events in El Salvador in an effort to argue that its policies are in fact promoting human rights. This is what prompts officials to attack the motives and methods of human rights organizations with a gloomier view of the situation.

It is also unfortunate because, in the process of misrepresenting developments, the administration places itself in a position where, to save its face, it cannot take the positive actions within its power. This is why the administration delayed so long before putting pressure on the Salvadoran armed forces to curb death squad activity and only did so when there appeared a real danger that Congress would cut off funds. This is also why the administration now refrains from using its clout to stop indiscriminate attacks on civilians in guerrilla-controlled zones. It is difficult or impossible to square apologies for the practices of the Salvadoran armed forces with credible efforts to get those forces to change their ways.

The Reagan administration would have done far less damage to human rights in El Salvador if it frankly acknowledged all abuses but claimed that U.S. security interests were so overriding as to justify extensive military assistance to the Salvadoran armed forces despite their abuses. Most likely, it did not take this course because it feared it might lose the debate that would have ensued.

Some blame for the administration's choice of tactics can be placed on the law that required it periodically to certify compliance with human rights conditions in order to continue military assistance. Indeed, critics of the law pointed out at the time that the certifications were being made that the law did a disservice, for it put the administration in the position of having to misrepresent the human rights situation in order to maintain the flow of military assistance, which it was determined to provide under any circumstances. Though this argument may have some merit, it would be unfair to attach too much significance to the certification law in this respect. The law was not adopted by Congress until December 1981. By then, nearly a year after taking office, the administration had already charted the course it has followed with respect to El Salvador and, indeed, with respect to other countries. The certification law may have compounded the problem, but it was not the cause.

The Reagan administration's approach seems to be rooted in a philosophy that was stated in the introduction to the State Department's *Country Reports on Human Rights Practices for 1981*, the first of these annual volumes compiled by the Reagan administration. It asserts, "It is a significant service to the cause of human rights to limit the influence the U.S.S.R. (together with its clients and proxies) can exert. A consistent and serious policy for human rights in the world must counter the U.S.S.R. politically."[19] The key word is the last one. Though the introduction goes on to assert that this will be done by pointing out abuses of human rights in Soviet bloc countries and acknowledges that the United States must seek redress for abuses in friendly countries, it is at least implicit in this assertion that there is symmetry between promoting the geopolitical interests of the United States and promoting human rights. An insistence on perceiving such a symmetry in Central America has been a prescription for disastrous policy.

In circumstances in which geopolitical considerations do not seem overriding, the personal commitments of U.S. diplomatic personnel tend to have a significant impact on human rights performance. Some Reagan administration appointees, such as Ambassador Thomas Aranda in Uruguay and Ambassador James Theberge in Chile, * have demonstrated little or no concern for human rights. Others, such as Ambassador Clayton McManaway in Haiti and Ambassador Arthur Davis in Paraguay, have done a great deal to try to improve the human rights situation. The performances of diplomats such as McManaway and Davis exemplify what can be done for human rights through the day-to-day operations of our embassies.

In the case of Haiti, U.S. assistance is small and the tiny military aid program is restricted to drug interdiction. Repression by the government of President Jean-Claude Duvalier ebbs and flows in response to democratic stirrings from the press, the Church, or political independents. When violations occur, Ambassador McManaway has quietly but firmly made high-level protests to the government. The embassy staff stays in close touch with local human rights monitors. On at least one occasion, in July 1984, the ambassador invited independent journalists and oposition political figures—many of them victims of human rights abuses—to a reception at the embassy. Coming as it did at a time of heightened repression, the gesture so offended President Duvalier that all government officials were instructed not to attend. The point, however, was clear: The United States supports human rights in Haiti.

Similarly, Arthur Davis in Paraguay has regularly protested when newspapers are closed and opposition figures abused and intimidated. He, too, has invited both officials and opposition leaders to embassy functions. When the owner of a newspaper that was shut down by the government held an *asado* (barbeque) for his out-of-work journalists, U.S. embassy representatives joined them. Moreover, Ambassador Davis has enlisted the State Department Human Rights Bureau's support for his efforts. Assistant Secretary Elliott Abrams has vigorously supported actions on behalf of human rights in Paraguay.

* As noted above, in December 1984 it was announced that Mr. Theberge would be shifted to another diplomatic post.

In contrast, Ambassadors Aranda and Theberge distance themselves from human rights victims and human rights monitors. In the process, they convey the impression to the government to which they are accredited that the United States does not care about human rights. Thereby, their actions promote abuses. In addition, because they have little or no contact with those concerned with human rights, it seems unlikely that they keep the Department of State well informed about abuses, diminishing its capacity to take steps to promote human rights in those countries.

At times when governments themselves undertake efforts to promote human rights, the United States should provide support, both through symbolic diplomatic gestures and materially. One such opportunity presented itself to the Reagan administration in the case of Colombia, but it was not seized.

The government of President Belisario Betancur, although it has been beset by economic difficulties and vast social problems, has performed remarkably with respect to human rights: It has investigated and sought to punish abuses; it has asserted civilian authority in cases of human rights abuse by the armed forces; and it has negotiated fixed-term peace settlements with guerrilla groups that had carried on armed conflict for decades, opening a possibility for genuine dialogue. Yet the U.S. embassy in Bogota has been silent about these matters, and the only comment forthcoming from the State Department following the signing of the peace agreements was a noncommittal press guidance stating that the United States hoped the agreement would lead to the rule of law in Colombia. The achievements of the Betancur government have not been rewarded with the economic assistance that Colombia urgently requires. Such increases in economic aid as the Reagan administration sought from Congress were directed elsewhere. Similarly, Argentina, where human rights improved most dramatically, urgently requires economic assistance. Its chances of perpetuating decent democratic government would be greatly enhanced if it could overcome its economic difficulties. This has presented a great opportunity for the United States but, up to this writing, it has been bypassed.

At the other end of the spectrum are countries where the human rights situation is disastrous, such as Guatemala. Sadly, even if the United States took every diplomatic initiative to support human rights, suspended all aid and sales, and publicly condemned the Guatemalan government, these actions might have little effect. The Guatemalan military has little need for U.S. assistance, and the generals have appeared virtually impervious to international criticism. Further pressure should be considered.

When confronted with unprecedented slaughter in Uganda in 1978, the U. S. Congress enacted legislation banning the import of Ugandan products to the United States and the export of U.S. goods to Uganda. The loss of an important market for Ugandan coffee as well as much-needed U.S.-manufactured items contributed to the undermining of President Idi Amin, who was overthrown a year later. Similar action against Guatemala for abuses under successive military regimes, accompanied by efforts to enlist other nations in a boycott, would have been warranted.

Though drastic economic measures can be justified on human rights grounds in circumstances such as those in Guatemala, military intervention is quite another thing. Though exceptions might be warranted when crimes against humanity are committed on the scale of Nazi Germany or Cambodia under the Khmer Rouge, the rule should be that military invasion, either directly or by proxy, should not be undertaken to promote human rights. For one thing, it is likely that military intervention will worsen the human rights situation, as has happened in Nicaragua where measures restricting human rights are justified by the government because of the emergency resulting from the U.S.-sponsored invasion, and where the *contras* themselves have committed many serious abuses. For another, as is also exemplified by Nicaragua, the actual reasons for the invasion are likely to be rooted in political and geopolitical considerations. The use, or abuse, of a human rights rationale to justify military intervention can only degrade the human rights cause.

If the first rule in promoting human rights is to avoid doing harm, the second rule is that human rights should be promoted for their own sake, not as part of an effort to achieve some other end. It is the failure to distinguish between the other interests of the United States and concern for human rights that so frequently leads us into doing harm.

NOTES

CHAPTER 1

A RHETORIC OF CONVENIENCE

1. The Committee of Santa Fe, "A New Inter-American Policy for the Eighties," ed: L. Francis Bouchey, Roger Fontaine, David C. Jordan, Lt. General Gordon Sumner, and Lewis Tambs (Washington, D.C.: Council for Inter-American Security, 1980), p. 1. Several of the editors later were given administration posts: Fontaine on the National Security Council, Sumner as aide to Assistant Secretary of State Thomas Enders, Tambs as ambassador to Colombia, Jordan as ambassador to Peru.
2. Ibid., p. 9.
3. Ibid., p. 20.
4. Jeane Kirkpatrick, "Dictatorship and Double Standards," *Commentary*, Vol. 68, No. 5 (November 1979), pp. 34–45.
5. Speech to the Trilateral Commission, reprinted in "Excerpts from Haig's Speech on Human Rights and Foreign Policy," *The New York Times* (April 21, 1981), p. A6.
6. Richard Kennedy, under secretary of state for management, confidential "Memorandum for the Secretary" (October 27, 1981), p. 1.
7. Ibid., p. 4.
8. Ibid., p. 5.
9. Charles Maechling, Jr., "Human Rights Dehumanized," *Foreign Policy*, No. 52 (Fall 1983), p. 120.
10. "Text of President Reagan's Address to Parliament on Promoting Democracy," *The New York Times* (June 9, 1982), p. A16.
11. "The Media and Human Rights," transcript of debate between Hon. Christopher Dodd and Hon. Elliott Abrams, Center for Communication, Inc., New York (March 30, 1984), p. 30.
12. James H. Michel, senior deputy assistant secretary of state for

inter-American affairs, speech to the University of Arkansas (April 12, 1984).

13. "Memorandum for the Secretary," op. cit., p. 4.

14. U.S. Department of State, *Country Reports on Human Rights Practices for 1982* (Hereinafter *Country Reports*) (Washington, D.C.: GPO, 1983), p. 2.

15. *Country Reports for 1983* (Washington, D.C.: GPO, 1984), p. 3.

16. Ibid., p. 5.

17. Bernard Weinraub, "Reagan's Human Rights Chief: No 'Liberal Mole,' " *The New York Times* (October 19, 1982).

18. Quoted in Americas Watch, Helsinki Watch, and Lawyers Committee for International Human Rights, *Failure: The Reagan Administration's Human Rights Policy in 1983* (New York: Americas Watch, Helsinki Watch, and Lawyers Committee for International Human Rights, 1984), pp. 16–17.

19. Speech by Elliott Abrams to the Cuban-American National Foundation, Palm Beach (August 23, 1984).

20. "Arms to Argentina: A Human Rights Message," letter to the *Washington Post* (December 23, 1983).

21. Ibid.

22. "A Human Rights Message (Cont'd)," letter to the *Washington Post* (December 30, 1983).

23. Elliott Abrams, prepared statement for hearings ("The Phenomenon of Torture") before the House Subcommittee on Human Rights and International Organizations, of the Committee on Foreign Affairs (Washington, D.C.: May 16, 1984). In the printed record of the hearings, this statement appears slightly altered.

24. Adapted from "The Laws" section of *Failure: The Reagan Administration's Human Rights Policy in 1983* (New York: Americas Watch, Helsinki Watch, and Lawyers Committee for International Human Rights, January 1984), pp. 6–12.

25. *Quarterly Reports* by the Department of the Treasury, obtained from the Congressional Arms Control and Disarmament Caucus and the House Subcommittee on International Development Institutions and Finance of the Committee on Banking. By country, the loans amount to: El Salvador, $279.62 million; Argentina, $1,362.7 million; Guatemala, $396.7 million; Chile, $1,199.3 million; Uruguay, $313.9 million; Paraguay, $388.2 million.

26. For an examination of the campaign against this office since early 1982, see Americas Watch, *U.S. Reporting on Human Rights in El Salvador: Methodology at Odds with Knowledge*

(New York: Americas Watch, 1982), and *Protection of the Weak and Unarmed: The Dispute Over Counting Human Rights Violations in El Salvador* (New York: Americas Watch, 1984).

27. Testimony before the Senate Foreign Relations Committee (Washington, D.C., February 8, 1982).

28. Letter to Patricia L. Rengel, director, Washington office of Amnesty International (September 15, 1982).

29. Americas Watch, *Human Rights in Guatemala: No Neutrals Allowed* (New York: Americas Watch, 1982), p. 117; see pp. 101–18 and 123–33 for a detailed examination of the Enders letter and Amnesty International's methodology.

30. Confidential "Memorandum for the Secretary," op. cit., p. 1.

31. *Country Reports for 1983*, p. 14.

32. Ibid.

CHAPTER 2

THE LAW AND LAWLESSNESS

1. U.N. Charter, Art. 55.

2. U.N. Charter, Art. 56.

3. *The Paquete Habana*, 175 U.S. 677, 700 (1900).

4. *Filartiga* v. *Pena*, 676 F. 2d 876, 884 (2d Cir. 1980).

5. U.S. Department of State, *Country Reports on Human Rights Practices for 1981* (Washington, D.C.: GPO, 1982), p. 5.

6. Ibid., p. 6.

7. Sec. 502B, Foreign Assistance Act of 1961 (amended).

8. Ibid., Sec. 116.

9. Sec. 701, International Financial Institutions Act.

10. Sec. 116(a), Foreign Assistance Act of 1961.

11. Sec. 728, International Security Development Cooperation Act of 1981.

12. Ibid., Secs. 725 and 726.

13. See Art. 4 of the International Covenant of Civil and Political Rights (1966).

14. Ibid.

15. Protocol II, Art. 1 (1).

16. Ibid., Art. 1 (2).

17. Protocol II, Art. 13 (2 and 3).

18. See cable from U.S. embassy in San Salvador to U.S. Department of State, January 25, 1984, reproduced in Americas Watch, *Protection of the Weak and Unarmed: The Dispute Over Counting Human Rights Violations in El Salvador* (New York: Americas Watch, 1984), pp. 14–28.

19. Common Art. 3 (1) and Protocol II, Art. 4.

20. Common Art. 3 (2) and Protocol II, Arts. 7, 8, 10, 11, and 12. Under Art. 10 of Protocol II, the convention provides, "Under no circumstances shall any person be punished for having carried out medical activities compatible with medical ethics, regardless of the person benefiting therefrom."

21. Aryeh Neier, personal interview with a deputy assistant secretary of state for human rights (May 1983).

22. Protocol II, Art. 17 (1).

23. Tayacan, *Psychological Operations in Guerrilla Warfare*, translation from the Spanish by Congressional Research Service, Library of Congress, (Washington, D.C., 1984) p. 14.

24. Ibid., pp. 14–15.

25. Ibid., p. 14.

26. Ibid., p. 33.

27. Ibid., p. 35.

28. "Casey's Letter on Nicaragua Manual," *The New York Times* (November 2, 1984), p. A3.

CHAPTER 3

"TRANSITIONS" TO DEMOCRACY: THE SOUTHERN CONE

CHILE

1. *U.S. News & World Report* (March 2, 1981), p. 50.

2. Address by James H. Michel, senior deputy assistant secretary of state for inter-American affairs, to the University of Arkansas (April 12, 1984) on United States support for democracy in Chile. Michel explicitly declines to deal with U.S. policy toward Allende.

3. Seymour M. Hersh, *The Price of Power: Kissinger in the Nixon White House* (New York: Summit Books, 1983), p. 259.

4. The $4 million figure is cited by the Senate Select Committee to Study Governmental Operations in Respect to Intelligence Activities ("the Church committee"), which released an extensive staff report in December 1975 titled *Covert Action in Chile 1963–1973*. The $20 million amount is cited as a base figure by Seymour Hersh in his Kissinger biography *The Price of Power*, op. cit., p. 260.

5. Hersh, op. cit., p. 270.

6. United Nations, *Report of the Economic and Social Council*, A/34/583 (November 21, 1979), p. 12.

7. United Nations, *Report of the Economic and Social Council*, A/36/594 (November 6, 1981), p. 183.

8. Amnesty International's September 1974 report uses this range. Lars Schoultz, *Human Rights and United States Policy Towards Latin America* (Princeton, N.J.: Princeton University Press, 1981), p. 12.

9. United Nations, *Report of the Economic and Social Council*, A/34/583 (November 21, 1979), p. 79.

10. The U.N.'s *Ad Hoc* Working Group on Human Rights in Chile reported a total of 180,000 detained for periods ranging from a few hours to 14 months. See United Nations, *Report of the Economic and Social Council*, E/CN.4/1188 (February 4, 1976), p. 29.

11. The Chilean Commission on Human Rights (CCDH) uses two figures on exile: 37,000, whom it counts as formally forced out of the country by expulsion decree, commutation of prison sentence to exile, or other specific act; and 200,000, whom it estimates to include workers whose livelihood was politically denied them, the families of those in formal exile, etc.

12. These numbers derive from the Vicariate of Solidarity, which has placed 644 cases before the courts; and from CCDH—1,644 being its conservative minimum, 2,500 being the figure used colloquially by CCDH. The larger figure has also been acknowledged by Amnesty International.

13. *Ad Hoc* Working Group on Human Rights in Chile, United Nations, *Report of the Economic and Social Council*, A/10285 (October 7, 1975), p. 74.

14. CCDH, *Informe Anual 1983*, pp. 20–21.

15. This analysis of the lists was made by the Comite pro Retorno (Committee for the Return of Exiles), a human rights group

concentrating on the exile issue, which works closely with CCDH.
16. CCDH, *Informe Anual 1982*, p. 64.
17. Maria Loreto Castillo case. Cf. CCDH, *Informe Mensual* No. 29 (May 1984), pp. 13–14.
18. Hector Patricio Sobarzo case. Cf. *Solidaridad* (newpaper of the Vicariate of Solidarity) (July 14–27, 1984), p. 6.
19. Juan Mejias and Erika Sandoval. Cf. CCDH, *Informe Mensual* No. 27 (March 1984), p. 11.
20. Sec. 701, International Financial Institutions Act.
21. James H. Michel, speech (April 12, 1984), op. cit. Following quotations are from the same source.

URUGUAY

1. See, generally, Junta de Comandantes en Jefe R.O. del Uruguay, *La Subversion: Las Fuerzas Armadas al Pueblo Oriental*, Tomo 1 (Montevideo, 1977).
2. See William Wipfler, "Uruguay's 'Liberty' Vote," *The New York Times* (November 28, 1980), p. A27; WOLA Press Release "Confidential Report Documents Brutal Conditions in Uruguayan Libertad Prison" (November 5, 1980).
3. Inter-American Commission on Human Rights, *Report on the Status of Human Rights in Uruguay* (hereinafter called *Uruguay Report*), OEA/Ser. L/V/11.43, doc. 19, corr. 1 (Washington, D.C.: January 31, 1978).
4. International Commission of Jurists, *The Review*, No. 24 (June 1980), p. 23.
5. See Amnesty International, *Report on Human Rights Violations in Uruguay*, AMR 52/35/83 (November 1983), pp. 25–28.
6. Committee to Protect Journalists and PEN, *Uruguay: Does Democracy Include Freedom of the Press?* (June 1983), p. 14.
7. Inter-American Commission on Human Rights, "Update on the Situation of Human Rights in Uruguay," 1979–80 Annual Report, OEA/Ser. L/V/II.50, doc. 13, rev. 1 (October 1, 1980), p. 128.
8. This proposal was outlined in *Events in the Republic That Justify a New Constitutional Text*, published by the armed forces (May 1983).
9. U.S. Department of State, *Country Reports on Human Rights Practices for 1980* (Washington, D.C.: GPO, 1981), p. 547.
10. Paris AFP in Spanish, 3:49 P.M. GMT, August 31, 1984, VI

Foreign Broadcast Information Service (September 4, 1984), K1.

ARGENTINA

1. For example, Vice President Henry Wallace said in January 1944 that "the next war will come via that country." Blum, *The Price of Vision: The Diaries of Henry Wallace* (Boston: 1973, p. 294), quoted in Carlos Escude, *Gran Bretana, Estados Unidos y la Declinacion Argentina* (Buenos Aires: Editorial de Belgnano, 1983), p. 62 (double translation).
2. Note by Richard Allen, AS 3471/12/2, FO 371/44687, quoted in Escude, op. cit., p. 51 (double translation).
3. John M. Goshko, "Administration Reiterates Aim of Scuttling Carter Policies," *Washington Post* (July 10, 1981), p. A12.
4. Congressional hearings on this subject suggest the extent of the interrelationships among Reagan advisers, conservatives in Congress, and the Argentine government. One public witness favoring the change of policy was James Theberge, formerly ambassador to Somoza's Nicaragua and a member of the Reagan transition team, who later became ambassador to Chile, but speaking in this instance as an independent international consultant. Also speaking in favor of the administration's proposed repeal was Joseph Karth, former Democratic congressman from Minnesota, who represented his own public-relations firm, KBS Associates, Inc., a foreign agent for the Argentine government.
5. This argument was widely reported in Argentina's progovernment press at the time.
6. "Defense Secretary Weinberger and National Security Advisor Richard Allen variously described [Galtieri] as 'a magnificent person' and an 'impressive general' at a gathering of military men in Washington, D.C." *Latin America Weekly Report* (November 13, 1981).
7. U.S. Department of State, *Country Reports on Human Rights Practices for 1982* (Washington, D.C.: GPO, 1983), p. 386.
8. Americas Watch—CELS, *The State Department Misinforms: A Study of Accounting for the Disappeared in Argentina* (New York: Americas Watch, 1983).
9. Henry Kamm, "Vatican Assails Argentine Junta Over Its Report on War on Leftists," *The New York Times* (May 4, 1983). The

full text of the letter is quoted in *The Argentine Military Junta's 'Final Document'—A Call for Condemnation* (New York: Americas Watch, 1983), pp. 8–9.

10. Anthony Lewis, "Gently with Gangsters," *The New York Times* (May 22, 1983). On May 17, 1983, this statement was released as a press guidance—that is, an unsigned, prepared response to press questions—rather than receiving the emphasis that would have attended a press release or other special effort.

CHAPTER 4

GEOPOLITICS AND HUMAN RIGHTS: CENTRAL AMERICA

1. Alan Riding, "The Central American Quagmire," *Foreign Affairs*, Vol. 61, No. 3 (Spring 1983), p. 641.

EL SALVADOR

1. Alexander Haig, *Caveat: Realism, Reagan and Foreign Policy* (New York: Macmillan, 1984).
2. Jeane Kirkpatrick, "Reagan Appointed Democrat Speaks Her Mind on World Domestic Politics," *Tampa Tribune* (December 25, 1980), p. 23A.
3. U.S. Department of State, *Country Reports on Human Rights Practices for 1980, 1981, and 1982* (Washington, D.C.: GPO, 1980, 1981, and 1982).
4. Americas Watch and American Civil Liberties Union, *Report on Human Rights in El Salvador* (New York: Vintage Books, 1982), p. 70; Americas Watch and American Civil Liberties Union, *First Supplement to Report on Human Rights in El Salvador* (New York: Americas Watch, 1982), pp. 208–12.
5. Robert J. McCartney, "Fraud Alleged in 1982 Salvador Vote," *Washington Post* (February 25, 1984).
6. Union Comunal Salvadorena, "El Salvador Update: The Land to the Tiller Program" (December 10, 1982), p. 1.

7. Personal interview with Dr. Benjamin Cestoni, San Salvador (June 29, 1983).

8. Personal interview with embassy official, San Salvador (June 28, 1983).

9. Ibid.

10. Lydia Chavez, "Salvadoran Tied to Killings Now in Job," *The New York Times* (July 9, 1983).

11. Ronald Reagan, certification of El Salvador, message to the U.S. Congress (July 27, 1982).

12. Americas Watch and American Civil Liberties Union, *Second Supplement to Report on Human Rights in El Salvador* (New York: Americas Watch and American Civil Liberties Union, January 20, 1983), pp. 115–16.

13. Americas Watch and American Civil Liberties Union, *Third Supplement to Report on Human Rights in El Salvador* (New York: Americas Watch and American Civil Liberties Union, July 19, 1983), pp. 82–87.

14. Americas Watch, *U.S. Reporting on Human Rights in El Salvador: Methodology at Odds with Knowledge* (New York: Americas Watch, June 1982), pp. 20–21 and 63–65.

15. *The Wall Street Journal* (February 10, 1982).

16. Ambassador Deane Hinton, "A Statistical Framework for Understanding Violence in El Salvador," San Salvador, cable from U.S. embassy (January 15, 1982), p. 8. See Americas Watch, *U.S. Reporting on Human Rights in El Salvador*, op. cit., p. 19.

17. Ibid.

18. U.S. Department of State, *Country Reports on Human Rights Practices for 1982* (Washington, D.C.: GPO, 1982), p. 493.

19. *The Christian Science Monitor* (August 3, 1983).

20. Francis X. Clines, "Reagan Explains Salvador Action," *The New York Times* (December 3, 1983), p. 3.

21. Thomas Pickering, U.S. ambassador to El Salvador, in an address before the American Chamber of Commerce in San Salvador (November 25, 1983), p. 7.

22. Americas Watch, *Protection of the Weak and Unarmed* (New York: Americas Watch, 1984), pp. 14–29.

23. Americas Watch, personal interview, embassy spokesman (July 11, 1984). The embassy official said Americas Watch had "misunderstood" its previous position, though this is contradicted by the text of the embassy cable quoted in *Protection of the Weak and Unarmed*, op. cit.

24. Chris Hedges, *The Christian Science Monitor*, series of stories filed throughout 1984.
25. Americas Watch and Lawyers Committee for International Human Rights, *Free Fire: A Report on Human Rights in El Salvador* (New York: Americas Watch, August 1984).

HONDURAS

1. Philip Taubman, "Honduras Seeks Looser Alliance and Rise in Aid," *The New York Times* (October 9, 1984).
2. In April 1984, local press embarrassed the government by revealing that U.S. ambassador John D. Negroponte had been involved in a meeting of the Foreign Ministry to discuss Honduran policy with respect to the Contadora peace process. See Lucy Komisar, "Honduran Anger at the U.S.," op ed, *The New York Times* (October 11, 1984).
3. Philip Taubman, op. cit.
4. Americas Watch, Lawyers Committee for International Human Rights, and Washington Office on Latin America, *Honduras: On the Brink* (New York, February 1984).
5. U.S. Department of State, *Country Reports on Human Rights Practices for 1983* (Washington, D.C.: GPO, 1984), p. 615, gives the fiscal year 1983 military assistance total as $48.3 million, but this is contradicted by both the State Department's Honduras desk officer and by the Central American History Institute's "Summary of Foreign Assistance Decisions on Central America, FY83–85" (Washington, D.C.: Central American History Institute, Georgetown University, 1984).
6. U.S. Department of State, *Country Reports on Human Rights Practices for 1982* (Washington, D.C.: GPO, February 1983), p. 555.
7. Ibid., p. 554.
8. Refugee Policy Group, "Refugees and Displaced Persons in Central America" (Washington, D.C., March 1984), p. 5.

NICARAGUA

1. Inter-American Commission on Human Rights, *Informe Sobre la Situacion de los Derechos Humanos en Nicaragua*, OEA/Ser. L/V/II.45, doc. 16, rev. 1 (Washington, D.C. November 17, 1978).

2. "Dictatorships and Double Standards," *Commentary*, Vol. 68, No. 5 (November 1979). Reprinted in *El Salvador: Central America in the New Cold War*, ed. M. E. Gettleman et al. (New York: Grove Press, 1981), p. 24.

3. *Communist Interference in El Salvador*, Special Report No. 80, U.S. Department of State (Washington, D.C.: February 23, 1981).

4. Jonathan Kwitny, "Apparent Errors Cloud U.S. 'White Paper' on Reds in El Salvador," *The Wall Street Journal* (June 8, 1981).

5. "A Secret War for Nicaragua," *Newsweek* (November 8, 1982), pp. 42–55.

6. U.S. Department of State, *Country Reports on Human Rights Practices for 1982* (hereinafter called *Country Reports*) (Washington, D.C.: GPO, 1983), p. 634.

7. Ibid.

8. *The Indigenous Peoples of Nicaragua's Eastern Coast: Their Treatment by the Junta of National Reconstruction* (February 1982). The close connections between the administration and certain private groups on the Miskito issue is suggested by the fact that Bruce McColm, author of the above report, later became the U.S.-sponsored member of the Inter-American Commission on Human Rights of the OAS.

9. See, for example, IACHR, *Informe Sobre La Situacion de los Derechos Humanos de un Sector de la Poblacion Nicaraguense de Origen Miskito*, OEA/Ser. L/V/II.62, doc. 26; Americas Watch, *Report(s) on Human Rights in Nicaragua* (May 1982, November 1982, April 1984); publications by the Board of Missions of the Moravian Church in the U.S.A.

10. *Country Reports*, p. 485.

11. Ibid., p. 580.

12. *Country Reports*, p. 635.

13. Ibid.

14. Cable by Ambassador Anthony Quainton (July 16, 1983) as quoted by Robert Parry, Associated Press dispatch (September 20, 1983).

15. Robert McCartney, "Nicaraguan Villagers Report Rebels Killed Noncombatants," *Washington Post* (August 7, 1984).

16. See, for example, Joshua Muravchik's article, "Manipulating the Miskitos," *The New Republic* (August 6, 1984).

17. Francis X. Clines, "U.S. Says Study Found Manual Broke No Law," *The New York Times* (November 11, 1984). p. 1.

18. Ibid.

19. "Week in Review," *The New York Times* (July 22, 1984).

256 NOTES

GUATEMALA

1. *Central America Report* (Guatemala City, July 6, 1984), p. 198.
2. Don Oberdorfer, "After the Killing Stops," *Washington Post* (April 18, 1982).
3. *Central America Report* (Guatemala City, June 15, 1984), p. 177.
4. Ibid.
5. FBIS, "Rios Montt on State of Siege, Death Penalty" (July 2, 1982), p. P5. The urban death squads had already succeeded in decimating the leadership of the moderate popular organizations. By the time Rios Montt came to power they had become politically counterproductive. The squads were revived later in Rios Montt's tenure and stepped up their activities under Mejia Victores.
6. Marlise Simons, "Guatemalans Are Adding a Few Twists to 'Pacification,'" *The New York Times* (September 12, 1982).
7. Pastoral letter, Episcopal Conference of Guatemala (May 27, 1982).
8. Gordon Mott, "Guatemala's Villagers Flee Rising Terror, *Miami Herald* (August 23, 1982).
9. Amnesty International, "Massive Extrajudicial Executions in Rural Areas Under the Government of General Efrain Rios Montt" (London, July 1982).
10. Allan Nairn, "The Guns of Guatemala," *The New Republic* (April 11, 1983), pp. 17–21.
11. Ibid.
12. Raymond Bonner, "Guatemala Enlists Religion in Battle," *The New York Times* (July 18, 1982).
13. IACHR, "Report on the Situation of Human Rights in the Republic of Guatemala, OEA/Ser. L/V/II.61, doc. 47, rev. 1 (October 5, 1983), pp. 66–67. See also Alan Riding, "Guatemalans Tell of Murder of 300," *The New York Times* (October 12, 1982).
14. Americas Watch, *Guatemala: A Nation of Prisoners* (New York, January 1984), Appendix D.
15. Americas Watch, *Creating a Desolation and Calling It Peace: May 1983 Supplement to the Report on Human Rights in Guatemala* (New York), p. 20.
16. *A Nation of Prisoners*, op. cit., p. 108.
17. *Prensa Libre* (Guatemala City, October 15, 1983).
18. *Prensa Libre* (Guatemala City, September 29, 1983).

19. Zoriana Pysariwsky, "Rights Inquiry on Guatemala Heavily Criticized," *The Times* (London) (March 21, 1984).

20. For example, in November 1983 the chief military commissioner, Rigoberto Ramırez Zepeda, told the press that "drastic measures will be taken against those who do not present themselves for duty in the civil patrols. . . . Anyone who refuses to participate is investigated to see if he has any relationship to groups that want to alter the established order." See *Prensa Libre* (November 4, 1983).

21. Special Rapporteur on Guatemala, Viscount Colville of Culross, *Introduction of the Report on the Situation of Human Rights in Guatemala*, United Nations, A/38/485 (November 30, 1983).

22. Editorial, "Guatemala Gain," *The New Republic* (September 10, 1984), p. 7.

23. Associated Press, "U.S. Leans Toward Arms for Guatemala," *Washington Post* (May 5, 1981).

24. U.S. embassy cable to Department of State (May 29, 1962) (No. A-125 "secret"), cited in Michael McClintock, "Disappearances in Central America," discussion paper for seminar on disappearances, Amnesty International—U.S.A. (June 22, 1980), p. 21.

25. "Guatemala and the Dominican Republic," staff memorandum prepared for the Subcommittee on Western Hemisphere Affairs, U.S. Senate Committee on Foreign Relations (Washington, D.C., December 30, 1971).

26. Brian Jenkins and Cesar D. Sereseres, "U.S. Military Assistance and the Guatemalan Armed Forces," *Armed Forces and Society* 3(4) (1977). Cited in Washington Office on Latin America, "Guatemala: The Roots of Revolution," *Special Update* (February 1983), p. 10. A "rapid reaction force" similar to the one developed in Guatemala in the 1960s was created in El Salvador in 1981, when U.S. advisers began teaching these techniques.

27. *Time* (January 26, 1968); cited in Washington Office on Latin America, op. cit.

28. Jenkins and Sereseres, op. cit.

29. See Michael McClintock, op. cit., p. 30.

30. Adapted from "Social and Economic Consequences of Repression," *Guatemala: A Nation of Prisoners* (New York: Americas Watch, 1984), pp. 50–51, 63–70.

31. Mark Thompson, *Fort Worth Star-Telegram* (December 15, 1982). The helicopters were sold as civilian goods under a license first granted during the final days of the Carter adminis-

tration. The Pentagon and the CIA had been pressing for renewal of Guatemalan aid since late 1977. State Department human rights officials blocked those efforts until late 1981, when the military advocates gained the upper hand. Under Reagan, the Department of State stopped resisting the aid initiatives and indeed became a proponent.

32. Hon. Michael Barnes, press release (January 7, 1983).

33. This array of aid became known, piecemeal, through the press: Allan Nairn, "Despite Ban, U.S. Captain Trains Guatemalan Military," *Washington Post* (October 21, 1982), p. 1 (on the Green Beret); "Illegal U.S. Aid to Guatemala Charged," *The New York Times* (November 15, 1982) (on the spare parts sale); and Richard H. Meislin, "U.S. Military Aid for Guatemala Continuing Despite Official Curbs," *The New York Times* (December 19, 1982) (on the instructor's role).

34. Prepared statement by Langhorne Motley, assistant secretary of state for inter-American affairs, before the Subcommittee on Western Hemisphere Affairs of the House Committee on Foreign Affairs (May 2, 1984); reprinted in U.S. Department of State, "U.S. Central American Policy at a Crossroads," *Current Policy*, No. 572 (Washington, D.C., May 2, 1984), p. 6.

35. Testimony of Stephen Bosworth before House Banking Subcommittee (August 5, 1982).

36. Author's interview (Washington D.C., October 13, 1982).

37. Daniel Southerland, "Administration Defends Plans to Aid Guatemalan Military," *The Christian Science Monitor* (January 10, 1983).

38. Author's interview (Guatemala City, October 7, 1982).

39. Christopher Dickey, "Haig's Emissary, in Guatemala, Discounts Charges of Rights Abuse," *Washington Post* (May 14, 1981), p. A16.

40. U.S. Department of State, *Country Reports on Human Rights Practices for 1981* (Washington, D.C.: GPO, 1982), p. 442.

41. Prepared statement of Stephen W. Bosworth and Stephen E. Palmer before the Subcommittee on Inter-American Affairs, House Committee on Foreign Affairs (Washington, D.C., July 30, 1981).

42. Assistant Secretary of State Thomas Enders, quoted in Alan Riding, "U.S. Is Said to Plan Aid to Guatemala to Battle Leftists," *The New York Times* (April 25, 1982).

43. "National Security Council Document on Policy in Central America" (reprint of complete text), *The New York Times* (April 7, 1983).

44. Reuters, "Guatemalan Is Said to Pledge Elimination of Death Squads," *The New York Times* (December 7, 1982).
45. Reuters, "Guatemalan Vows to Aid Democracy," *The New York Times* (December 6, 1982).
46. Juan Vasquez, "Guatemala Now Deserves Aid, U.S. Ambassador Says," *Miami Herald* (April 17, 1982).
47. Ricardo Chavira, "Guatemalan Indians Said Slain," *San Diego Union* (May 5, 1982).
48. U.S. Department of State, *Country Reports on Human Rights Practices for 1982* (Washington, D.C.: GPO, 1983), p. 517.
49. Bosworth, op. cit., 1982.
50. Americas Watch interview (Guatemala City, October 29, 1982).
51. Americas Watch, Helsinki Watch, and the Lawyers Committee for International Human Rights, *Failure: The Reagan Administration's Human Rights Policy in 1983* (New York: Americas Watch, Helsinki Watch, and the Lawyers Committee on International Human Rights, 1984), p. 37.
52. Philip Taubman, "Guatemalan's Remarks Applauded by U.S.," *The New York Times* (August 10, 1983).
53. *Country Reports on Human Rights Practices for 1983* (Washington, D.C.: GPO, 1984), p. 578.
54. *Central America Report* (Guatemala City, July 6, 1984).
55. Philip Taubman, "Slaying Case in Guatemala Angers U.S. Aides," *The New York Times* (September 11, 1983).
56. Allan Nairn, "Guatemala Can't Take Two Roads," op ed, *The New York Times* (July 20, 1982).
57. Ibid.
58. Prepared statement of Stephen W. Bosworth and Stephen E. Palmer, op. cit.
59. Ibid.
60. *MacNeil/Lehrer Report* (January 10, 1984), transcript.
61. FBIS, "Official Rejects Bishops' Recent Criticism" (November 18, 1983), p. P6. A government spokesman said, "there are malicious interests behind the bishops' statements" and that "when they return from Rome [where they were visiting the pope], they should clarify their remarks, since they have been harmful and have formed part of the campaign to discredit Guatemala."
62. Loren Jenkins, "Guatemalan Murders," *Washington Post* (November 28, 1983). Another Guatemalan AID employee had been murdered in February, along with three associates. These cases provoked the only strong public U.S. criticism of Guatemalan human rights violations made during the Reagan years.

63. UPI, "A U.S. Official Fled Guatemala in Fear According to Report," *The New York Times* (December 20, 1983).

64. FBIS, "Deputy Foreign Minister on U.S. Measures" (January 5, 1984), p. P3; FBIS, "Weapons Shipment" (January 24, 1984), p. P13.

65. Report of the National Bipartisan Commission on Central America (the Kissinger commission), cited in Americas Watch, *Guatemala: A Nation of Prisoners*, op. cit., p. 140.

66. Author's interview (Guatemala City, October 7, 1982).

CHAPTER 5

DEMOCRACIES UNDER FIRE

PERU

1. Americas Watch interview with then Minister of Justice Ernesto Alayza (December 15, 1983).

2. *La Republica* (Lima, July 22, 1984).

3. "Caso Oropeza, Una Hora Despues," *Caretas*, No. 812 (Lima, August 13, 1984), p. 10.

4. Enrique Zileri, "Tragedia en Huanta . . . y el caso de Ayala," *Caretas*, No. 813 (Lima, August 20, 1984).

5. "The Royal Hunt of the Sol," *The Economist* (November 26, 1983), p. 77.

6. Marlise Simons, "In Peru Prisons, Rebels Offer Some Clues to 'Shining Path,' " *The New York Times* (September 7, 1984), p. 1.

7. See, for example, Mario Vargas Llosa, "Inquest in the Andes," *The New York Times Sunday Magazine* (July 31, 1983), p. 18.

8. "Los herederos andinos de Mao y Pol Pot," *Informe Latinoamericano*, IL-84-32 (London, August 17, 1984), p. 382.

9. Marlise Simons, op. cit.

10. Amnesty International, "Peru: Torture and Extrajudicial Executions" (London, August 1983), p. 45.

11. Ibid.

12. Marlise Simons, "Peru Adopts Severe Tactics to Combat Guerrillas," *The New York Times* (August 18, 1984), p. 1.

13. See Marlise Simons, "Peruvian Military Fights Terrorists with Terror," *The New York Times* (September 2, 1984).

14. "Este es el Reino del Terror," *La Republica* (Lima, November 25, 1983).
15. Amnesty International, op. cit.
16. "Curas, calor y politica," *Caretas*, No. 733 (Lima, January 31, 1983), p. 10.
17. Fernando Gonzales Vigil, "Opinion: More on Human Rights in Peru," *LASA Forum* (Winter 1984), p. 24.
18. Interview (Lima, December 15, 1983).
19. "E.E.U.U. reitera apoyo a democracia peruana," *El Comercio* (Lima, August 31, 1984), p. 1.

COLOMBIA

1. U.S. Department of State, *Country Reports on Human Rights Practices for 1983* (Washington, D.C.: GPO, 1984), p. 515.
2. Cristina de la Torre, ed., *Amnistia, hacia una democracia mas ancha y profunda*, Editorial Oveja Negra (Bogota, May 1983), p. 21.
3. FEDEFAM (Federacion de Familiares de los Desaparecidos), *Informe Sobre Colombia* (Caracas, January 1984).
4. Figure and comparison appear in Americas Watch, *Human Rights in the Two Colombias: Functioning Democracy, Militarized Society* (New York: Americas Watch, October 1982), p. 6.
5. See description of "the MAS case" in following material and in Americas Watch, *The "MAS Case" in Colombia: Taking on the Death Squads* (New York: Americas Watch, July 1983).
6. See Gabriel Garcia Marquez, "In Which Country Do We Die?" *El Espectador* (Bogota, August 31, 1983).
7. *Area Handbook for Colombia* (Washington, D.C.: American University, 1976), pp. 321–27.
8. *Human Rights in the Two Colombias*, p. 4.
9. Gabriel Garcia Marquez, op. cit.
10. Numerous testimonial statements accusing the army of torture were compiled by the Permanent Committee for the Defense of Human Rights, the Committee in Solidarity with Political Prisoners, and the Jesuit research organization CINEP in their 1982 report *Muerte y Tortura en Caqueta*. One example is reprinted, in English, in "Human Rights in the Two Colombias," op. cit., pp. 9–10.
11. Cited in *Human Rights in the Two Colombias*, p. 8.
12. Permanent Committee for the Defense of Human Rights, "Iti-

nerario de la Represion Oficial, Militar y Paramilitar, Agosto 1982–Agosto 1983" (Bogota, November 1983).

13. *Cromos* (weekly) (Bogota, August 12, 1983).

14. Permanent Committee for the Defense of Human Rights (Bogota, February 3, 1984).

15. *El Tiempo* (Bogota, January 14, 1984).

16. *The New York Times* (June 2, 1982).

17. "Informe de una Mision de Amnistia Internacional a Colombia" (January 15–31, 1980), p. 38.

18. Jaime Sanchez Torres, "Colombia Represion, 1970–1981," (Bogota: CINEP, 1982), p. 35.

19. See *The "MAS Case" in Colombia: Taking on the Death Squads*, op. cit.

20. Reported in Permanent Committee for the Defense of Human Rights, "Cuadro Sinoptico de la Represion Oficial, Militar y Paramilitar durante los Siete Primeros Meses de 1981–82–83 y 84" (Bogota, August 1984).

21. Ibid.

22. For one foreign witness's account, see George Rogers, "Protecting Colombia's Peace," op ed, *The Christian Science Monitor* (September 21, 1984).

23. Former Colombian President Alfonso Lopez Michelsen, for example, said acidly, "Ambassador Tambs . . . has a habit of saying things attacking our internal policies." *El Tiempo* (July 29, 1984).

24. "Balance de la Situacion de los Derechos Humanos Durante Los Anos del Gobierno Actual," paper presented at the IV National Forum on Human Rights, Bogota (August 24–26, 1984).

25. Press briefing issued by the U.S. Department of State (September 4, 1984).

CHAPTER 6

RECOMMENDATIONS

1. John M. Goshko, "Administration Reiterates Aim of Scuttling Carter Policies," *Washington Post* (July 10, 1981), p. A12.

2. Edward Schumacher, "Latins Get Taste of Kirkpatrick Style," *The New York Times* (August 5, 1981), p. A3.

3. Jeane Kirkpatrick, speech to Third Committee of the U.N. (December 1, 1981).

4. "Reagan Supports Rios Montt," *The New York Times* (December 6, 1982).

5. Raymond Bonner, "Chilean Exiles Appeal to Mrs. Kirkpatrick for Help," *The New York Times* (September 22, 1981), p. A16.

6. *Washington Post* (July 10, 1981).

7. James Nelson Goodsell, "Galtieri's Power: Only as Firm as His Grip on Economy?," *The Christian Science Monitor* (December 18, 1981), p. 3.

8. Colin Campbell, "Wiesenthal Denies Slighting Timerman," *The New York Times* (June 14, 1981), p. A23.

9. "Rights Group Asserts Guatemala Kills Indians," *The New York Times* (May 8, 1983).

10. Americas Watch, *U.S. Reporting on Human Rights in El Salvador: Methodology at Odds with Knowledge* (New York: Americas Watch, 1982).

11. U.S. Department of State, *Country Reports on Human Rights Practices for 1983* (Washington, D.C.: GPO, 1984), p. 504.

12. Elliott Abrams, testimony before House Subcommittee on Western Hemisphere Affairs, of the Committee on Foreign Affairs (August 3, 1983).

13. "Fleeing Salvador's Truth," editorial, *Boston Globe* (November 15, 1983).

14. Ibid.

15. See, for example, the report on El Salvador in U.S. Department of State, *Country Reports on Human Rights Practices for 1982* (Washington, D.C.: GPO, 1983).

16. Elliott Abrams, interview, *The Christian Science Monitor* (August 3, 1983).

17. "Fleeing Salvador's Truth," editorial, *Boston Globe*, (November 15, 1982).

18. Ibid.

19. See, for example, U.S. Department of State, *Country Reports on Human Rights Practices for 1982.* (Washington, D.C.: GPO, February 1983).

INDEX

Abrams, Elliott, 5, 9–10, 11, 14,
  131, 198, 202–3, 234–35, 240
  Congress and, 11, 13
Acevedo, Sebastian, 61
ADO (Colombian guerrilla group),
  225n
Afghanistan, Soviet invasion of,
  119
AFL-CIO, 22n, 123
Agosti, Brigadier, 96
agrarian reform, 210, 211n, 212,
  224n, 225
agriculture:
  in Argentina, 93, 94
  in Guatemala, 194
AID, U.S. (Agency for
  International Development),
  17, 191, 203
Albania, 213
alcaldes indigenas, 195
Aleman, Cristobal, 124
Alfonsin, Raul, 21, 28, 33, 108,
  109
alguaciles, 195
Allende, Salvador, 45–46, 47, 64,
  65, 70
Alliance for Progress, 45, 223, 224n
Alvarez Martinez, Gustavo, 143,
  144, 147, 153–55, 160
Americas Watch, 8, 18, 37, 107,
  186, 199, 210n, 218, 225
  El Salvador and, 124, 126, 128,
    134, 136, 137
  Nicaragua and, 162, 165–66,
    168–69, 170–71
Amin, Idi, 242

amnesty, 49–50, 66, 84, 228
  of Argentine military, 103, 108,
    109
  in Nicaragua, 173
Amnesty International (AI), 17–19,
  60, 76, 183, 202–3, 204, 215,
  217
amparo, writs of, 50, 58
ANAPO movement, Colombian,
  224
anti-Semitism, 16, 174
APRA Party, Peruvian, 212
April 19 Movement (M-19), 224,
  229–30, 232
Aranda, Thomas, 89, 240, 241
Arbenz Guzman, Jacobo, 157
ARDE (contra group), 163
ARENA (Nationalist Republican
  Alliance), 121n, 138
Argentina, 7, 92–111, 144, 233,
  234
  Alfonsin administration in,
    108–11
  British influence in, 93, 94
  Carter administration and, 92,
    96, 99–101, 103
  certification law and, 32, 33,
    102–3, 105, 108
  Chile compared to, 48
  Chile's relations with, 46n
  Colombia compared to, 206
  Constitution of, 96, 108
  controversy over jurisdiction to
    try crimes in, 28–29, 109–10
  Country Reports for, 106
  democracy in, 19, 42, 84, 92–111

Committee of Peasant Unity, Guatemalan (CUC), 195
Committee of Santa Fe, 3, 23, 101
Committee to Protect Journalists, 79n
Communism, Communist Party, 45, 94, 116, 142, 213
 in Colombia, 223, 226
 in Guatemala, 190, 192, 199, 203
 in Nicaragua, 158, 159, 162
 in Uruguay, 73, 81n
 see also Soviet Union
concentration camps, 59
Congress, U.S., 5–6, 11, 12, 30, 219, 242
 Argentine policy and, 100, 102–3
 Chile policy and, 65, 103
 "country-specific" laws adopted by, 13–14, 31–32
 El Salvador policy and, 13–14, 119–20, 121, 125–26, 139, 235, 236, 239
 Guatemala policy and, 180, 196, 197
 Honduras policy and, 145
 Nicaragua policy and, 161, 176
 Uruguay policy and, 87, 88, 89
 see also House of Representatives, U.S.; Senate, U.S.
Conservative Party, Argentine, 93, 94
Conservative Party, Colombian, 222
Contadora group, 231n
contras (contra-revolucionarios), 36, 112, 128n, 163, 175, 177, 242
 Argentine support of, 98, 110
 Boland Amendment and, 38–39
 Catholic Church and, 172
 CIA manual for, 38, 176
 in Honduras, 141, 152, 155, 160
 Miskitos recruited by, 152, 155n, 164, 165, 166, 173–74
Convention on Political Rights of Women (1952), 29n

cooperatives, Guatemalan, 194, 195
Coordinadora Democratica Nicaragüense, 178
Costa Mendez, Nicanor, 104
Costa Rica, 143, 145, 155, 178n
Country Reports on Human Rights Practices, 8–9, 10, 14, 15, 19n, 21, 29, 68, 89, 90n, 106, 239
 on El Salvador, 130–31
 on Guatemala, 15, 198, 199, 200
 on Honduras, 148–50
 on Nicaragua, 163–64, 168–69, 170, 175
Court of Appeals, U.S., 33n
Covadonga, executions in, 17
CPDDH (Permanent Committee for the Defense of Human Rights), 226–27, 228, 232
CPDH (Permanent Commission on Human Rights), 128n, 163, 168, 169, 170
crimes:
 common vs. government, 34–35
 jurisdiction to try, 28–29, 78–79, 109–10, 228
Cronica, 127
Cruz, Arturo, 178
Cuba, 95, 115, 157, 159, 191, 213, 230
Customs, U.S., 203

D'Aubuisson, Roberto, 22n, 121, 138
Davis, Arthur, 240
death squads, 32
 in Argentina, 97, 99
 in Colombia, 221–22, 226–27, 228
 in El Salvador, 10, 12, 23, 33, 115, 116, 130–33, 233, 234–36, 238
 in Guatemala, 182, 183, 188
Deaver, Michael, 101
Deaver and Hannaford, 101
Declaration of Independence, U.S., 25, 29

Nicaragua (*cont.*)
National Guard in, 157, 158
open hostility and covert war in, 159–64
political parties in, 178
relocation of Indians in, 38, 156, 165–67
Salvadorans in, 135
Sandinista human rights violations in, 16, 156, 162–70, 179
Sandinista regime in, 20, 38, 98, 113, 128n, 144, 148, 158, 161–74
Sandinista response to critics in, 172–74
Somoza dynasty in, 156, 157–58
state of emergency in, 167–68, 171
Supreme Court of, 167
torture in, 16, 168–69, 175
U.S. aid to, 34, 159
U.S. double standard in, 174–76
U.S. Marines in, 156, 157
see also contras; Miskito Indians
Nicolaides, Cristino, 105–6
Nixon administration:
Chile policy of, 46, 64–65
Uruguay policy of, 86
Noel, General, 215
nonaligned movement, 96, 110
Nuremberg trials, 27, 28, 29

OAS (Organization of American States), 15, 76, 95, 105, 230
Charter of, 161n
General Assembly of, 76, 86
Human Rights Commission of, 76, 77, 90n, 164–65, 172–73, 174, 185–86
O'Mara, Denis, 59
Ongania, General, 95
On the Law of War and Peace (Grotius), 27
Operation Laso, 223
ORDEN (El Salvador paramilitary network), 116

Organization of American States, *see* OAS
Oropeza Chonta, Jesus, 209–10

Pakistan, 34
Panama, 231n
elections in, 21–22
Panzos incident, 182–83, 186, 191
Paraguay, 6, 233, 240
loans to, 13, 102
torture in, 27
Partido Liberal, Honduran, 142
Partido Liberal Independiente, Nicaraguan (PLI), 178
Partido Nacional, Honduran, 142
PASOH (Socialist Party of Honduras), 142
PCN, Salvadoran (National Conciliation Party), 138
PDC, Salvadoran (Christian Democratic Party), 116–17, 122
PEN, 98, 102
PEN American Center, 79n
Percovich, Luis, 210n
Permanent Commission on Human Rights (CPDH), 128n, 163, 168, 169, 170
Permanent Committee for the Defense of Human Rights (CPDDH), 226–27, 228, 232
Peron, Isabel, 96
Peron, Juan Domingo, 94, 95, 97
Peronism, 94, 95, 96
Peronist Party, Argentine, 96
Pertini, Sandro, 107
Peru, 208–19
antiterrorist law in, 208–9
Belaunde government in, 217–18
Colombia compared to, 218, 220
democracy under fire in, 205–7, 208–19
disappearances and murders in, 209–10, 216–17
economy of, 210, 211–12, 217
elections in, 21–22, 205, 212–13

With friends like these : the America
watch report on human rights and
U.S. policy in Latin America /
edited by Cynthia Brown ; preface b
Jacobo Timerman ; introduction by
Alfred Stepan. — New York : Panthe
on, 1985.
 p. cm.

 Includes index.
 ISBN 0-394-72949-8

(Cont. on next card
84-2641